LGBTQ CATHOLIC MINISTRY

PAST AND PRESENT

JASON STEIDL JACK

FOREWORD BY
JAMES MARTIN, SJ

Paulist Press
New York / Mahwah, NJ

Cover design by Joe Gallagher
Book design by Lynn Else

Library of Congress Cataloging-in-Publication Data
Names: Steidl, Jason, author.
Title: LGBTQ Catholic ministry : past and present / Jason Steidl ; foreword by James
Martin, SJ.
Description: New York / Mahwah, NJ : Paulist Press, [2023] | Includes bibliographical
references and index. | Summary: "Argues that LGBTQ Catholics and their allies have
been struggling for recognition and pastoral care in the U.S. Catholic Church since
the 1940s, using a variety of strategies to integrate their faith and sexuality and navigate
the institutional church"— Provided by publisher
Identifiers: LCCN 2022027448 (print) | LCCN 2022027449 (ebook) | ISBN
9780809155699 (paperback) | ISBN 9781587689680 (ebook)
Subjects: LCSH: Church work with sexual minorities. | Church work—Catholic
Church. | Catholic Church—United States.
Classification: LCC BX2347.8.H65 S74 2023 (print) | LCC BX2347.8.H65 (ebook) |
DDC 261.8/35766—dc23/eng/20220909
LC record available at https://lccn.loc.gov/2022027448
LC ebook record available at https://lccn.loc.gov/2022027449

ISBN 978-0-8091-5569-9 (paperback)
ISBN 978-1-58768-968-0 (e-book)

Published by Paulist Press
997 Macarthur Boulevard
Mahwah, New Jersey 07430
www.paulistpress.com

Printed and bound in the
United States of America

Dedicated to the great cloud of witnesses who have struggled for LGBTQ acceptance, representation, and affirmation in the Roman Catholic Church.

But you are a chosen race, a royal priesthood, a holy nation, God's own people, in order that you may proclaim the mighty acts of him who called you out of darkness into his marvelous light.

—1 Peter 2:9

CONTENTS

Contents

FOREWORD

The Joys and Hopes, the Griefs and Anxieties of the LGBTQ Catholic

By James Martin, SJ

When I wrote *Building a Bridge*, a book about the Catholic Church's need to reach out to the LGBTQ community, in 2017, I was completely unprepared for the strong reactions it would provoke, both positive and negative.

To begin with, the Catholic *Catechism*'s simple call for "respect, compassion, and sensitivity" toward gays and lesbians was a decided challenge for many people, even though the book did not challenge any church teaching. Within a few weeks of the book's publication, I received hate mail and death threats and was accused of heresy and apostasy by Catholic commentators, fellow priests, and even a few bishops. Talks and lectures were cancelled at Catholic parishes and colleges, and many of those that did proceed were marked by protests. It was a vivid reminder of the kind of treatment that LGBTQ Catholics experience on a day-to-day basis.

But alongside those negative reactions, which were in the minority, were the overwhelmingly positive ones: standing ovations at parishes and long lines of people waiting to give me tearful hugs and share their stories (and their children's and grandchildren's stories). I heard from countless LGBTQ and allied Catholics who were grateful for the book. Many were eager for words of welcome and affirmation from a priest. Their stories of struggle and perseverance in the Church continue to inspire my ministry, which I hope amplifies their voices within a community of faith that needs to hear from them. In time, the book would be supported by many in the Catholic hierarchy, and two years after its publication, I was invited by Pope Francis to meet with him at the Vatican to discuss the book and LGBTQ ministry in the Church more generally.

All of this was a reminder of the need for a more open conversation about the place of LGBTQ Catholics in the Church and the Church's response to that place—and a conversation about the history of this kind of ministry.

In 2017, as *Building a Bridge* was going to print, I met Jason Steidl, then a PhD student in theology at Fordham University and a member of the ministry team for Out at St. Paul, the LGBTQ ministry of St. Paul the Apostle in New York City and one of the largest and most vibrant LGBTQ communities in the entire Catholic Church. Coincidentally, my Jesuit community had just moved next door to the parish.

Jason and others on the St. Paul's ministry team invited me to a dialogue with their community that both affirmed and challenged what I had written. Some asked about next steps. Others shared their frustrations with my "bridge-building" attempts. In fact, Jason himself challenged me in the most fruitful of ways by reminding me that it is the Catholic Church that has marginalized the LGBTQ community, and not the other way around. In other words, both lanes in this admittedly "two-way bridge" are not equal, and the onus to begin bridge-building belongs to the Church. Thanks to my conversations with Jason and the Out at St. Paul team, the second edition of the book was much revised. Since then, we've continued the conversation.

As I got to know Jason better, I saw that he was eager to share his knowledge of the ministry and advocacy that preceded *Building a Bridge,* which was, after all, just a small contribution to this ministry. For decades, communities such as Dignity and ministries such as Fortunate Families built a foundation for the work that is taking shape today. Leaders like Fr. John McNeill, Sr. Jeannine Gramick, and Fr. Robert Nugent sacrificed much to affirm the dignity of LGBTQ people. More broadly, LGBTQ Catholics have always been a part of the Church. As baptized believers, they possess innumerable spiritual gifts, enrich the faith, and share in the Christian call to live as "priest, prophet, and king."

It is no surprise that Jason's first book, *LGBTQ Catholic Ministry,* expands on these themes. It is a beautifully written, well-researched, and important book, and I know of none other like it.

His writing focuses on the work of grassroots and lay Catholics to change the Church from the bottom up. The book spans three-quarters of a century, beginning with George Hyde and the Eucharistic Catholic Church in 1946 and concluding with newly formed ministries such as the internet-based Vine & Fig. Over the past few years, I've gotten to know many of these organizations as allies and these individuals as friends. Each story is unique and exemplifies the creativity and passion of those committed to LGBTQ ministry. Relationships to the hierarchy and strategies for change differ from organization to organization, but each possesses an unwavering commitment to pastoral care for those who feel themselves on the margins.

Jason himself is certainly no stranger to LGBTQ advocacy. Today, he is a board member for Fortunate Families and professor who works with pastoral leaders. I rely on his insights, perspective, and counsel often. As an openly gay man, Catholic theologian, and lay minister, he has wrestled with his own relationship to the Church and Catholic tradition. The fruit of his many years of discernment, reflection, and participation in the Church are evident in his gifted writing and ability to tell a complex story with clarity and grace. Jason's history-conscious account of LGBTQ Catholic ministry in the United States balances his love for the Church with honesty and sensitivity for LGBTQ perspectives. He discovers within these stories a call to transforming action.

The history that Jason shares in *LGBTQ Catholic Ministry* is not always comfortable. Many in the Church have failed to treat LGBTQ Catholics with the dignity they deserve. Knowledge of this painful past must be faced, but it can also help us build a better future. Recognizing that LGBTQ people have remained in the Body of Christ through the highs and lows is the first step to building bridges between the community and church leaders.

The Church is now catching up as it learns more about the "joys and the hopes, the griefs and the anxieties" of LGBTQ people, to quote the Second Vatican Council's document *Gaudium et Spes*. The last few decades bear witness to the triumphs and tragedies of those who struggled to reconcile their sexual and gender identities with Catholic community. Nevertheless, LGBTQ Catholics and their allies remain a wellspring of hope in parishes, schools, and other Catholic institutions, as well as in society at large. Many of those whom I have met are sensitive to the movement of the Holy Spirit and eager to engage their fellow Catholics. Their stories of faith and perseverance are a treasure for the Church.

In his first apostolic exhortation, *Evangelii Gaudium*, Pope Francis encouraged Catholics to "go forth and preach the Gospel to all: to all places, on all occasions, without hesitation, reluctance, or fear. The joy of the Gospel is for all people: no one can be excluded." Above all else, this may also be the animating message of LGBTQ Catholic ministry: all people are welcome in the Family of God. In our divided world, Catholics need to hear this message more than ever. The Church is a home for everyone. To quote the popular hymn, "all are welcome."

LGBTQ Catholic Ministry is a vivid testimony to God's work in the lives of LGBTQ Catholics and God's faithfulness to the Church through them. I hope that this beautiful new book will encourage LGBTQ Catholics, their families, allies, lay and ordained ministers, and everyone else striving to build a church where all are truly welcome.

ACKNOWLEDGMENTS

This book is a fruit of my growth in multiple grace-filled communities.

For several years, the Out at St. Paul (OSP) ministry in Manhattan has helped me embrace my calling to engage the Church as an LGBTQ Catholic. The Paulists are agents of the Holy Spirit, and the parish of St. Paul the Apostle bears the good fruit of affirming spiritual community. Fr. Gil Martinez has been a channel of healing and reconciliation for hundreds of LGBTQ Catholics, myself included. Fr. Mark-David Janus has been a mentor who helped me recognize and develop my gifts. Marianne Palacios, Ian Rogers, and so many other OSP members are family. They kept me grounded through the writing of this book, much of which took place during a global pandemic.

Many thanks are due to the Fordham Theology Department, where I first reconciled my faith and sexuality. Friends and colleagues Paul Schutz, Eric Martin, and John Gleim, among countless others, manifested God's unconditional love and showed me the meaning of Christian discipleship. Publicly gay mentors Patrick Hornbeck and Bryan Massingale taught me the power of socially engaged theology and encouraged me to press on when I struggled or was attacked. I cannot overstate how great an impact the department had on my academic, spiritual, and personal growth. I am forever indebted.

I am thankful for those who have enabled my ministry and advocacy. Fr. James Martin, SJ, amplified my voice and modeled courage in the face of opposition. Stanley "JR" Zerkowski invited me to leadership in Fortunate Families and offered the best example of dialogue-based advocacy. Jamie Manson recommended my work to editors and showed me the power of pride in being an openly dissenting Catholic.

This book would have been impossible without the support of the St. Joseph's University community, where I was assistant teaching professor during the writing of this book. Tom Petriano welcomed me to an academic and faith community that is rooted in integrity and grows toward the peripheries. University grants helped fund travel to conferences and archives where the ideas for this book took shape.

Thanks are due to Caitlin McCarthy of the LGBTQ Community Center in Manhattan and Brendan Faye for their assistance with archives. Murray Watson, Eric Martin, and Diane Vescovi, my editor, read drafts of my work and offered invaluable feedback.

Aurelio Matheu, a dear friend, admonished me to be smart and keep writing. My husband, Damian Jack, helped me dream big dreams. Joe Steidl and Mary Haynes, my parents, raised me with a passion for justice, humility to acknowledge my limitations, and the certainty of my immeasurable dignity.

Finally, all thanks to God, who willed me and this book into existence. As Psalm 139:14 declares, "I praise you, for I am fearfully and wonderfully made. Wonderful are your works; that I know very well."

INTRODUCTION

No Such Thing as an LGBTQ Catholic?

In 2018, Charles Chaput, then archbishop of Philadelphia, surprised many when he told the Synod on Youth, "There is no such thing as an LGBTQ Catholic." Using the acronym in official church teaching, he suggested, would imply "that these are real, autonomous groups, and the Church simply doesn't categorize people that way."[1]

His claim would be laughable were it not such a brazen attempt to erase LGBTQ Catholics. If there is no such thing as an LGBTQ Catholic, after all, their objections to homophobia and transphobia can go unanswered. If there is no such thing as an LGBTQ Catholic, there is no need to show them compassion.

Chaput must know that church teaching does, in fact, categorize people by their sexuality. The *Catechism* labels same-sex desire as a "condition" and homosexual acts as "intrinsically disordered."[2] The Vatican bans men from seminary if they "practice homosexuality, present deep-seated homosexual tendencies or support the so-called 'gay culture.'"[3] Chaput, along with other bishops, endorses Courage, a ministry for those who "experience same-sex attractions and those who love them."[4] These are real categories with real consequences.

For many Catholic leaders, only certain groups categorized by their sexuality can be acknowledged: those who are ashamed of their "intrinsic disorder" and struggle against their "homosexual inclinations." The hierarchy's antiqueer rhetoric adds to the Church's long history of institutional erasure, manipulation, and spiritual abuse of LGBTQ people.[5]

But this is not the only side of the story. For many decades, LGBTQ Catholics and allies have asserted their place within a religious institution that often denies their existence. They have done so by creating ministries of hospitality and affirmation that reflect their unique spiritualities and traditions. Due to social and ecclesial homophobia and transphobia, they also present unique pastoral needs.

Today, the LGBTQ Catholic movement is gaining momentum. Grassroots attitudes are shifting and ministries are flourishing. The pope himself seems to be on board with many initiatives. It may be a time for cautious optimism, but we must also remember the painful past. LGBTQ apostolates are precarious and face opposition from authorities at local, diocesan, and universal levels of the Church. As long as leaders like Charles Chaput try to erase LGBTQ Catholics, it is all the more necessary to share their stories of perseverance.

THE JESUIT WHO MOVED NEXT DOOR

The story of this book begins with the Society of Jesus. In February 2017, a group of Jesuits moved near my parish, the Church of St. Paul the Apostle in Manhattan. Shortly after they arrived, the Out at St. Paul (OSP) ministry team (which I was part of) received an unsolicited email from Fr. James Martin, SJ. He wanted to speak with us about *Building a Bridge*, the new book he had written in response to the Pulse nightclub shooting.

At first, we questioned Fr. Martin's intentions. Who was he, and why did he deserve our time? As proud New Yorkers, we were curious but not starstruck. Our ministry was already successful. We had our own voice, community, and heroes. We did not want to be used as a promotional opportunity.

Despite our misgivings, we gave Fr. Martin a chance. He was a superstar priest and had a great deal of influence, after all. At his first talk with our community, we were floored by the dozens of visitors who came to hear him speak. So many longed to hear a priest say that they were created in God's image and deeply loved.

Over the next few months, we watched as *Building a Bridge* exploded in popularity. Martin's speaking events and media appearances made it clear that he had tapped into a powerful spiritual and cultural moment. We were amazed at the shockwaves that his simple message sent throughout the Church. The advocacy that OSP took for granted was dangerously charged for many committed to maintaining the status quo. At times, his allyship came with a heavy cost—vicious personal attacks, threats, and attempts at manipulation from the highest levels of the Church.

HARD QUESTIONS AND HISTORIES

The controversy surrounding *Building a Bridge* continues to this day, but so has the advocacy it inspires. Family and friends of LGBTQ people ask how they can make the Church more hospitable. Lay folks show up in droves to support parishes with affirming ministries. Priests, often risking their own careers, create spaces for LGBTQ parishioners to serve as CCD leaders, eucharistic ministers, and members of the choir. Even some bishops are building better relationships with the LGBTQ Catholic community. There are reasons for optimism.

There is also much work that remains to be done. Since *Building a Bridge* was published, I've spoken with countless Catholics who are passionate about LGBTQ ministry but feel stymied by a lack of resources. Fr. Martin's book is a helpful conversation starter, but what does community and pastoral care look like in the real world? How do ministers navigate the complexities of church teaching and institutions?

Unfortunately, in a church that sees queer sexuality and gender as a source of shame, LGBTQ ministry is often discussed in hushed tones and coded language. What if an unfriendly priest hears? Should we fear reprisal from alt-right Catholic websites such as Church Militant? What will the bishop say? The news is full of stories about LGBTQ and allied Catholics fired from their jobs in schools and parishes for coming across as too friendly to the movement.

Unlike many, I've had the privilege of belonging to an affirming parish where it is safe to be openly gay and minister. I've also served on the board of directors for Fortunate Families, a national ministry dedicated to equipping the Church for the pastoral care of LGBTQ people. More importantly, my experiences as a gay Catholic and theologian shape how I understand the Church's relationship to the LGBTQ community.

Sometimes, the history of this relationship is hard to recount. The Church's mistreatment of queer Catholics is heartbreaking. Nevertheless, a painful history opens up to hope for the future. LGBTQ Catholics and their allies are tenacious. Decades of ministry provide a vision for what is possible in communities committed to justice and mercy. This book will share some of their experiences.

AUDIENCES

I offer this work with three audiences in mind.

First, I write for LGBTQ Catholics. Most of us were raised in homes and parishes that taught us we were strange and did not belong. Homophobia and transphobia perpetuated our isolation and shame. There were few, if any, queer mentors, role models, or saints. It took many of us years to integrate our faith and sexuality and find our place within the broader LGBTQ community.

Once we arrived, however, we discovered a people ennobled and emboldened by generations of struggle. We found ourselves surrounded and supported by a great "cloud of witnesses," those saints — canonized or not — who lived with integrity and helped others to do the same. Queer believers belong to a proud movement that is making the Church more Christlike. This book affirms that we are not, and have never been, alone.

Second, I write for allies and ministers. The Church can be terrifying for advocates of queer people. LGBTQ ministry is dangerous, and many have greatly suffered for their solidarity with the queer community. Is it worth it? When will change come?

You are not the first to ask these questions, and you will not be the last. Your efforts, nevertheless, matter a great deal. You help LGBTQ Catholics hold on to their faith. The burdens you take upon yourself make their burdens more bearable. Your solidarity and allyship are invaluable, and I write with examples of perseverance to encourage you to press on.

Third, I write for an academic audience. I am a liberation theologian by training. My approach employs history in the service of theology, defined by Gustavo Gutiérrez as a "critical reflection on Christian praxis in light of the word of God."[6] Especially important to liberationist thought is the experience of the poor and marginalized as a *locus theologicus*, a fruitful space to reflect on God's work in the world. This book explores LGBTQ experience as one such site.

This book is also a work of pastoral theology. In recent decades, the discipline has exploded with subfields dedicated to families, women, children, youth, racial and ethnic communities, and other groups. Ministry to LGBTQ people is a new but rapidly expanding area of interest within this milieu. More often than not, however, the conversation is *about* LGBTQ Catholics rather than *with* them. I offer a history that prioritizes LGBTQ perspectives to encourage dialogue and greater understanding.

NAVIGATING THIS BOOK

This work is divided into eight chapters.

The first chapter examines the origins of LGBTQ Catholic ministry in the Eucharistic Catholic Church (ECC), an independent Catholic community founded by George Hyde, an ex-seminarian from Atlanta, in 1946. Throughout the mid- to late twentieth century, ECC grew into an international organization committed to caring for its socially ostracized members. The denomination was part of the Homophile Movement, which encouraged gays and lesbians to integrate into mainstream society as best they could. As a church of gay and straight and black and white parishioners, ECC established a powerful precedent for diverse and affirming ministry.

The second chapter traces the meteoric rise of DignityUSA, an influential ministry founded in 1969 by an Augustinian priest from San Diego. At times, Dignity succeeded in winning the support of lay Catholics, priests, and even bishops. The group's unapologetically LGBTQ-affirming theology, however, set it on a crash course with the Vatican, which in 1986 expelled Dignity and similar groups from Catholic parishes around the world. Today, the community is a prophetic force that lobbies for change outside traditional parish and diocesan structures. The model of ministry that DignityUSA established decades ago remains a powerful example for LGBTQ-affirming communities today.

Chapter 3 recounts the history of New Ways Ministry (NWM), a national organization that has navigated ministry at the edges of the institutional Church. Launched in 1977 by Sr. Jeannine Gramick and Fr. Robert Nugent, NWM today is well known for its workshops, retreats, newsletters, and book publishing. Opposition from the hierarchy has been severe over the course of more than half a century, but NWM has survived by blurring the line between outsider and insider status. Today, many of its leaders are laypeople, and it continues to be one of the most influential voices on LGBTQ Catholic issues.

Chapter 4 tells the story of Fortunate Families (FF), which emerged in the 2000s as a ministry by and for allied parents struggling to accept their children's sexuality. In addition to providing pastoral support for families, founders Casey and Mary Ellen Lopata harnessed parents' love for their children in the struggle for LGBTQ liberation. In recent years, FF has pursued a more reconciling relationship with the institutional church by obtaining the blessing of Bishop John Stowe, OFM Conv., of Lexington, Kentucky, where FF's national headquarters are located. The bishop's endorsement has enabled the group, now led by JR Zerkowski, to serve within parishes, dioceses, schools, and religious orders across the United States.

Chapters 5 and 6 turn to the LGBTQ community of St. Paul the Apostle, an urban parish in New York City that is also the mother church of the Paulist Fathers, a missionary order committed to evangelizing U.S. culture. The Gay and Lesbian Catholic Ministry (GLCM) at St. Paul began in the early 1990s at the height of the AIDS epidemic, a time when gay activists were locked in conflict with the Archdiocese of New York. Donald Maher, a gay activist and member of St. Paul, created a ministry of hospitality, compassion, and affirmation to overcome the divide between gays and lesbians and the institutional church. After a brief hiatus in the early 2000s, LGBTQ ministry returned to St. Paul under the leadership of its pastor, Fr. Gil Martinez, and a ministry team of lay leaders. Today, Out at St. Paul (OSP) is a thriving apostolate that reflects the cultures and charisms of Hell's Kitchen, the parish's gayborhood to its south.

Chapters 7 and 8 follow the evolution of Fr. James Martin's ministry with LGBTQ Catholics. A Jesuit like Pope Francis, Martin emulates Christ's outreach to social and religious outcasts, provoking praise and criticism from around the world. Although Martin does not dissent from church teaching and enjoys his superiors' approval, his challenge for the institutional church to "build a bridge" to the LGBTQ community has elicited robust responses in recent years. Today, he is one of the most recognizable allies of the LGBTQ Catholic movement.

The ninth chapter concludes with observations and reflections on the present state of LGBTQ ministry. Why would anyone hope that the institutional church will change? Queer ecclesiology shows a way forward. Rather than relying on the hierarchy, Catholics must look to LGBTQ people and their allies for salvation from homophobia and transphobia. At the grassroots level, Catholics are among the most affirming Christians in the United States, and apostolates are springing up in Catholic parishes around the country. The chapter concludes with short profiles of three new ministries that prove God is transforming the Church through LGBTQ and allied Catholics.

FOR FURTHER INVESTIGATION

Unfortunately, there are many stories and perspectives that are absent from this work. First, the geographic scope of this book is limited to the United States. The Catholic Church extends around the world, with local, national, and international LGBTQ ministries that merit further study. Second, it is limited by its historical timeline (1946–2021). Queer Catholics have been part of the Church since its founding, yet this book will examine ministries from only the mid twentieth to early twenty-first centuries. Third, my approach privileges the stories of lay and grassroots actors and communities on the margins of the institutional church. In the future, I hope to write about the rise and fall of LGBTQ ministries in dioceses and archdioceses such as Cleveland, Los Angeles, Chicago, and Baltimore. These histories offer invaluable insights into the clerical and hierarchal cultures of a Church that has wrestled with its identity since Vatican II. Fourth, while the present book at times focuses on the experiences of women, BIPOC, and other marginalized and minoritized groups, their perspectives are far underrepresented, and much work remains to be done discovering, recovering, and amplifying their voices. Sexism, racism, ableism, agism, and other structural sins dominate history-telling as much as other forms of human culture. This is an area of growth for my own scholarship and academic scholarship more broadly.

LGBTQ CATHOLIC MINISTRY IS HERE AND QUEER

For LGBTQ people, coming out is a prophetic act of resistance against erasure. Harvey Milk, one of the first openly gay politicians in the United States, told activists, "We will not win our rights by staying quietly in our closets....We are coming out! We are coming out to fight the lies, the myths, the distortions! We are coming out to tell the truth about gays!"[7]

As a political, spiritual, and relational tool, coming out functions in the Church as well as it does in society. Queer Catholic honesty and vulnerability change hearts. In Catholic communities, telling the history of LGBTQ Catholics reveals that Chaput and hierarchs like him are gravely mistaken. LGBTQ Catholics exist and have been a "real, autonomous" group for more than three-quarters of a century.

From a theological standpoint, LGBTQ Catholic stories are also sacred. They possess God-given power to challenge Christian homophobia and transphobia by revealing the innumerable ways that God moves outside of traditional family, relationship, and even church structures. LGBTQ people belong to the Body of Christ, and they call the Church to be more faithful to Christ's mission of hospitality, compassion, and accompaniment.

At the start of the gay liberation movement, a popular activist refrain proclaimed, "We are here. We are queer. Get used to it." As LGBTQ Catholics and allies continue to struggle for recognition, affirmation, and justice, their advocacy in the Church echoes their forebears' message: LGBTQ Catholic ministry is here. LGBTQ Catholic ministry is queer. And it's time for the Church to get used to it.

Chapter 1

OUT OF SPIRITUAL CLOSETS

George Hyde and the Eucharistic
Catholic Church

> Now faith is the assurance of things hoped for,
> the conviction of things not seen.
>
> —Hebrews 11:1

THE BEGINNINGS OF LGBTQ-INCLUSIVE CATHOLIC COMMUNITY

What we might now call LGBTQ Catholic ministry began in the United States as an act of resistance against spiritual abuse.[1]

On a Saturday afternoon in late 1945, a "festive" young man entered the confessional at Sacred Heart Roman Catholic Church in downtown Atlanta. According to one euphemistic account, he went to ask pardon for "having engaged in an unacceptable form of lovemaking."[2]

The confession would have been routine were it not for the confessor, who refused mercy and called the young man an abomination. The priest would grant absolution only if the young man agreed that the biblical slur was true. Growing defensive, the young man refused to condemn himself, provoking the priest to threaten a lifetime ban from the Eucharist. When the young man again refused to repent, the priest shouted, "Get the hell out of my church!"

The next day, the young man gathered his courage to attend Sunday Mass. Toward the end of the liturgy, he went up to receive the Eucharist with everyone else. The priest, recognizing him, made good on his threat and denied communion. The young man returned to his pew without making a show. There was always next week.

The young man returned to church yet again the following Sunday. This time, when the priest passed him by, he stood in silence at the front of the congregation until Mass ended. People noticed the young man's protest, and it became the talk of the town. Within a few weeks a group of supporters, including a former seminarian named George Hyde, joined him in solidarity.[3] Hyde channeled publicity from the spectacle to launch the Eucharistic Catholic Church (ECC), the first LGBTQ-affirming Catholic ministry in the United States.[4]

The story of ECC, like many LGBTQ Catholic ministries, reveals a complex relationship to the institutional church. While members embraced Catholic faith and found their inclusive vision for community in Catholic tradition, there was no room for them within traditional parochial or diocesan structures. Homophobia was a powerful force that disfellowshipped LGBTQ Catholics from Christ's table. Many left the Roman Catholic Church for communion with independent Catholic churches, where it was much easier to find support for their lives and loves. Gay and lesbian Catholics wanted to be part of the Roman Church, but the Roman Church wanted nothing to do with them.

As the twentieth century progressed and new LGBTQ Catholic ministries emerged, they too struggled through questions of spiritual identity and pained relationships with the institutional church. Some, despite all the obstacles, flourished within the Church. Others flourished without it. Many ministries disappeared or separated from Catholic community, unable to reconcile affirming practices and formal affiliation.

This chapter and the next will share some of their stories, revealing the complex ways that LGBTQ ministries navigated Catholic traditions and struggled for institutional support. The opportunities for, and limitations to, LGBTQ ministry have always depended on the time, place, and personalities involved. No two stories are the same, but they all reveal a fervent desire to foster inclusive spiritual community patterned after the ministry of Jesus Christ. Depending on the context, LGBTQ Catholics found varying levels of support from the Church that claims to follow Christ.

FORMER SEMINARIAN GEORGE HYDE'S PROPHETIC STAND

In late 1945, George Hyde was a twenty-two-year-old former seminarian with an already colorful history. Hyde grew up Southern Baptist but converted to the Catholic Church as a young man. In the process, he developed a special relationship with Gerald P. O'Hara, the bishop of Savannah-Atlanta, who sponsored him to attend St. Mary's of the Barrens Seminary in Perryville, Missouri.[5] Hyde's seminary formation did not last long.

At St. Mary's, students routinely met in the chapel to publicly work out their grievances with one another. These Chapters of Faults often turned into forums for seminarians to accuse each other of sin. At one such meeting in the early fall of 1945, one of Hyde's classmates accused him and "Deacon So and So of fondling each other in an immoral way." Hyde, who was already thinking of leaving the seminary, took the accusation as an opportunity to deliver what he described as a "little Martin Luther speech."[6]

Why, he asked, did the Church tolerate open adultery and fornication among heterosexual Catholics yet immediately expel seminarians who were merely suspected of homosexuality?[7] Instead of drawing people to Christ, the seminary had built "spiritual closets…in every nook and corner of the church for the purpose of shutting away those who do not measure up to the standards of your dysfunctional self-righteousness." It was time, Hyde proclaimed, for the Church to embrace those with "same-gender sexual and affectional orientation.… I have nothing more to say," he concluded, "except, perhaps, to pray that the Spirit of the Living God will fall afresh on you and your pastoral outreach."[8]

After speaking his peace, Hyde returned to his room and found his bags already packed for him. He left the seminary and returned to Atlanta to stay with Bishop O'Hara until he could discern his future.

That's where he heard the news about the young man's plight at Sacred Heart Church and decided to join in solidarity.[9]

On the third Sunday of the "festive" young man's protest, Hyde went up to the altar rail with him. As one of the bishop's favorites, Hyde imagined that he could pressure the pastor into compliance. He was wrong; the priest denied him communion together with the young man.[10] Afterward, the pair regrouped and decided to invite others to join the cause.[11] Their plan succeeded, and in the following weeks more and more arrived to protest the Mass. By the spring of 1946, Hyde had gathered a small, yet diverse, community of eighteen people who objected to the church's exclusion of the young gay man. Thus was born the first Catholic community dedicated to gay ministry. At a time when anti-sodomy laws were being enforced in Georgia and across the United States, Hyde's advocacy was daring and prophetic.[12]

THE AFFIRMING COMMUNITY OF THE EUCHARISTIC CATHOLIC CHURCH

After several weeks of protests, George Hyde's group decided to meet of their own accord for Bible study and worship. Institutional strictures could not impede their commitment to each other and living out their faith and sexuality with integrity. From that moment on, they were independent Catholics, one of many splinter groups that maintain Catholic traditions apart from the formal authority of the Roman Catholic Church.[13]

At first, Hyde's community struggled to affiliate with a new denomination. Members yearned for spiritual leadership, but who would accept them? In the late spring of 1946, Hyde met John Kazantks, an Atlanta school teacher and Greek Orthodox bishop who had been suspended from ministry in Greece for his own homosexual proclivities.[14] Hyde asked the bishop to preside over the group's liturgies, but Kazantks objected because he struggled with English and felt he was too old. Instead, the bishop agreed to ordain Hyde so that he could minister himself.[15]

Hyde's ordination to the priesthood took place on July 1, 1946, at the Winecoff Hotel in Atlanta. His nascent community received financial support from the Cotton Blossom Room, a bar in the hotel frequented by gay men, and took the name Blessed Sacrament.[16] Many of its members knew the pain of exclusion from the Lord's Supper, but their Catholic faith was grounded in a eucharistic table open to all Christians, gay or straight.

The small church held its first Christmas Eve service in 1946 in a house that members had converted into a worship space, office, and living quarters. The group was diverse, welcoming people of color, gay and lesbian sexualities, and allies. Hyde was committed to inclusion, often telling congregants, "If kneeling side by side in prayer next to a black person or a gay person is a problem, know that it is you who has a problem, not them."[17]

The group was controversial. The Ku Klux Klan singled out members for harassment, and outsiders regularly interrogated Hyde as the "pastor of that queer church."[18] After the church's first Christmas Eve service ended, protestors hurled slurs and pelted parishioners with stones as they left the building. Hyde was struck in the head and carried a scar for the rest of his life. He saved the rock that hit him as a sign of hope for a better future.[19]

That future arrived soon. By the end of 1947, Blessed Sacrament, which changed its name to Holy Eucharist (and later became known as the Eucharistic Catholic Church [ECC]) to avoid confusion with Episcopal and Roman Catholic parishes of the same name, could boast more than two hundred members.[20] ECC became a haven for gay believers. Just a couple of years after its founding, the church provided housing and jobs for several men who had been caught up in an Atlanta police raid of a "homosexual party" at the Cox-Carlton Hotel.[21] Prioritizing ministry to social and religious outcasts, ECC expanded to Macon, Savannah, and Athens, Georgia, and eventually to cities as far away as Cleveland, New York, Washington, D.C., Toronto, and Vancouver.

In ECC's early years, sacramental and ministerial support came from a variety of men, including Episcopal and Roman Catholic priests. According to Hyde, several clerics left active ministry in their own denominations to join the gay-affirming church's ranks. With gifted spiritual leaders, ECC innovated new forms of ministry. In Washington, D.C., Hyde began a house of formation for "Domestic Missionaries" who took on secular jobs and "by exercising good work and social habits exhibited that gay people were basically good, decent, and responsible persons." In addition to providing much-needed funds for the church, the initiative evolved into a ministry that supplied chaplains on call for the Holiday Inn hotel chain.[22]

TRADITIONAL CHRISTIAN ETHICS AND SAME-SEX RELATIONSHIPS

While ECC affirmed same-sex partnerships, Hyde insisted that the community not become a gay enclave. He explained that "a gay church is just as wrong as an exclusively heterosexual church....You cannot discriminate anyway whatsoever."[23] From the forties to the sixties, ECC could best be characterized as part of the Homophile Movement, which encouraged homosexuals to fit in as best they could with the heteronormative culture around them.[24] As the leader of ECC, Hyde condemned an "anything goes" sexual ethic and believed that "God legislated certain definite confessional, ethical, moral codes for us. We (Christians) have to make an effort to live according to those."[25] In a 1975 interview, he distinguished ECC from other gay Christian groups such as Dignity (Roman Catholic) and Integrity (Episcopalian) that had embraced the sexual revolution of the sixties. Members of these organizations, Hyde explained, "thought of their sexuality as little more than a series of glandular experiences punctuated by a cigarette." True Christianity, on the other hand, "was 'death' to the practice on Saturday nights of multiple sex partners in the men's room and bushes."[26]

Although Hyde discouraged promiscuity among ECC members, he was sensitive toward the challenges they faced as queer folks, knowing that many were traumatized from years of spiritual abuse. A 1954 advertisement in ONE Magazine, a publication of the homophilic movement, welcomed newcomers to try a "church truly one and catholic, embracing any and all....We do not attempt to judge."[27] As priest, Hyde promised to accompany members of his congregation when they stumbled on the journey of faith. "So you fall down flat on your face," he assured, "I'll pick you up and brush you off and we'll go on again. But you've got to try."[28]

Hyde took a holistic approach to caring for the spiritual, relational, and emotional needs of his parishioners, but he prioritized spiritual well-being above all the others. "If we get the spirituality balanced," he maintained, "everything else will take care of itself!"[29]

Hyde's pastoral solicitude meant that same-sex couples were welcomed and integrated in the church, where they could serve alongside other members. He considered homosexuality a gift from God to be celebrated and embraced within the safety of committed relationships. Disaffirming theologies that denied God's gift of sexuality to homosexuals revealed that "somebody is mixed up somewhere." Hyde was certain the doctrinal mistake belonged to others, not the gays and lesbians who carefully discerned God's will for their lives.[30]

A SPIRITUAL HOME

After many years of independent ministry, the Eucharistic Catholic Church affiliated with what would later become known as the Orthodox Catholic Church of America (OCCA), a denomination described by historian Julie Byrne as a "small but enduring jurisdiction that combines eastern and western Catholicisms."[31] Hyde was mentored by Archbishop Clement Sherwood, the small denomination's leader from 1932 until 1962, for three years before being ordained a bishop himself in 1957. The pair's relationship flourished because Sherwood never questioned the significant number of homosexuals active in ECC. After Sherwood's death in 1969, Hyde was elected OCCA's metropolitan archbishop and became the spiritual leader of the denomination.[32]

Throughout the decades, Hyde's ministry inspired countless others, and the independent Catholic movement became known for its gay-affirming doctrine and practice.[33] Among those mentored by Hyde was Bishop Michael Francis Augustine Itkin, a controversial visionary described by some as the "gay pope." Ordained by ECC in 1957, Itkin was active in gay liberationist circles of the sixties and seventies and today is celebrated as St. Mikhael of California by the Moorish Orthodox Church in America.[34]

In addition to Michael Itkin, Hyde also worked with and supported Robert Clement, who in 1968 founded the Church of the Beloved Disciple, a gay-affirming Christian community in Manhattan. Clement marched as an openly gay priest in New York City's first Gay Pride Parade and, in 1970, officiated the first public Catholic "holy union" ceremony.[35] A few years later, Hyde appointed Clement as head of both the American Catholic Church and the ECC. As gay liberation advanced in the twentieth century, independent Catholicism gave believers such as Hyde, Itkin, and Clement the structures and supports they needed to foster vibrant queer-affirming communities.[36]

The community that Hyde served was eclectic and often divided by differences of doctrine, politics, and practice. In 1959, for example, Itkin began his own church after accusing Hyde of neglecting the more demanding call to faith-based political activism. Hyde himself schismed from OCCA in 1995 when the denomination began to ordain women.[37] Like many gay Catholic men, his passion for diversity in Christian leadership ended at representation for gay men.

Despite Hyde's limitations, he remained committed to pastoral sensitivity and hospitality, the affirmation of same-sex relationships, and eucharistic devotion until his death in 2010. His Catholic faith gave him a lifelong vision for ministry that would have been impossible without the Roman Catholic formation he received.

FROM ASSIMILATION TO PRIDE

After George Hyde's establishment of the Eucharistic Catholic Church in 1946, it would be more than two decades before a second national LGBTQ ministry emerged from within the Roman Catholic Church. By then, circumstances in society and the Church had changed. Movements for gay and lesbian civil rights shifted from the assimilationism of the fifties and sixties to the Gay Pride that openly challenged traditional sexual norms in the seventies.

In the final decades of the twentieth century, gay and lesbian Catholics burst out of the closet with new demands for pastoral care, theology to reflect their experiences, and ecclesiastical support for their civil rights. The most prominent ministry that pushed for change was DignityUSA, an organization that, at its peak, had more than ten thousand members spread across the United States and world. Decades prior, however, it was George Hyde's ECC that first set the mold for gay- and lesbian-affirming Catholic community.

Chapter 2

SOME VERY SPECIAL PEOPLE

DignityUSA, Gay Pride, and the Struggle for Catholic Affirmation

> But we are not among those who shrink back
> and so are lost, but among those who have faith
> and so are saved.
>
> —Hebrews 10:39

SOCIAL REVOLUTION AND CATHOLIC MINISTRY IN THE 1960S

DignityUSA rose to prominence as the sixties came to an end. It had been a heady decade for civil rights and liberation movements. Democratic revolutions in the developing world threw off the yokes of colonial oppression. In the United States, the black and Chicano movements challenged the racism that had pervaded society from the nation's founding. Women, awakened to the evils of patriarchy by the feminist revolution, demanded equal rights and social and economic opportunities alongside men. The summer of 1969 saw LGBTQ people in the United States come out against the homo/transphobia that silenced them before. A new era of pride characterized by radical honesty and political activism beckoned queer folks out of the closet and into the streets.[1]

The Roman Catholic Church was not unaffected by the social transformations taking place around it. Underrepresented and marginalized groups organized to challenge social sin in the Church. New fields of contextual and political theologies grew from Catholic engagement with modernity and experiences of oppression at the grassroots. The Black and Latinx civil rights movements confronted racism in the hierarchy. Catholic women questioned the centuries-old misogyny that denied their gifts and prohibited their full participation in ministry.[2] Within this tumultuous social and ecclesial milieu, it was only a matter of time before LGBTQ Catholics began to demand reform of the communities and institutions that refused them pastoral care.

Within the Church, Vatican II had initiated a sea tide of change. John XXIII described the Council as an *aggiornamento*—an opening up of the Church to the world. *Gaudium et Spes*, the Pastoral Constitution on the Church in the Modern World, called Catholics to identify with "the joys and the hopes, the griefs and the anxieties of the men of this age, especially those who are poor or in any way afflicted" (no. 1).[3] Ideally, this meant that the world would no longer be considered a threat to faith, but a springboard for greater understanding and evangelization.

The Council had an immense impact on pastoral ministry. Theologians, church leaders, and ministers paid closer attention to the "signs of the times" as they discerned, in the words of theologians Robert Imbelli and Thomas Groome, "the social and historical contexts in which Christians are called to live out the full responsibilities of their faith."[4] This included a turn to the experiences of the poor, excluded, and suffering as a source for theological reflection. In Latin America, liberation theologian Gustavo Gutiérrez, a priest who ministered in Peruvian slums, defined theology as a "critical reflection on Christian praxis in light of the word of God."[5] Many Latin American bishops, such as San Salvador Archbishop (and now Saint) Oscar Romero, reoriented their ministry and leadership to reflect the Church's new social, political, and spiritual priorities.[6]

Culture became a focal point for evangelization. Catholic ministers searched for what *Ad Gentes*, the Council's Decree on the Mission Activity of the Church, described as the "genius and the dispositions of each culture" (no. 22).[7] Vatican II affirmed the good in every society and recognized God's work among the unevangelized. How could ministers cultivate the seeds of faith already planted in human hearts? Where was God moving in the world, and how could culture serve as a vehicle for, rather than an impediment to, the Church's mission?

Some Catholics looked to the sciences and humanities to inform their ministry and theology. Vatican II acknowledged that the Church had much to learn from fields such as psychology, anthropology, and sociology in its mission to communicate the gospel. The Council fathers believed that human knowledge could "elevate the human family to a more sublime understanding of truth, goodness, and beauty, and to the formation of considered opinions which have universal value" (*Gaudium et Spes* 57). *Ad Gentes* advised that evangelists be well trained in the sciences and humanities to support their divine calling (no. 16). The Church's dialogue with these disciplines yielded fresh approaches to theological reflection and new opportunities for pastoral applications.

A SUPPORT GROUP FOR CATHOLIC GAYS AND LESBIANS

One priest who took the Council's admonition to engage culture and science seriously was Fr. Pat Nidorf, an Augustinian living in San Diego. Ordained in 1962, Nidorf was an artist who attended seminary in the years leading up to Vatican II.[8] As a professional psychologist and minister, Nidorf, known as Fr. Pat, witnessed the exclusion that LGBTQ Catholics experienced within a tradition ill-equipped to care for their needs. He later recounted,

> The Catholic gay people whom I had met were frequently bothered by ethical problems and identity with the church. It seemed obvious that the church wasn't meeting the needs of the gay community. In counseling gay Catholics, there always seemed to be an excessive and unreal problem of guilt that was sometimes reinforced in the confessional instead of being resolved.[9]

At a provincial meeting in early 1969, he proposed a support group for gay and lesbian Catholics, and his brother priests backed the project.[10]

Nidorf's new ministry met once a month in San Diego before it moved to Los Angeles, where gatherings took place in private homes. Fr. Pat advertised in the *Los Angeles Free Press* and the *Advocate*, a U.S. gay-interest magazine.[11] He named the group Dignity, he said, "since one of our basic goals was to bring dignity into the spiritual and social lives of some very special people."[12] An early list of Dignity's priorities included working "for the development of [the Church's] sexual theology and for the acceptance of Gays as full and equal members of the one Christ," "justice and social acceptance through education and legal reform," and affirming the dignity of gay Catholics "to aid them in becoming more active members of Church and society."[13]

The ministry came with risks. To prevent critics from interfering and to foster a community of honesty and vulnerability, Nidorf required that early members pay a fee, carry a membership card, and, at times, interview in person before he would give them access. A newsletter informed members of where they would meet from month to month.[14] In their interactions together, most members used only their first names or pseudonyms to protect their identities.[15]

Dignity's first constitution, written in May 1970, pushed for an evolution in the Church's moral teaching and theological anthropology, contending that "homosexuality is a natural variation on the use of sex."[16] Three years prior to the American Psychiatric Association's decision to de-pathologize homosexuality, Dignity destigmatized same-sex desire as healthy, natural, and moral. The organization argued that gays and lesbians—like everyone else—possessed a natural right to "responsible and fulfilling" sexual intimacy that could be exercised "with a sense of pride."[17]

On September 26, 1970, Dignity moved its meeting to the basement of St. Brendan's in Los Angeles, the first parish to accept the organization.[18] As Dignity spread across the United States in the early seventies, it found other gay-friendly parishes and priests who opened their doors to welcome the group. Many of the parishes that would welcome Dignity, such as St. Francis Xavier in Manhattan, belonged to religious orders that had more latitude for bold pastoral initiatives than diocesan parishes. Some chapters offered a prearranged donation in exchange for the space.[19]

In coordination with parish leadership, Dignity held support groups, Masses, prayer meetings, and social events. Unlike parish-based gay and lesbian ministries that emerged later, Dignity maintained its independence from parochial oversight. Still, Dignity members intended to remain in the Church, a choice that allowed them to build trusting relationships within the institutional church. A network of priests emerged to support the community's sacramental and pastoral needs. As late as 1989, James Bussen, Dignity president from 1985 to 1989, claimed that 99 percent of Dignity Masses had "at least some form of ordained, facultied priests saying Mass for them at least some of the time."[20]

Throughout the seventies and eighties, homophobia was still the rule in most of the Church and society. This meant that Dignity had a complicated relationship with parts of the hierarchy. Many bishops tolerated Dignity in parishes if members did not raise a ruckus or openly challenge church teaching.[21] Other bishops were more suspicious. In Los Angeles, for example, Dignity was welcome at St. Brendan's until the archdiocese learned about the group. In February 1971, the newly appointed Archbishop Timothy Manning summoned Fr. Nidorf and his provincial to the chancery, where the prelate complained about their lack of communication and disrespect for his authority. Manning made it clear that Nidorf, an Augustinian, was unwelcomed to minister in the archdiocese without his permission.[22] After telling the pair that an organization like Dignity was "untenable" in the Catholic Church, Manning forbid Fr. Pat from any contact with the group.[23] On February 20, 1971, Nidorf announced his resignation from Dignity leadership at a community potluck.[24]

GROWING INTO A NATIONAL NETWORK

Lay leaders were prepared to take Nidorf's place. By the time Fr. Pat resigned, several were already exercising pastoral and organizational ministry. So began Dignity's long tradition of lay leadership. If members of the hierarchy would not care for LGBTQ Catholics, they would care for each other. More than twenty years after the group's founding, then DignityUSA President Patrick Roche acknowledged, "We grew up as a community that self-ministered....There was never really a period of complete acceptance."[25]

In Fr. Nidorf's place, Dignity members elected Bob Fournier (Pelletier) to become the group's first general chairman. Fournier

---

oversaw many of the functions that would become fundamental to Dignity's mission. In March 1971, he edited the national newsletter in which he vowed that "Dignity will continue. Why? Because there is a need. As Gay Catholics, we love the church. We want the sacraments."[26] Fournier employed developing understandings of theology and psychology to defend gay and lesbian sexualities as moral and natural expressions of human nature.[27] Under his leadership, the group began a monthly speaker series that welcomed academic, social, and spiritual leaders. The first to be invited in March 1971 was Dr. Evelyn Hooker, a UCLA psychologist whose field-defining research argued that homosexuality was not a mental illness.[28]

Spiritual ministries were not forgotten, either. In August 1971, Dignity held its first retreat at St. Andrew's Benedictine Priory in Valyermo, California. With Fournier and others freed from episcopal constraints, Dignity began reaching out to LGBTQ Catholics around the United States with their inclusive message. Before the internet, much of the group's work was a ministry of correspondence with those who were struggling to reconcile their faith and sexuality. Dignity volunteers answered thousands of inquiries from around the country and world.[29]

Dignity's work bore fruit, and the group's first chapter outside of Southern California formed in Louisville, Kentucky, in November 1971. This reflected a general pattern that would continue in the decades to come. While LGBTQ ministries tended to thrive in coastal metropolitan areas with sizable LGBTQ populations, they also flourished when welcomed in more rural, Midwestern, and Southern contexts. LGBTQ ministry, like every work of God, came with many surprises.

Dignity's first annual meeting was held in Los Angeles on February 19, 1972. At that time, there were 198 members, including twenty-five priests, four brothers, and two seminarians.[30] Prior to the Vatican crackdown in the 1980s, Catholic priests, religious, and seminarians were much freer to openly support the gay and lesbian movement, a fact that was evident in the founding of Dignity/New York (Dignity/NY). In September 1972, Joe Gilgamesh (Killion), the newly elected Dignity president, embarked on a nationwide campaign to raise support for local Dignity chapters and begin a national network. While in New York, he met with Fr. John McNeill, a Jesuit moral theologian teaching at Woodstock College. Two years earlier, McNeill had published a series of groundbreaking articles in the *Homiletic and Pastoral Review* titled "The Christian Male Homosexual."[31] As current DignityUSA executive Marianne Duddy-Burke wrote in her memorial reflection after McNeill's death, "These pieces were articulating the very same concepts the founders of Dignity were developing, only in much more learned and compelling language."[32]

At their meeting in New York City, McNeill gave Gilgamesh permission to reprint his work, and Gilgamesh asked McNeill to begin a Dignity chapter there. With fellow Jesuit Fr. Bob Carter, McNeill obliged Gilgamesh's request. The new group's purpose, according to McNeill, "was to bring the message of God's love and acceptance to Catholic gays and lesbians."[33]

Nearly a year after Gilgamesh's visit, close to one hundred people attended Dignity/NY's first meeting in the West Village.[34] By 1976, Dignity/NY was so well-established that Fr. Leo Gallant, an ambitious Marist priest who supported the ministry, sought to offer daily "gay Masses" across the boroughs.[35] Additional Dignity chapters soon formed in Chicago, Washington, D.C., Boston, San Francisco, and Seattle, and before long Dignity had enough grassroots collaboration to sustain a national office in Boston.[36]

SUPPORT FROM PRIESTS, BROTHERS, AND SISTERS

Throughout the 1970s, encouragement for gay and lesbian Catholics came from unexpected places. In March 1972, the National Federation of Priests' Councils (NFPC), an organization founded after Vatican II to represent priests in grassroots ministry, voted to create a taskforce on ministry to gays and lesbians. Two years later, the priests' organization approved a resolution calling for the decriminalization of homosexuality and objecting to discrimination against homosexuals in "employment, governmental services, housing, and child rearing involving natural or adoptive parents."[37]

The NFPC was not alone among church leaders. In 1974, the National Coalition of American Nuns condemned social and legal discrimination of homosexuals as immoral, and within a decade both the National Assembly of Religious Brothers (NARB) and National Assembly of Women Religious (later NARW, "of Religious Women") had issued their own statements expressing solidarity with gay, bisexual, and lesbian people.[38]

Communities of priests and men and women religious were lightyears ahead of the United States Conference of Catholic Bishops, which to this day campaigns against LGBTQ civil rights. The priesthood and religious life, these communities suggested, were compatible with being a good ally to the LGBTQ community. Even if most bishops remained silent or opposed Dignity, priests, pastors, and men and women religious knew that the Church needed to do a better job supporting LGBTQ Catholics.

DIGNITY, ETHICS, AND THE SEXUAL REVOLUTION

From its start, Dignity contributed to the Church's reflection on sexual ethics. At the height of the sexual revolution, Catholics were discerning the relationship between their faith and sexuality. Which parts of traditional Catholic teaching were fundamental to sexual flourishing, and which needed to be reinterpreted in light of contemporary experience and new understandings of human sexuality?

By the early seventies, many believed that the Church's official teaching needed to be reevaluated. In 1968, Pope Paul VI had released his controversial encyclical, *Humanae Vitae*, which maintained traditional prohibitions against the use of contraception for married couples. Upsetting many Catholics, the encyclical came despite the counsel of a Vatican commission that recommended the Church's approval of contraception. After the encyclical's release, most married Catholics rejected *Humanae Vitae* and continued using artificial birth control anyway, opening a deep chasm between the experiences of grassroots believers and the Church's authoritative teaching.[39]

Responding to the crisis that *Humanae Vitae* and the sexual revolution provoked, the Catholic Theological Society of America (CTSA) convened a Committee on Sexuality to investigate these issues more closely. Dignity members took the opportunity to offer their input. If new theological models for understanding human sexuality were needed for straight couples, the development of teaching for gay and lesbian believers was even more critical. As Bob Fournier had articulated years earlier, "Theologians must hear our voices and must realize that we are flesh and blood. We are not abstract moral cases."[40] Over Labor Day weekend of 1974, gay and lesbian Catholics met in Detroit to prepare a communique destined for the committee's consideration.[41]

Dignity's impact on the committee's reflections is unclear, but, nearly three years later, CTSA published *Human Sexuality: New Directions in American Catholic Thought*. The book dedicated more than thirty pages to homosexuality. Rather than prescribing a simple answer to whether same-sex relationships were morally acceptable, it offered a lengthy consideration of the scientific, historical, theological, and pastoral questions involved before providing twelve pastoral guidelines "offered with some degree of moral certitude." The fifth guideline affirmed that "homosexuals have the same rights to love, intimacy, and relationships as heterosexuals," a position very similar to Dignity's own statement of purpose from years before.[42]

Dignity encouraged other theologians to reflect on LGBTQ Catholic experience as well. In 1973, Fr. Pat Nidorf, who was still tangentially involved in Dignity's mission, sent a copy of the group's faith statement to Gregory Baum, a Canadian Augustinian priest, theologian, and ethicist who had contributed to Vatican II's documents on ecumenical and interreligious dialogue. Nidorf's letter inspired Baum to write an article titled "Catholic Homosexuals" for *Commonweal*, a lay Catholic publication.

Baum's piece was groundbreaking because it argued that same-sex relationships are not violations of God's plan for human sexuality, as the Church traditionally taught, but challenges to cultural norms, which could change according to time and context. For that reason, he contended, church teaching on homosexuality was more malleable than many supposed. Baum also argued that the Church, patterning its ministry after Christ's own, ought to love and welcome LGBTQ people rather than persecute and ostracize them. The theologian's praise for Dignity's compassionate ministry to homosexuals spread word of the group to a much wider Catholic audience.[43]

With more and more grassroots Catholics considering the spiritual needs of gays and lesbians, Dignity promoted its own printed materials. In March 1975, the group compiled and distributed a series of articles titled "Theological/Pastoral Resources." The booklet's authors were a who's who of names familiar to LGBTQ ministry today: Sr. Jeannine Gramick, then a member of the School Sisters of Notre Dame, professor of mathematics, and cofounder of Dignity/Baltimore and

Washington; Fr. Robert Nugent, originally a priest from the Archdiocese of Philadelphia who later joined the Salvatorian order and ministered alongside Sr. Jeannine Gramick; and Fr. Tom Oddo, a Holy Cross priest and professor at Stonehill College who would go on to become president of the University of Portland before his untimely death in 1989.[44] The early to mid-seventies were auspicious years full of hope and new possibilities for gay and lesbian Catholics. Dignity led the way.

FINDING DIGNITY IN FLOURISHING COMMUNITIES

As theological debates on homosexuality quickened in the Catholic Church, Dignity focused on building local communities. Members regularly met inside and outside of parishes, at regional gatherings and national conventions. Days and Weekends of Recollection provided a time for spiritual renewal and retreat. The line between prayer and socializing was often blurred, and alcohol played a role in both. An August 1976 newsletter from Dignity/NY thanked attendees for the "great cooperation in our friends bringing wine, etc. for the Liturgies," but then reminded that the socials afterward functioned "on a byo basis!"[45]

By 1979, there were eighty-one chapters across the United States, with some in unlikely places such as Lubbock, Texas; Cheyenne, Wyoming; Sioux City, Iowa; and Birmingham, Alabama.[46] Local chapters held independent charters but supported the regional and national levels of the organization with a percentage of members' dues. A charter gave local communities at least two representatives in the national House of Delegates, DignityUSA's governing body, in addition to other delegates awarded based on proportional representation.[47]

Chapters often had very different relationships with the hierarchy. In the 1980s, for example, Dignity/Detroit was known for its closeness to Most Holy Trinity, the parish that hosted it, and its support for archdiocesan fundraising initiatives.[48] The relationship between Dignity/NY and its archdiocese, by contrast, was far more antagonistic. In 1984, the *New York Times* reported Dignity's protest at the cathedral after Cardinal John O'Connor refused to sign a statement "required by the city's Executive Order 50 that groups receiving city funds not discriminate in employment or hiring because of 'sexual orientation or affectional preference.'"[49] Regional and national gatherings of Dignity delegates, meetings of the national officers, and DignityUSA's biennial conventions provided opportunities for elected representatives to discuss and discern the ministry's position on these pressing issues, not the least of which was the tension between Dignity's prophetic and conciliatory stances vis-à-vis the hierarchy.[50]

Local chapters supported committees with evocative names: liturgy, prayer, social action, priests, couples, consciousness-raising.[51] Outreach included ministries to prisoners, the elderly, women in shelters, the homeless, and, later, AIDS patients.[52] As in the broader LGBTQ community, affinity groups flourished. A subcommunity known as the Defenders "sought to educate the Dignity membership relative to the concerns and needs of those of us in the Levi/Leather scene" and was "dedicated to the principle that it is not incompatible to be both Roman Catholic AND active in the Levi and Leather scene."[53]

Dignity events reflected gay life. Chapters gathered in bars and clubs. Members danced in parish halls and competed against other gay and lesbian Christian communities in volleyball tournaments. Some sang in choirs and acted in plays, such as the 1973 performance of *The Fantasticks* by Dignity/Los Angeles.[54] Community filled vacation calendars. In August 1979, one group of East Coasters organized a temporary chapter on Fire Island, the well-known gay destination off Long Island.[55] A second summer "mission" in gay-friendly Provincetown, Massachusetts, began in the early 1980s and lasted through the early 2000s.[56]

Ongoing discernment about the relationship between Christian faith and sexuality remained a fundamental part of Dignity's mission. In 1984, Dignity's Task Force on Sexual Ethics began a years-long investigation to discover how members lived out their sexuality in relationship to their faith. After five years of surveys and several visits to Dignity communities around North America, the task force published a report that included: (1) an overview of the experiences of Dignity members; (2) pastoral resources for gay and lesbian Catholics; and (3) a hopeful and challenging vision for the future. The document, approved by the national House of Delegates in 1989, affirmed Dignity's "work to develop a common understanding of sexual ethics, to be Church in the lesbian and gay community, to integrate spirituality and sexuality, and to achieve the deeper communion that is the gift of the Spirit."[57]

Each member of DignityUSA received a copy of the task force report to serve as a resource for "conscience formation and spiritual growth."[58] Not all Dignity members approved of the study, however. In a missive to DignityUSA, Patti O'Kane of Dignity/Brooklyn described it as "long," "rather bland," and inconsistent. "There is nothing profound or novel about it," she explained, "that it took ten people and six years to complete."[59] O'Kane's response to the task force report revealed Dignity's perpetual struggle to represent a wide range of membership. Disagreement in the group was common, especially on matters of great personal and pastoral import.

Fostering Ecclesial Partnerships

As a vulnerable minority community in the Church and society, Dignity members recognized the value of partnerships with other LGBTQ ministries and groups. One of Dignity's early partners was the Salvatorian Gay Ministry Task Force, an initiative of the order's Peace and Justice Taskforce. The Salvatorians were vocal critics of the National Conference of Catholic Bishops' (NCCB) stance on gay and lesbian issues who, by 1974, had established their own National Center for Gay Ministry in Milwaukee and published a booklet on gay and lesbian ministry.[60]

As Dignity's reputation spread, it also networked with queer Catholics around the world. The group's first international offshoot was Acceptance, an Australian ministry founded in 1971 by lay leader Garry Pyle after he attended a Dignity gathering in the United States. Within a few years of its founding, Acceptance had chapters in major cities across Australia that supported a professional telephone counseling service, medical clinic, and choir, among other pastoral initiatives.[61] More recently, Dignity has affiliated with organizations such as the Global Network of Rainbow Catholics, founded in 2014 to advance LGBTQ civil rights and access to pastoral care around the world, and Equal Future, a humanitarian campaign to raise awareness in the Catholic Church about the abuse of LGBTQ children.[62]

"Other Places to Be on a Saturday Night": Dignity and Women

One of Dignity's ongoing areas of growth has been the inclusion of women in leadership and ministry. According to current DignityUSA executive Marianne Duddy-Burke, "There is and has a been a rampant sexism within Dignity that has had to be confronted."[63]

From its first ad for *Advocate* magazine in 1970, Dignity presented itself as a community for both men and women.[64] Unfortunately, membership rolls failed to reflect this ideal. Minutes from a 1973 steering committee meeting of the New York/New Jersey chapter gave voice to Dignity women who "felt that the large number of men attending our meetings would not exactly make the women feel at ease."[65] Three years later, a 1976 *New York Times* article revealed that Dignity/NY had 180 members but only a few women.[66] Some blamed visiting priests for the shortage of lesbians. In 1985, Dignity/NY's Feminist Issues Committee disclosed, "Maybe it is too much to expect attitudes to change quickly, but until we get the attitudes changed on the part of the priests ministering to us, women will find other places to be on a Saturday night."[67]

The exclusion of women from Catholic ministry and leadership did not preclude some Dignity members from identifying the struggle for gay equality as part of the struggle for women's liberation. In Dignity's early years, a few local chapters attempted to foster community for lesbians and bisexual women through women's groups. By the late 1970s and early 1980s, there was a blossoming of feminist consciousness in the national organization. In 1979, Deenie Dudley became the first regional director for Dignity/Atlanta. That same year, DignityUSA issued guidelines for gender-neutral theological language in its liturgies.[68]

Dignity leadership prioritized educating its grassroots members about women's issues. The February 1981 edition of the national newsletter provided a special insert titled "Women in Dignity" that highlighted women's experiences and celebrated their contributions to the ministry.[69] Around the same time, Women's Concerns became one of the most important national standing committees, its status reinforced by a monthly column in the newsletter titled "Moving the Mountains—Not for Women Only."[70]

The mid-eighties saw measured progress on women's issues. The National Committee on Women's Concerns took the lead with a study of women's needs in the organization. When Marianne Duddy-Burke submitted the group's report in 1985, there was only one woman—a straight ally—on the national board, and there had been no lesbians in national leadership for more than a decade. Duddy-Burke and other women vowed to challenge the all-male leadership, and they succeeded. Within a couple of years, DignityUSA's board of directors included several women, and a later revision to Dignity's national constitution mandated gender parity (later, called "gender diversity") in leadership.[71]

The Ups and Downs of Dialogue

Through its dozens of communities, Dignity sparked a movement. Like other marginalized Catholics, its members knew the power held by bishops to transform the Church. They found ready allies in Thomas Gumbleton and Joseph Imesch, auxiliary bishops in the Archdiocese of Detroit. In July 1974, Brian McNaught, then president of Dignity/Detroit, became embroiled in a public quarrel with *The Michigan Catholic*, Detroit's archdiocesan paper, after the publication dropped his column due to his advocacy on behalf of gay issues. In response, McNaught went on a hunger strike to raise awareness of homophobia in the Church.[72] Dignity members from around the country supported his cause, as did the two bishops. In a letter to McNaught, Gumbleton and Imesch promised to use their power on his behalf, saying, "We have a serious obligation to root out those structures and attitudes which discriminate against homosexuals as persons."[73]

Other ecclesiastical jurisdictions were not so amenable to Dignity's cause. On April 10, 1975, Dignity leaders met with representatives from the Archdiocese of New York to discuss their spiritual needs. According to those who attended, church officials were hesitant to offer church space for Dignity gatherings because they feared it could serve as an endorsement of homosexuality. Later in the meeting, the archdiocese's representatives offended the Dignity leaders by asking if the ministry's members were celibate.[74]

Dignity/NY was disappointed by dialogue and intensified pressure on the archdiocese by organizing a series of monthly vigils outside St. Patrick's Cathedral.[75] Still, the archdiocese remained unmoved. When a *New York Times* reporter asked for the archdiocese's opinion of Dignity's ministry, a chancery spokesperson responded that the group had a moral duty to discourage homosexuality. Anything else, the archdiocese claimed, was un-Catholic.[76]

In addition to local advocacy, Dignity leaders developed a plan to influence bishops at the national level. Part of the impetus for this venture may have come in February 1974, when the Pastoral Research

Committee of the NCCB published its "Principles to Guide Confessors in Questions of Homosexuality." Although the manual urged pastors to consider the origins of, and an individual's ability to "control," the homosexual tendency when providing counsel, it also reiterated traditional teaching that "genital sexual expression between a man and woman should take place only in marriage."[77]

On June 17, 1975, Dignity representatives met with bishops on the NCCB Liaison Committee in Washington, D.C., to discuss the pastoral guidelines. The meeting took months to plan and included those interested in gay and lesbian ministry from both organizations. After hearing Dignity's presentation, which called on the bishops to support gay and lesbian civil rights and pastoral care, Bishop Warren Boudreaux, the committee's leader, promised to communicate Dignity's concerns to the rest of the bishops at the NCCB's annual meeting to be held the following month.[78]

The gathering seems to have gone well and opened possibilities for future dialogue. A few months later, Dignity promoted a national day of fasting and prayer "with a theme of reconciliation of the Gay Catholic with their church." The event culminated in a trip to the NCCB meeting in Washington, D.C., where Dignity members spoke with Archbishop Joseph Bernardin of Chicago and Bishop James Rausch of Phoenix, then president of the NCCB. A subsequent DignityUSA report called on readers to

> rejoice with us in a very successful weekend....We cannot overemphasize the significance of this visit (with the bishops). It was not so much what was said by either of us, but the concrete expression of openness, dialogue, and their own recognition that we are, indeed, a reality to be contended with, ministered to, and sensitively understood.[79]

Following their meeting with NCCB representatives, Dignity members received an invitation to attend Call to Action, a conference for grassroots Catholic leaders to be held in Detroit in October 1976. The meeting, inspired by Paul VI's and Vatican II's calls for the laity to be more involved in the Church, brought together 1,400 delegates and ministers from across the country. Among these, Brian McNaught was the only openly gay representative, although other Dignity supporters attended to draw attention to their cause.

During the gathering, Call to Action attendees drew up a long list of proposals for action on issues such as clericalism, racism, feminism, and, thanks to Dignity's presence, homophobia. Dignity's contribution exhorted bishops to fight systemic discrimination against gay and lesbian people and promote pastoral initiatives.[80] Although the NCCB disregarded many of the recommendations that came from the Call to Action conference, Dignity's participation showed that gay and lesbian Catholics had a place within progressive Catholicism.[81]

Ecclesial advocacy continued in the years that followed. Dignity members attended the 1976 Eucharistic Congress in Philadelphia, where they distributed twenty thousand leaflets and held their own inclusive Mass apart from the official liturgies. When the Catholic Committee on Urban Ministry met for its annual conference at the University of Notre Dame in late October 1978, Dignity representatives attended to represent the interests of gay and lesbian believers.[82]

Dignity's activism even reached the highest echelons of the hierarchy. During John Paul II's first visit to the United States as pope, scores of Dignity members met him at every stop with their banners proudly unfurled. The pope's visit, one participant described, was a moment of both "ecstasy and agony"—ecstasy for the excitement that his visit engendered; agony at the Church's ongoing exclusion of gays and lesbians.[83] Dignity's visibility during John Paul II's visit did not endear him to the group's cause, but a few years later someone at the Vatican mistakenly sent a proclamation of the pope's apostolic blessing to Dignity's national headquarters. Church officials later claimed that the blessing had been sent in error and formally revoked it, but it hung in Dignity's national office until the organization went fully remote in 2007.[84]

In addition to its attempts to reach Pope John Paul II, Dignity leadership continued to dialogue with U.S. bishops throughout the late seventies and early eighties. There were meetings with representatives of the NCCB to follow up on the Call to Action conference but also with prelates such as Cardinal Timothy Manning of Los Angeles and Archbishop John Quinn of San Francisco to discuss local initiatives. In their effort to communicate with bishops, Dignity members took advantage of mass mailings. After the group published Brian McNaught's A Disturbed Peace: Selected Writings of an Irish Catholic Homosexual in 1981, it sent copies to every U.S. bishop.[85]

ACTIVISM, POLITICS, AND PUBLIC ADVOCACY

Beyond its lobbying of bishops, Dignity's advocacy spread to the public sphere, where the group's organizing activities reflected members' commitments to activism. Local chapters invited political activists to speak, and newsletters regularly updated Dignity members on the gay civil rights movement. Community education campaigns bore fruit in shared actions. In January 1977, Dignity lobbied for a national gay rights bill by sending letters to Catholic members of the House of Representatives.[86] Later that year, Dignity intervened in Dade County, Florida, where conservative singer Anita Bryant and religious leaders such as Coleman Carroll, the archbishop of Miami, were leading a crusade to overturn a local gay and lesbian civil rights ordinance. Their homophobic "Save Our Children" campaign succeeded by slandering gay people as child abusers and pederasts. Dignity, with other gay and lesbian groups, did not let the calumny go unanswered. Marching in South Florida's first gay pride parade, Dignity members carried signs that retorted, "Hi Mom! Hi Dad! We ARE Your Children."[87]

Following the setback for gay civil rights in Florida, Dignity representatives met with activist groups at the National Gay Leadership Conference in Denver to strategize their next steps. Turning to California, Dignity helped defeat Proposition 6, a 1978 ballot initiative that tried to ban homosexuals from working in public schools due to the threat they supposedly posed to children. Close to a year later, around 250 Dignity members attended the National March on Washington for Lesbian and Gay Rights.[88] It seemed as if gay liberation was in sight, and Dignity was present on several fronts to see it through.

The "Gay Disease"—Dignity and the AIDS Crisis

In February 1980, Dignity established a national office in Washington, D.C., where the organization's leadership would be close to U.S. political leaders and the NCCB headquarters. Just as Dignity and other groups were gaining momentum for gay civil rights, however, the first reports of AIDS began circulating in the media. On July 3, 1981, the *New York Times* reported forty-one cases of Kaposi's Sarcoma diagnosed

---

among homosexuals.[89] The rare skin cancer was a telltale sign of AIDS and warning of the public health calamity to come. Months after the *Times* report, the fall 1981 issue of Dignity's national newsletter covered the growing epidemic in an article titled "Gay Disease."[90] Little did Dignity members know how great an impact HIV would have on their community.

Over the next several years, AIDS decimated the LGBTQ population. By the time that effective antiretroviral therapies became widely available in 1995, more than 260,000 people in the United States had died from the disease.[91] The loss was overwhelming for LGBTQ communities.

Amid so much suffering and death, Dignity responded as best it could. Since many families rejected those diagnosed with HIV/AIDS, the ministry became a spiritual family for the dying. To those living with HIV/AIDS, Dignity distributed grants for food, housing, medicine, and doctors' bills. Local Dignity chapters helped provide spiritual care and sacraments for those suffering in hospitals. Working with, and often including, clergy, Dignity members visited the sick and organized public prayer services. In New York City, more than five hundred attended a Dignity Mass of Healing led by then Jesuit Fr. Bill McNichols to anoint those struggling with the disease.[92] As a final act of mercy for the dead, Dignity ensured that they received Catholic funerals. At a time when many parishes refused to bury AIDS victims, Dignity found priests who would preside at funeral Masses.[93]

Throughout the eighties and nineties, Dignity also welcomed the families of AIDS victims. Parents and other family members often learned about their children's (usually) gay sexuality when the latter were close to death. Marianne Duddy-Burke recalled,

> Dignity members embraced families who were devastated by this news and who often faced judgment when they sought out their own priests. More straight people became part of the Dignity community during and in the immediate aftermath of the AIDS crisis than at any other time. Moms, dads, siblings, and grandparents of AIDS victims became woven into the fabric of Dignity communities, often remaining friends for life of the frontline Dignity caregivers.[94]

Women were a fundamental part of Dignity's response to the AIDS crisis. As the disease decimated the numbers of healthy men in the group, Dignity women stepped up to provide care. It was a turning point in their relationship with the organization. The women's compassion, Marianne Duddy-Burke remembered, "helped build deep friendships and transformed many men's attitudes towards the women in their communities."[95]

Dignity prioritized compassion, but education was also a fundamental part of the group's AIDS ministry. Local chapters welcomed medical experts to discuss the disease's prevention and management. The community recognized its members' needs for holistic care and encouraged them to pursue therapy as a way of caring for their mental health.[96] Fr. John McNeill issued a Theological Statement on AIDS that provided a counternarrative to prevalent interpretations of the crisis. AIDS was not God's punishment for gays, he explained, but a theodicy that could not be explained. The Christian response to the epidemic was to join with the God of Jesus Christ in suffering with and ministering to those who were sick, cast out, and dying.[97] In the worst years of the AIDS crisis, Dignity did just that. To raise awareness and minister to the spiritual wounds of the LGBTQ community, Dignity held annual World AIDS Day Masses, liturgies, and services for healing.[98]

The Halloween Letter and Dignity's Expulsion from the Church

In 1986, Dignity was grappling with the AIDS epidemic as it continued to assert its presence in the institutional church. Despite its careful investment in relationships and dialogue with the Catholic hierarchy, nothing could safeguard the organization from the attack that would come from the Congregation for the Doctrine of the Faith (CDF), then headed by Cardinal Joseph Ratzinger, on October 30, 1986.

Earlier in the year, the Vatican's clampdown on dissent, especially regarding questions of sexual morality, was already taking shape. In the spring, Charles Curran, a well-known priest and moral theologian who had long dissented from church teaching on a number of sexual issues, lost his position as a professor of moral theology at the Catholic University of America. Although his job was supposedly protected by tenure, the Vatican decreed that Curran's dissent disqualified him as a professor of moral theology. The ecclesiastical order firing him came to the U.S. bishops from Cardinal Ratzinger, one of John Paul II's most trusted advisers, so there was no use arguing.[99]

The CDF proclamation had a chilling effect on theological discourse, but it would pale in comparison to the catastrophe awaiting gay and lesbian Catholic ministry on October 30, 1986, the day when the CDF publicly released its infamous "Letter to the Bishops of the Catholic Church on the Pastoral Care of Homosexual Persons." Also known as The Halloween Letter, both for the date of its release and the fear it instilled in the hearts of gay and lesbian Catholics, the missive sought to clarify official church teaching on "homosexual acts" by claiming the authority of magisterial tradition and speaking on behalf of God. While the letter struck a pitiable note for those suffering from the homosexual "condition," it offered no mercy for those proudly "living out of this orientation in homosexual activity."[100]

The missive stated, in unequivocal terms, that same-sex relationships were neither morally justifiable nor a part of God's plan for humanity.[101] The letter also heaped opprobrium on Catholics who undermined church teaching, especially if they claimed that gays and lesbians were oppressed by "unjust discrimination" in society. These homosexual advocates, Ratzinger maintained, had used propaganda to manipulate the Church and its pastors for purposes "so profoundly opposed to the teaching of the Church."[102] The hierarchy, the letter warned, was being exploited for political ends that ran contrary to the gospel.

Although the CDF proclamation paid lip service to the fact that "homosexual persons have been and are the object of violent malice in speech or in action," it also gaslighted them for the persecution they faced. The document said that when gay people and their allies organized for civil rights in secular society, "neither the Church nor society at large should be surprised when other distorted notions and practices gain ground, and irrational and violent reactions increase." Gay and lesbian activists, the letter asserted, brought violence upon themselves.[103]

The Halloween Letter was addressed to Catholic bishops around the world but was released in English.[104] It may have just as well been an attack on everything that Dignity stood for: the inherent goodness of gay and lesbian sexualities; the holiness of same-sex relationships; the necessity of fighting back against oppression in the Church and society.

The teaching stung gay and lesbian Catholics, and Dignity members refused to accept it without a response. James Bussen, Dignity's president, gave a series of rapid-fire media interviews. In remarks to the *Chicago Tribune*, he called the Vatican letter "an appalling and abysmal step backward."[105] On November 1, he went on CBS's *This Morning* to defend Dignity's work before flying to Washington, D.C., for a protest and press conference outside the apostolic nuncio's residence.[106] The following April, DignityUSA took out a full-page ad in *Newsweek* that contrasted the Church's homophobic teaching with Jesus's silence on the issue.[107] Dignity's message to the world was clear: Jesus sided with gays and lesbians, not the hierarchy.

MOVING FORWARD BY CHALLENGING EXCLUSION

The year of 1987 was a painful one for Dignity. In addition to the suffering and death that piled on from the AIDS crisis, dioceses and parishes began enforcing the Halloween Letter, which prohibited dissenting groups from meeting on church property. David Pais, a member of Dignity/NY, recounted, "When we were asked to leave the parish, I felt like I was being thrown out of my home. I had just lost my lover [to AIDS], so it was like a double whammy."[108] The first expulsion took place in Syracuse just two weeks before Christmas in 1986. According to James Bussen, by 1989 all but ten Dignity groups had been expelled from Catholic parishes, and those that remained kept "a low profile about it."[109]

Faced with a harsh new reality, Dignity began to evolve. In early February 1987, the national board issued guidelines for chapters to begin searching for new worship spaces.[110] Within local communities there were passionate debates about whether the organization should resist the CDF directive or try to appease Vatican leaders. Mark Jordan writes,

> Some stayed with the national organization, which became a kind of temporary government-in-exile. Others submitted to the official Vatican line and resumed their places in

regular parishes or joined an officially approved "diocesan outreach program." Yet other members perceived an opportunity to seek out "conservative" protest groups of one sort or another.[111]

Feelings at the 1987 national convention were raw when one delegate provocatively asked, "If we don't stand up for ourselves, who will?"[112] After much debate, the delegates voted to adopt what became known as the Bal Harbour Resolution, named after the Miami suburb where they met. New language added to DignityUSA's Statement of Position and Purpose openly flouted the CDF, affirming that "we can express our sexuality physically in a unitive manner that is loving, life-giving, and life-affirming."[113]

The Bal Harbour Resolution marked a clear departure from Dignity's earlier strategy of reconciling with the institutional church. James Bussen explained, "Dignity had been a go-along, get-along organization, but when someone throws stones at you, you react."[114] Many who were uncomfortable with Dignity's new position left the organization, but some saw it as a positive change. Patrick Roche, who became Dignity's president just a couple of years later, described the convention as the pivotal moment when Dignity finally embraced its identity as church outside of the institutional church.[115]

Two years after Bal Harbour, delegates to the 1989 national convention in San Francisco reaffirmed the ministry's new trajectory. Gay and lesbian sexuality, they proclaimed, was

> the holy gift of God. The overwhelming majority of us are able to say we are both sexually active and comfortable in our relationship with Christ. Being sexually active enables us to be more at ease with ourselves, more fulfilled in our relationships, more productive in our work and service.[116]

For more than thirty years since its expulsion, Dignity has continued building its original charisms. Many chapters now meet in Protestant spaces. Whenever the Catholic hierarchy takes an action that affects LGBTQ people, Dignity responds with a public statement holding spiritual leaders to account.[117] Although Dignity remains a community non grata in official church spaces, Dignity representatives have continued meeting with Catholic priests and bishops in private.[118]

Dignity also remains a thorn in the side of the hierarchy. In the wake of the 1986 expulsion, a *National Catholic Reporter* headline announced, "Dignity Leaders Take Up Cudgels after Eviction." In the same article, James Bussen warned church leaders, "If they're going to disrupt our lives, we're going to disrupt theirs."[119]

Dignity made good on the threat. In New York City, some members participated in the Cathedral Project, a years-long publicity campaign that included press releases and protests against Cardinal O'Connor.[120] Emerging from the cultural and political milieu that gave rise to ACT UP, Dignity held monthly demonstrations at the 10:15 a.m. Mass in St. Patrick's Cathedral. Just as the homilist would begin his homily, Dignity members would stand up in silent protest. Activists wore pink triangles—the mark given to homosexuals in German concentration camps during the Nazi regime—on lavender armbands to mark their identity.[121]

After a few weeks of protest, police began removing protestors from the cathedral, and the archdiocese took legal action. Eventually, some Dignity members were charged with disrupting a religious service and barred from entering the cathedral.[122] Dignity leaders remained undeterred and started holding their own Masses outside the building. Even to this day, a form of their protest continues. Each year during Pride, Dignity/NY holds a vigil on the sidewalk outside of St. Patrick's, a right won by the group in a case that went to the Supreme Court.[123]

Dignity's separation from the institutional Church has yielded substantial fruit, though at a significant cost. Freedom from the hierarchy has allowed Dignity to build an inclusive Catholic community that recognizes, affirms, and celebrates the gifts of women just as much as men. Unlike in the institutional church, women in Dignity regularly preside over Mass and preach. The current executive director and chief spokesperson is Marianne Duddy-Burke, who has served in that role since 2007.

A ministry freed from CDF oversight also allows Dignity to respond much more quickly to changing social mores and pressing social justice issues. As the gay and lesbian movement has blossomed into the much larger LGBTQIA+ movement, DignityUSA has been at the forefront of trans-, queer-, intersex-, and asexual-affirming theologies and ministries.[124] The group's unconditional acceptance of all sexual orientations and genders sets it apart from much of the institutional

Catholic Church, which remains hostile to non-cisgender and/or non-heterosexual people.

Dignity's outsider status brings its own challenges as well. Many members bear emotional and spiritual wounds from decades of conflict with the institutional church, and these do not heal easily. Separation from traditional parishes also means that Dignity communities may sometimes appear, in the words of Mark Jordan, as a "sliver of a church" or a "'special interest' congregation," lacking the diversity and charisms of the entire body of faith.[125] Finally, questions remain over Dignity's Catholic identity. Is reconciliation possible or even desired? What can the institutional Catholic Church offer a community that has become self-sufficient and confident in its own vision of Catholic spirituality, ethics, and community?

For more than half a century, Dignity has negotiated Catholic faith and LGBTQ identities. It went from bridge-building with ecclesiastical leaders and seeking acceptance in parishes and dioceses to creating and sustaining its own communities on the margins of the Church. The process has been fraught for Catholic leaders and Dignity members alike. Sometimes the lines dividing them were clear; other times they were not.

Indeed, in the early seventies, one of Dignity's most steadfast supporters and sought-after speakers was Sr. Jeannine Gramick, a member of the School Sisters of Notre Dame. In 1977, with the help of Fr. Bob Nugent, a Salvatorian priest, she founded New Ways Ministry, a national organization to educate Catholics on gay and lesbian issues. Like Dignity, New Ways Ministry has been controversial and drawn rebuke from the Catholic hierarchy. Still, more than half a century later, Gramick and her supporters continue to inspire advocacy for LGBTQ people. The following chapter will share New Ways Ministry's story of survival and hope.

Chapter 3

CLOSENESS, COMPASSION, AND TENDERNESS

New Ways' Half Century of Advocacy and Pastoral Care

> I am about to do a new thing;
>   now it springs forth, do you not perceive it?
> I will make a way in the wilderness
>   and rivers in the desert.

—Isaiah 43:19

SOWING AND REAPING FOR THE KINGDOM OF GOD

In the Synoptic Gospels, Jesus tells the parable of the sower who wantonly throws seed to the wind. Some gets eaten by birds. Some shoots up among rocks but withers with the noonday sun. A third batch sprouts and is choked out by thorns. Some of the seeds, though, fall on good soil and reach maturity.[1]

The story is an apt image for God's work in the world. God generously sows, and sometimes, improbably, the seeds take root and grow, multiplying the sower's investment many times over.

Such was the case with LGBTQ Catholic ministries from the late 1980s until the early 2010s. Some were nonstarters; others flourished for a while then withered away; many adapted to survive a harsh environment; and a lucky few fell onto well-cultivated ground that was ready to receive them. In each case, God's goodness to LGBTQ Catholics was apparent. The seeds may have germinated in surprising places. The conditions were less than ideal. But grace was manifest in ministries that showed the Spirit moving among the people of God.

After the Vatican released its 1986 Halloween Letter, Dignity, the most prolific and best organized LGBTQ Catholic ministry in the world, no longer had a physical home in the Church. The process of expelling local Dignity chapters from parishes was excruciating. As the AIDS epidemic ravaged the LGBTQ community, the hierarchy enforced a no-tolerance policy for dissenting voices.

Dignity's expulsion, however, did not mean the end of LGBTQ Catholic ministry. The resilience of God's growing kingdom among queer folks and their allies took many forms. Some, like New Ways Ministry (NWM) and Fortunate Families, became national organizations. Others, like Manhattan's Gay and Lesbian Catholic Ministry at the Church of St. Paul the Apostle, were local initiatives that flourished under the care of supportive pastors and communities. Throughout the many decades of John Paul II's and Benedict XVI's papacies, these communities had to carefully balance their public Catholic identities with the pastoral care they provided for LGBTQ people. Survival demanded careful negotiations and a deft ability to maneuver the many levels of ecclesial authority.

NWM is the longest-running and most well known of the national organizations that thrives on the edges of the institutional church. Cofounded in 1977 by Sr. Jeannine Gramick, SSND, and Fr. Robert Nugent, SDS, NWM has helped build a more affirming church through decades of education, advocacy, and ministry initiatives.

A Nun, a Priest, and a Risky Apostolate

NWM's story begins with Jeannine Gramick, who left her Philadelphia home in 1960 to join the School Sisters of Notre Dame in

Baltimore. She taught high school mathematics before becoming a professor at the College of Notre Dame Maryland and earning her PhD in mathematics education from the University of Pennsylvania in 1975.[2]

While in graduate school, Gramick befriended Dominic Bash, a flamboyant gay man, former seminarian, and hairdresser who would go on to become a prominent AIDS activist. Bash's story of marginalization in the Church was emblematic of what many LGBTQ Catholics experienced. "I was brought up as a Roman Catholic and taught to love one another," he said. "Yet, they couldn't love me and I couldn't live a lie."[3] When Bash asked Gramick, "What is the Catholic Church doing for my lesbian and gay sisters and brothers?" she interpreted his question as a call from God to act.[4]

At the time, there were scarce resources for gay and lesbian ministry so Gramick proceeded on her own. She began by coordinating a gay- and lesbian-inclusive Mass for Bash's queer Catholic friends in his living room and, after returning to Baltimore in 1972, hosting group discussions and counseling in her convent.[5] Her ministry blossomed. With the encouragement of her religious superiors, Gramick helped start the Washington, D.C., and Baltimore chapters of Dignity in 1972 and 1973, respectively. As a woman religious who recognized the limits of Catholic teaching on homosexuality, she quickly became a sought-after speaker and writer within these communities.[6]

Fr. Robert Nugent grew up in Norristown, Pennsylvania, just outside Philadelphia's city limits. He was ordained for the Archdiocese of Philadelphia in 1965 and saw himself as "a typical Irish Catholic priest."[7] His career trajectory, however, was anything but ordinary. In 1971 he was serving at a hospice for the homeless when he read about Gramick's work in the *Philadelphia Bulletin*. He wrote to her with a casual offer to assist, and she responded with an invitation to attend a meeting of gay Christians.[8] Sensing a new mission to counseling and pastoral work, Nugent left parish ministry and began serving with Gramick. In 1975, he separated from a rocky relationship with the Archdiocese of Philadelphia to affiliate with the Salvatorians, a religious order at the forefront of progressive causes. "Jesus went to the bars and restaurants to help," Nugent said, "and that's the kind of calling I had."[9]

Gramick and Nugent were well prepared for pastoral work. Both shared a profound capacity to listen, empathize, and learn from gays and lesbians. Decades after meeting, they reflected on how "the Lord called us in different ways to engage in a public ministry with and on behalf of a group of people who have traditionally been neglected or abused by some segments of the Church."[10] They were also willing to challenge the status quo. Nugent admitted they "knew it was risky, because Catholics weren't talking and writing about sexuality," but they persevered, believing that the Church could change.[11]

Educating the Church

Around that time, there were signs of hope in the wider Church. In 1978, Gramick and Nugent wrote to supporters, "Statements from Catholic bishops, diocesan newspaper editorials, peace and justice groups, organizations and communities of religious women and men all indicate that we are in the initial state of a courageous response to a sensitive and complex but vital ministry."[12]

One promising sign came from Bishop Francis Mugavero of Brooklyn, who in 1976 addressed a letter to those struggling with the Church's teaching on sexuality. Mugavero characterized homosexuals as hurting and confused but also lamented the way they were mis-understood and "at times" suffered from unjust discrimination. "We pray," he said, "that through all the spiritual and pastoral means avail-able they will recognize Christ's and the Church's love for them and our hope that they will come to live in his peace."[13]

Mugavero's pastoral approach encouraged Gramick and Nugent in their own work. In 1976, the pair joined the Quixote Center, a Catholic social justice organization outside of Washington, D.C., and began offering workshops named after a line from Mugavero's letter that pledged to "find *new ways* to communicate the truth of Christ."[14] The following year, they opened an office in Mount Rainier, Mary-land, and founded NWM as an independent nonprofit organization dedicated to educating the Church on homosexuality.

In addition to providing spiritual support and counseling for gays and lesbians, NWM gave workshops for parishes and dioceses. In the summer of 1978, a series of three Los Angeles workshops, supported by archdiocesan leaders, drew more than two hundred participants.[15] Discussions focused on gay and lesbian experiences and the need for pastoral care, not moral absolutes. "The real moral problem," Gramick asserted in 1979, "is the lack of justice and love shown in dealing with gay people. It is time for the Church to make recompense for this situation."[16]

To this day, NWM workshops remain one of the ministry's most popular programs and are offered for church staff, LGBTQ Catholics, family members, and allies alike. The daylong gatherings cover everything from biblical interpretation to queer spirituality. According to NWM, Building a Bridge workshops have taken place in more than 90 percent of U.S. dioceses over the last half century. Usually, group facilitators work with faith communities that are in the earliest stages of reaching out to LGBTQ people by helping participants understand their own gifts and callings while also exploring new opportunities for evangelization outside the parish.[17]

A chief goal of the workshops is to provide space for LGBTQ Catholics to share their experiences. By focusing on "storytelling and dialogue,...many walls of ignorance and fear are broken down, and bridges are built right in the course of the workshop."[18] Attendee evaluations reveal NWM's effectiveness. After participating in a 1984 workshop, one woman religious shared,

> My own very limited knowledge of homosexuality led me to misunderstand much of the problem. It was only because of the injustices perpetrated that I gave any thought to the issue at all. Your own faithfulness to church teaching coupled with a sensitivity to the plight of the homosexuals and the scientific data you presented has helped my own attitudes to open up considerably.[19]

A Flurry of Publications

Nugent and Gramick made an immediate impact on the gay and lesbian Catholic movement through their prolific writing. Even prior to NWM's founding, the pair collaborated for Dignity's 1975 publication of *Homosexual Catholics: A Primer for Discussion*, a booklet that would affectionately become known as the "gay catechism."[20] There was more to come in the years ahead. In 1978, Nugent and Gramick co-edited *A Time to Speak: A Collection of Contemporary Statements from U.S. Catholic Sources on Homosexuality, Gay Ministry and Social Justice*, which offered positive assessments of gays and lesbians from Catholic and civil rights leaders. Written for "social action days, workshops, and large gatherings," the booklet was so successful that it required a second printing a few months after the first.[21] Two decades later, their 1995 volume, *Voices of Hope: A Collection of Positive Catholic Writings on Gay and Lesbian Issues*, expanded NWM's affirming moral, theological, and pastoral evaluation of LGBTQ people, their relationships, and the gifts they bring to the Church.[22]

Many NWM books were responses to Vatican teaching. Following the CDF's 1975 *Persona Humana: Declaration on Certain Questions Concerning Sexual Ethics*, Nugent edited *A Challenge to Love: Gay and Lesbian Catholics in the Church*, which called for solidarity and new approaches to pastoral care.[23] When the CDF expelled Dignity from Catholic parishes in 1986, Gramick, with the help of coeditor Pat Furey (a pseudonym), published *The Vatican and Homosexuality: Reactions to the "Letter to the Bishops of the Catholic Church on the Pastoral Care of Homosexual Persons."*[24] At one of the most perilous times for LGBTQ Catholic ministries, NWM fearlessly amplified twenty-five voices that challenged the Church's exclusion of sexual minorities.

Other works were educational. In 1983, *Homosexuality and the Catholic Church* came out of NWM's first national symposium and traced changing social, scientific, and ecclesial attitudes toward gay and lesbian people.[25] By 1992, Gramick and Nugent were combining their wisdom from decades of ministry to write *Building Bridges: Gay and Lesbian Reality in the Catholic Church*.[26] Recognizing how fraught the book could be within a church that struggled with questions of sexual identity and morality, spiritual guru Richard Rohr hailed the authors for being "courageous enough to stay in with their church on this perilous path to wisdom."[27]

In addition to these volumes, Gramick and Nugent regularly contributed to dialogue in secular and religious journals. At the height of the AIDS epidemic, they opened a special issue of the *Journal of Homosexuality* with an essay on the perils of advocacy in religious spaces.[28] In 1987, Gramick lamented the maltreatment of lesbians in *Concilium*, a European Catholic journal known for its progressive theology. The article raised such a ruckus that several European dioceses filed complaints with the Vatican.[29]

Other pieces were directed toward nonacademic audiences. Over the years, both Gramick and Nugent wrote for publications such as *America*, *National Catholic Reporter*, and *The Christian Century*. Topics were diverse. Sometimes Gramick and Nugent provided counsel for hurting families.[30] Other times, they criticized Courage, a Catholic ministry that treats same-sex attraction as an illness.[31]

Of all its published resources, one of NWM's most impactful forms of outreach was its quarterly periodical *Bondings*, which delivered detailed reports of news affecting gay and lesbian Catholics. An early issue from the fall of 1979, for example, covered the National Dignity Convention, gay ministry in England and Holland, Gramick's ongoing study of lesbian experience, updates on civil rights actions, and NWM's annual budget.[32] The newsletter, now under the direction of NWM executive director Francis DeBernardo and managing editor Robert Shine, continues *Bondings'* original mission through an active online presence and email LISTSERV.

NEW WAYS FOR LESBIANS

From NWM's earliest years, Gramick and Nugent focused on ministry to lesbians, a group that had been neglected by many male-dominated Catholic ministries. In 1978, Gramick won a $38,000 grant from the National Institute of Mental Health for a three-year "Study of the Coming Out Process and Coping Strategies of Lesbian Women." More than one hundred volunteers participated, and data gathered from the study reinforced NWM's capacity to serve women.[33] Subsequent to the study, Gramick explained how Catholic lesbians face unique challenges because they "bear the double social disadvantage of being female and homosexual in patriarchal, heterosexist institutions" and "must constantly struggle to maintain church allegiance and to challenge their church's persistent blindness to lesbianism."[34]

Spirituality and leadership development were key elements of NWM's work with lesbians. The same year that Gramick won funding for a study of lesbian experiences, NWM partnered with Dignity to offer a retreat for lay lesbians, one of the first of its kind.[35] Many of the retreat attendees coalesced into a new group dedicated to women's issues and lesbian Catholic visibility. The organization became known as the Conference of Catholic Lesbians (CCL) and began holding regular gatherings where members came to hear women speakers, participate in women-led liturgies, and organize against the mutually reinforcing realities of homophobia and misogyny in the Church.[36]

LESBIAN NUNS AND GAY PRIESTS

In 1979, NWM again expanded its ministry to gay women, but this time with a retreat in Hyattsville, Maryland, for women religious. The event, sensationalized by the prospect of "lesbian nuns," brought NWM one of its first major controversies. Upon learning of the retreat, the Archdiocese of Washington, then led by Cardinal William Baum, notified U.S. bishops and heads of religious orders that NWM did not have his permission to hold the retreat. A second intervention came from the Vatican, which ordered Gramick's and Nugent's superiors to cancel the event altogether. Although Nugent bowed out from planning, Gramick did not, and five women attended the retreat, including Charlotte Doclar, SSND, who would go on to work with NWM for a year after the retreat.[37]

NWM's ministry to women religious grew through the mid-eighties with regional conferences and symposia.[38] Since 1990, NWM has also facilitated Womanjourney Weavings (WW), "a program of support and education for lesbian sisters, congregational leaders, and formation/vocation ministers."[39] As a leader in many of these initiatives, Gramick has spoken extensively and written on the identities, gifts, and experiences lesbian women religious bring to the Church.[40]

More recently, NWM has also offered annual retreats for gay priests and brothers. Decades after the first retreat for lesbian women religious, these gatherings remain controversial. In 2018, a retreat hosted at the Siena Retreat Center in Racine, Wisconsin, drew the ire of Milwaukee Archbishop Jerome Listecki, who warned, "This event is not in line with Catholic Church teaching and is in no way connected to or endorsed by the archdiocese, and New Ways Ministry is not a Catholic organization."[41]

After Listecki's disavowal, alt-right Catholic media piled on with their own criticisms. On the weekend of the retreat, more than two dozen protestors gathered outside the retreat center, which was maintained by the Dominican Sisters and doubled as a retirement home for elderly sisters.[42] To mitigate the threat of violence from protestors, the sisters had to hire extra security to protect their community and retreat attendees. NWM executive director Francis DeBernardo responded to criticism that the retreat encouraged gay priests to be sexually active. "Our programs," he said, "are designed to help people who want to live out their goal of celibacy in authentic ways and also ways that respects their individuality. Celibacy doesn't mean pretending to be heterosexual. Celibacy can also mean being affirming of who you are as a gay man."[43]

GATHERING TOGETHER

For nearly half a century, NWM has been an unrivaled clearinghouse for LGBTQ Catholic-related news, networking, and resources. A chief method of disseminating information and fostering new ministries has been its quinquennial symposia. The first national symposium, held in Washington, D.C., in November 1981, was attended by more than two hundred people and endorsed by more than forty Catholic organizations. The meeting's aim was to provide "basic and solid information regarding homosexuality from the perspective of sociology, moral, pastoral and feminist theology, religious life and celibacy, as well as from the experience of lesbian and gay persons themselves."[44]

As with NWM's retreat for lesbian sisters two years before, the Archdiocese of Washington again sent out letters condemning the organization. The archdiocese may have also interfered with the symposium venue.[45] After applying to rent the National 4-H Center in Bethesda, Maryland, NWM leaders were shocked to find out they could not host the gathering there due to the symposium's sensitive topic. NWM chose to move the meeting to a nearby hotel and sued 4-H for violating its constitutional rights. Although the lawsuit was unsuccessful, NWM gained helpful publicity in the process.[46]

Since its first controversial gathering, there have been several other NWM national symposia with themes such as "From Water to Wine: Lesbian/Gay Catholics and Relationships" and "Justice and Mercy Shall Kiss: LGBT Catholics in the Age of Pope Francis." The meetings welcome LGBTQ Catholics, allies, celebrated theologians, and public figures from around the world. In 2012, for example, speakers included Sidney Auxiliary Bishop Geoffrey Robinson, ethicist Patricia Beattie Jung, and Maryland Governor Martin O' Malley. The symposia typically generate headlines but, more importantly, provide community, vision, and support for LGBTQ ministry leaders.

ON THE FRONT LINES OF THE FIGHT FOR CIVIL RIGHTS

One of NWM's most distinctive features has been its advocacy for LGBTQ civil rights. While many LGBTQ Catholic ministries avoid explicit involvement in U.S. politics, NWM has made the political a central part of its pastoral mission. For that reason, the group's activism often puts it at odds with diocesan and Vatican authorities.

Nugent's and Gramick's political work predated NWM's founding. In 1975, Nugent, then serving as a Dignity chaplain in Philadelphia, appeared before the Philadelphia city council to argue for a pro-gay civil rights ordinance. His public stand garnered good press but did not help his relationship with Cardinal John Krol, who opposed the measure and sent his own representative to publicly oppose him. The break in Nugent's relationship with Krol was one of the reasons he left archdiocesan ministry soon afterward.[47]

Half a decade later, Gramick and Nugent testified before the Baltimore city council in favor of another gay rights measure. Gramick's argument focused on civil liberties for those who disagreed with traditional Catholic moral teachings. "I support the civil rights of persons," she said,

> regardless of sexual orientation because of my own religious convictions even though the highest official representative of the Catholic Church here in Baltimore has expressed his opposition to the proposed amendment because the Catholic Church traditionally teaches that homosexual behavior is immoral. Such reasoning would logically imply support for the civil rights only of those persons whose personal life conforms to Catholic moral teachings. Such a posture is provincial at best; immoral, at worst.[48]

After Gramick gave her testimony, Archbishop William Borders, the prelate she referenced, signaled his disapproval in a letter to her provincial administrator, but no further action was taken.[49]

NWM's first *official* involvement in a civil rights campaign came in late 1977, when the ministry brought together U.S. Catholic leaders to defend a gay rights ordinance in Dade County, Florida. The measure, infamously opposed by the Archbishop of Miami and Anita

Bryant's *Save Our Children* campaign, "sparked the idea for a coalition of Catholics supporting civil rights for homosexual persons as an 'alternative Catholic voice.'"[50] The following year, NWM joined with Dignity and other groups to form the Catholic Coalition for Gay Civil Rights (CCGCR).

CCGCR's founding statement, which ran as an ad in the *Washington Star* and *National Catholic Reporter* in the fall of 1979, was eventually endorsed by more than three thousand Catholic individuals and organizations.[51] The manifesto held that "proclaiming the kingdom of God demands a vigorous public ministry of liberation from both personal and social forces that oppress people—persons with a homosexual orientation are oppressed people—they have a full and equal claim upon love and understanding and upon the pastoral concern of the Church." CCGCR employed Catholic social teaching to "support protective legislation (at all levels of society) that guarantee gay persons' basic human and civil rights relative to housing and employment."[52]

CCGCR was politically active for several years, resisting California's Proposition 6, a 1978 ballot initiative that would ban gays and lesbians from teaching in public schools, and supporting a civil rights measure in Wichita, Kansas, that was vigorously opposed by the local Catholic ordinary.[53] In 1979, the group urged Catholic members of Congress to expand the National Civil Rights Act to include sexual orientation and participated in the March on Washington for Gay Rights, an event that drew close to one hundred thousand gays, lesbians, and allies to mark the tenth anniversary of the Stonewall Riots.[54]

After CCGCR disbanded, NWM partnered with other Catholic organizations to make prophetic interventions. When Matthew Shepard was killed by a homophobic attack in 1998, for example, NWM and Pax Christi USA ran a full-page "Catholic Pledge to End Violence against Gay and Lesbian People" in the *New York Times*. Citing church teaching, the statement called on "all Catholics and people of goodwill to look into their hearts and weed out violent perceptions and behaviors."[55] Two thousand Catholics, including nine bishops, signed the statement.

NWM has also offered affirming Catholic perspectives in public debates on same-sex marriage, adoption, employment discrimination, and other issues. For several decades, the ministry has been one of only a few Catholic organizations to publicly oppose the Vatican. Take, for example, NWM's 1992 response to the CDF statement, "Some Considerations Concerning the Response to Legislative Proposals on the Non-discrimination of Homosexual Persons," which claimed "there is no right to homosexuality."[56] NWM's position paper, "A Time to Speak—Catholics for Lesbian and Gay Civil Rights," affirmed "the inherent dignity of lesbian and gay persons and we pledge our renewed support for their basic civil rights in the areas of employment, housing and public accommodations."[57] The prophetic statement ran in the *National Catholic Reporter* on November 13, 1992, and included three U.S. bishops among more than 1,500 other signatories.

More recently, NWM continues to offer an alternative Catholic voice to the homophobia and transphobia that are rife in Catholic institutions. In 2020, NWM worked with Dignity and other LGBTQ Catholic groups to submit an amicus brief to a federal court in support of Noel Koenke, a former campus minister at St. Joseph's University who sued for sexual harassment after the school urged her to remain in the closet. As a part of the Equally Blessed Coalition, NWM has met with Congressional leaders to lobby for pro-LGBTQ legislation and, in August 2021, NWM leaders spearheaded a theological defense for LGBTQ nondiscrimination in a position paper titled "A Home for All."[58]

ADVOCACY AND OPPOSITION IN THE CHURCH

Nugent and Gramick often succeeded in developing impactful relationships with the hierarchy. Although perpetually at odds with some ecclesial officials, there were moments when NWM broke through opposition to shape the institutional church. Measurable success came early when, in 1978, NWM served as a consultant to the U.S. Catholic Conference's Ad Hoc Committee for the Plan of Pastoral Action for Young Adults. Tasked with representing sexual minorities, NWM participated in the document's planning and later brought together a group of gay Catholics to respond to the first draft. The final draft appealed for the Church to "be with gay men and women, learn from them, and be their advocates."[59]

Nugent's and Gramick's work with the hierarchy carried them abroad. In 1979, the pair traveled to Europe to meet with English and

Dutch ministry leaders, including bishops. In the progressive Netherlands, the Catholic Council for Church and Society had just issued "Homosexual People in Society: A Contribution to the Dialogue within the Faith Community," a pastoral statement that reflected on gay and lesbian experiences in light of Scripture and Catholic teaching on human dignity.[60] In England and Wales, Nugent and Gramick worked with Quest, a group similar to Dignity, and met with church leaders who were then preparing "An Introduction to the Pastoral Care of Homosexual People." A final draft of the guidelines affirmed traditional church teaching on sexual morality but also noted the difference between unhealthy homosexual promiscuity and the stable, caring relationships of "two homosexual persons who feel incapable of enduring a solitary life devoid of sexual expression."[61]

After Gramick and Nugent's European tour, NWM published the Dutch and English and Welsh statements for U.S. audiences. The documents drew Vatican criticism, but they also served as templates for a few pastorally sensitive statements that were to come from U.S. dioceses and bishops in the years ahead.[62]

Closer to home, NWM worked with Catholics across a broad spectrum of the institutional church. In the fall of 1979, NWM representatives traveled to Richmond, Virginia, for the diocese's annual Christian Education Convention, attended the Eastern regional meeting of the Catholic Committee on Urban Ministry, and spoke to a women's group at St. Camillus parish in Silver Spring, Maryland, among other activities.[63]

Dialogue and Relationship Building with Bishops

Dialogue with U.S. bishops was a priority. Gramick and Nugent met privately with some prelates who were afraid of being outed as NWM supporters, and many opened their dioceses for their workshops. A few bishops offered their public support for NWM initiatives, often at the peril of their own ecclesiastical careers.[64] Richmond Bishop Walter Sullivan, for example, wrote the introduction to *A Challenge to Love* before Cardinal Ratzinger demanded Sullivan's name be removed from the book's cover.[65]

Other bishops were unphased by possible Vatican blowback. In 2002, retired Bishop Leroy Matthiesen of Amarillo, Texas, held a Mass for NWM at the fifth national symposium in defiance of the secretary of the CDF, who had written the local bishop with instructions to stop the eucharistic celebration.[66] Over the course of NWM's first twenty-five years, at least seven bishops bravely accepted invitations to speak at its symposia and other major programs.[67]

Of all NWM's allies, its strongest was Detroit Auxiliary Bishop Thomas Gumbleton. He had been a supporter of gays and lesbians since at least the mid-1970s, when he came to the defense of Brian McNaught, a gay writer who was fired by the archdiocesan newspaper for his public identification with Dignity. At the 1992 NWM symposium, Bishop Gumbleton shared his own story of struggle with homophobia and the need to reconcile with his brother, who had come out to him as gay. The speech was a turning point for his ministry. According to NWM, Gumbleton became the "'point bishop' for this issue, crisscrossing the nation, talking to Catholic groups about gay and lesbian issues." On several occasions, he even criticized the inadequacy of church teaching on homosexuality and the damage it caused to LGBTQ people.[68]

Always Our Children

Following Bishop Gumbleton's groundbreaking speech, NWM collaborated with him to influence the National Conference of Catholic Bishops (NCCB). In 1992, after the CDF published its criticism of gay civil rights legislation, Nugent and Gramick campaigned for the U.S. bishops' organization to address homosexuality as an urgent pastoral matter. Upon learning that only a member of the NCCB could introduce such a measure for consideration, Bishop Gumbleton agreed to champion NWM's cause. With the support of more than a dozen other bishops, he asked the NCCB Committee on Marriage and Family Life to explore issuing a document on homosexuality. Cardinal Joseph Bernardin, then chair of the committee, agreed to advance their proposal.[69]

The resulting NCCB document took nearly five years to complete, but *Always Our Children: A Pastoral Message to Parents of Homosexual Children and Suggestions for Pastoral Ministers* (AOC) was worth the wait. Both Fr. Nugent and Mary Kilbride, an NWM board member, consulted on early drafts. The bishops' message was a monumental victory for gay and lesbian Catholics, and NWM described AOC as a historic pastoral statement....This document, directed to parents and pastoral ministers, is one of the strongest affirmations of the goodness of lesbian and gay people in the Catholic Church. "In you, God's love is revealed," the bishops say to gay and lesbian people at the close of this document which calls Catholic parents and leaders to initiate dialogue, outreach, and affirmation of the gay and lesbian members of their families and parishes.[70]

In the years after AOC's publication, several parish and diocesan ministries developed from its vision for pastoral care. Making the most of the NCCB statement, NWM created a follow-up report and offered a presentation on its implementation at the NCCB's annual meeting in 1998.[71]

Trouble in the Archdiocese of Washington

For all its advocacy, NWM faced hostility from local, national, and international church leaders.

Throughout the seventies and eighties, Gramick and Nugent had an especially fraught relationship with the Archdiocese of Washington, the canonical territory in which NWM's office is located. The first salvo came in 1978, when Cardinal William Baum revoked Nugent's faculties to preach and hear confessions within the archdiocese. At first the chancery claimed it was because Nugent no longer resided in Washington but later admitted that his association with NWM was to blame.[72]

In 1980, Baum left the archdiocese to become prefect of the Congregation for Catholic Education in Rome. His replacement, Archbishop James Hickey, was even more dogged in his attempts to silence Nugent and Gramick. The pair's first encounter with the new archbishop came during preparations for NWM's first national symposium in 1981. On September 20, Hickey summoned Gramick and Nugent to a meeting in his private residence. The archbishop and his advisers dominated the agenda, making it clear that he was not interested in dialogue with them. Less than a month later, without further consultation, Hickey released a letter calling NWM's position on homosexuality "ambiguous."[73]

Over the next few years, Hickey tried to curtail NWM by any means possible. On numerous occasions, he contacted dioceses where NWM workshops were scheduled to prevent them from taking place.[74] In a meeting with Gramick in 1983, the archbishop urged the nun to give up her apostolate altogether. When that strategy did not work, he called on Gramick's and Nugent's superiors to remove them from gay and lesbian ministry and withdraw them from his archdiocese.[75]

The Salvatorians and School Sisters of Notre Dame stood by Nugent and Gramick throughout their ordeal, believing that their apostolate to gays and lesbians was pastorally and theologically sound. From the late seventies through the mid-eighties, the two religious communities conducted at least three in-depth studies of NWM with evaluations by canon lawyers, theologians, program participants, and NWM leadership itself. These investigations found no ambiguity in Gramick and Nugent's presentation of church teaching, which the pair communicated with as much clarity as criticism.[76]

Conflicts with the Hierarchy and the Vatican

After several failed attempts to silence NWM, Hickey had few options other than to ban the organization from the archdiocese, which he did in 1984. As part of his crusade against Gramick and Nugent, the archbishop appealed to the Vatican for assistance. In July 1984, at Hickey's urging, the Congregation for Religious and Secular Institutes (CRSI) threatened Nugent's and Gramick's superiors general with "further disciplinary action" if the pair refused to resign from NWM leadership.[77]

Nugent and Gramick complied with the letter, if not the spirit, of the CRSI order. They gave up official control of the NWM board to Sr. Helen Marie Burns of the Sisters of Mercy and control of NWM staff to layperson Kurt Schade. Nevertheless, they continued holding workshops under the auspices of the CCGCR and, later, the Center for Homophobia Education and the Catholic Parents Network.[78] Gramick and Nugent, after all, still had the support of many within the hierarchy. A snapshot of their calendar from August to September 1989 reveals a busy schedule in institutional Catholic spaces. On August 9, Gramick and Nugent facilitated a "Homophobia in Religion and Society" workshop in the Diocese of Sacramento at the invitation of Bishop

Francis Quinn. A month later, they organized a seminar outside of New York City titled "Our Lesbian and Gay Religious and Clergy." Noted Yale historian John Boswell was a guest speaker, and representatives from several religious orders and local dioceses, including the vicar for religious from the Archdiocese of New York, attended.[79]

In the wake of the 1984 CRSI order, Gramick moved to Brooklyn, where she continued ministering to gays and lesbians for five years under the protection of Bishop Mugavero and the Office of Social Action of the Brooklyn Sisters of Mercy. Nugent tried to establish himself in Brooklyn, but Bishop Mugavero refused to give him canonical authorization, so he moved to Newark, where he spent three years in ministry before the newly appointed Archbishop Theodore McCarrick revoked his faculties in 1987. Nugent returned to Baltimore that year to continue his work.[80] Although some bishops made Nugent and Gramick's ministry difficult, the pair were adept at preserving their vocations under the guise of different communities, ministries, and geographies.

THE MAIDA COMMISSION INVESTIGATES

Throughout the late eighties, Nugent's and Gramick's critics kept close watch over their activities and made numerous complaints to the Vatican. In 1988, CRSI, which had been renamed the Congregation for Institutes of Consecrated Life and Societies of Apostolic Life (CICLSAL), announced the formation of a committee to "render a judgment as to the clarity and orthodoxy of the public presentation of the two religious with respect to the church's teaching on homosexuality."[81] Green Bay Bishop Adam Maida, a canon and civil lawyer, soon to become cardinal archbishop of Detroit, was charged with the probe. For several years, the commission lay dormant and only sprang back to life after NWM tried to hold a workshop in a Detroit parish in the spring of 1994.[82] On May 11, 1994, the Archdiocese of Detroit issued a statement claiming that Nugent and Gramick's ministry "may have created an ambiguity which has caused confusion in the minds of some people."[83] The investigation was ready to proceed.

Within months, Gramick and Nugent were attending church hearings and providing written responses to questions about their ministry and then recent book, *Building Bridges*. Their attempts at dialogue, however, were in vain, as no one sympathetic to the ministry had been appointed to the investigative committee.[84] With cards stacked against Gramick and Nugent, the Maida Commission made quick work of its task and sent its critical evaluation to CICLSAL. The commission had concluded that Nugent and Gramick "merely *present* the Church's teaching but give no evidence of personal advocacy of it."[85] Authorized teachers of Catholic tradition, it implied, needed to give their full and enthusiastic assent to every element of Catholic teaching.

A Vatican Trial

Following the report's submission, Gramick and Nugent's case was transferred to the CDF due to its doctrinal implications.[86] As their case worked its way through Vatican bureaucracy, Nugent and Gramick continued their work from Baltimore, where they had both resettled. Their hope for the Church was boundless, as was their will-ingness to dialogue with church officials. Gramick likes to share the story of a flight from Rome to Munich in the late 1990s when she was on her way to pray at the grave of her congregation's founder for a miraculous resolution to the Vatican investigation. Glancing at other passengers on the plane, she realized that Cardinal Ratzinger was on board. Gramick believed that God had placed the CDF head in her path, so she approached him and started a conversation. When Ratz-inger realized who she was, he chuckled and said that he had been aware of her work for twenty years.[87]

The conversation between Gramick and the future pope may have had little impact on the CDF's verdict-in-waiting, but it demon-strated the nun's ability to befriend even her most hardened opponents. Throughout her long ministry, Gramick refused to "let ideological dif-ferences put a distance between Catholics." Those who stood against her and Nugent, she believed, were "just as sincere as we are."[88]

After several years and painstaking dialogue, Ratzinger finally issued his condemnation of Nugent, Gramick, and NWM on May 14, 1999. While the CDF announcement acknowledged the pair's pasto-ral mission, it criticized their dissent from church teaching and con-tinued disobedience to the 1984 order that forced them to resign from NWM leadership. The Vatican portrayed Nugent and Gramick as sow-ers of confusion and division in the Church. Catholics struggling with homosexuality, it stated, deserved genuine pastoral care that included the "truth" about their "intrinsic disorder," something that Gramick and Nugent refused to provide. For that reason, the CDF declared the pair were "permanently prohibited from any pastoral work involving homosexual persons and are ineligible, for an undetermined period, for any office in their respective religious institutes."[89]

Resistance to an Unconscionable Verdict

For nearly a year after the order, Gramick and Nugent complied with the Vatican directive by refraining from pastoral ministry. All the while, they continued speaking out about their ministry and experiences of the investigation.[90] Soon after the 1999 CDF order was released, Gramick began a publicity campaign to pressure the Vatican into reversing its decision.[91] She spelled out her opposition to the Vatican pronouncement at a Nebraska meeting of Call to Action, an organization of lay Catholics committed to social justice. "No one has the right to intrude on your conscience," she said, "to invade that sacred space between you and God."[92]

Along with speaking engagements and news conferences, Gramick organized a letter-writing campaign. Statements from theologians, church leaders, women religious, and LGBTQ Catholics flooded the CDF. In August 1999, the Leadership Conference of Women Religious (LCWR) passed a resolution largely inspired by Gramick's situation that signaled the group's intention to "initiate conversations with official leaders at all levels of the Roman Catholic Church to address a pattern in the exercise of ecclesiastical authority experienced as a source of suffering and division by many within the Catholic community."[93] Gramick and Nugent remained a thorn in Ratzinger's side.

In response to Gramick and Nugent's ongoing activism, the pair were summoned to Rome on May 23 and 24, 2000, for meetings with the superiors general of their religious orders. According to a *National Catholic Reporter* account, after years of contentious dialogue CICL-SAL had finally ordered them to refrain from

> Speaking or writing about the ban or the ecclesiastical processes that led up to it; Speaking or writing on matters related to homosexuality; Protesting against the ban or encouraging

the faithful to publicly express dissent from the official magisterium; Criticizing the magisterium in any public forum whatsoever concerning homosexuality or related issues.[94]

This time, the Sisters of Notre Dame and Salvatorians had little choice but to enforce CICLSAL's demand for formal obedience. The two communities had stood by Nugent and Gramick for decades, but the Vatican pressure grew too strong to bear.

New Realities and the Costs of Conscience

Following their trip to Rome, Gramick and Nugent responded very differently to their congregations' directives. In Nugent's case, Vatican harassment finally had its intended effect: the priest submitted in obedience to his superiors and stopped speaking about gay and lesbian ministry in public. After decades of bearing costly witness, he went back to parish ministry, serving for several years at St. John the Baptist in New Freedom, Pennsylvania. Even though Nugent stopped public ministry, he continued providing private counsel to LGBTQ Catholics, theologians, and ministry leaders.[95] He remained faithful to his priestly vow of obedience until his death from lung cancer in 2014, contending that he would someday be vindicated and his trial would contribute to the Church's transformation. "In order to have an effect on the house," he once said, "you must live in it."[96]

Gramick came to a different conclusion. In a May 25, 2000, statement, she explained her intention to disobey the CDF and her religious superiors. "After finding my voice to tell my story," she declared, "I choose not to collaborate in my own oppression by restricting a basic human right. To me this is a matter of conscience."[97]

Gramick knew the price of disobedience would be dismissal from the Sisters of Notre Dame. In September 2000, she announced that she was leaving her religious community of more than three decades to enter the Sisters of Loretto, a congregation with a mission to "bring the healing spirit of God into our world" and to "improve the conditions of those who suffer from injustice, oppression, and deprivation of dignity."[98] By joining the new religious order, Gramick was no longer obliged to obey the silence imposed on her by the Sisters of Notre Dame.[99]

Although Gramick found a new religious congregation to welcome her, the ordeal took a personal toll. In early 2001, Gramick shared that she was still "very much in a state of grieving" at the loss of her first community.[100] Neither did Vatican attacks against her stop. At least nine letters from the Vatican from 2000 to 2008 admonished the Sisters of Loretto to curb Gramick's advocacy or expel her from their community.[101] Her new congregation, however, held strong as a shelter from censure.

Ecclesiastical Consequences and Ministry Fallout

Vatican investigations and decrees were powerless to keep Gramick from fulfilling her vocation, but episcopal interventions limited NWM's activity throughout the 1990s and 2000s. Cancel culture was rife in the Church. In October 1997, Bishop Edward Egan of Bridgeport, Connecticut, canceled a retreat to be held by Nugent and Gramick for the Catholic parents of gays and lesbians in his diocese.[102] A year and a half later, Cardinal Maida banned the annual Pax Christi meeting from a Catholic parish because Nugent and Gramick were featured speakers at the gathering.[103] In 2002, the CDF secretary, Archbishop Tarcisio Bertone, tried to stop Mass from being celebrated at NWM's fifth national symposium in Louisville, Kentucky, and in February 2005, the Archdiocese of Detroit canceled a parish reception for Gramick after the debut of a documentary about her.[104]

Statements from powerful U.S. bishops showed they were in lockstep with the Vatican. Immediately after the CDF issued its 1999 ban, Bishop Joseph Fiorenza of Galveston and Houston and then president of the NCCB issued a statement on behalf of the conference in support of the Vatican decision.[105] In 2010, after NWM came out in support of same-sex marriage, Chicago Cardinal Francis George, Fiorenza's successor as president of the USCCB, reiterated the conference's opposition to NWM:

> No one should be misled by the claim that NWM provides an authentic interpretation of Catholic teaching and an authentic Catholic pastoral practice....Accordingly, I wish to make it clear that, like other groups that claim to be Catholic but deny central aspects of church teaching, New Ways

Ministry has no approval or recognition from the Catholic Church and that they cannot speak on behalf of the Catholic faithful in the United States.[106]

NEW DIRECTIONS

Despite ecclesiastical investigations, censorship, and disavowal, NWM continued to grow and evolve. In 1996, Francis DeBernardo, who had worked as a staff member since 1994, became executive director. DeBernardo is a Brooklyn native who began his career writing for *The Tablet*, the Diocese of Brooklyn's weekly newspaper. After graduate school at the University of Maryland, DeBernardo began volunteering and then working for NWM, a position he described as "exciting" and "natural" for him.[107]

As executive director, he has expanded NWM's online presence, continued facilitating NWM workshops, and organized countless political and theological responses to LGBTQ issues. In an interview with *National Catholic Reporter*, DeBernardo shared his vision for NWM's mission: "One thing that I like is that for a good part of our work, we are in the background. Our priority is to enable others to step forward. We encourage people to do the work of LGBT ministry and give them the support and tools to do so....I think that real education is a formation of people."[108]

"THIS POPE GIVES ME HOPE"

Since the election of Pope Francis in 2013, NWM's relationship to the institutional church has been undergoing a process of rehabilitation. Even though the 1999 and 2000 CDF and CICLSAL pronouncements against Gramick and NWM still stand, the Vatican has dramatically changed under the leadership of Pope Francis. Rather than enforcing doctrinal ideals like his predecessors, Francis has encouraged the Church to be a "field hospital" for those wounded on the battlefield of life. His pastoral orientation encourages ministries on the peripheries of the Church that care for those neglected in more traditional Catholic spaces.

Changes in the Vatican have been a boon for groups like NWM. No longer is the CDF the powerful and feared doctrinal watchdog that it once was. Moreover, the new papal regime has offered olive branches to many of the individuals and communities that were censured before. One such olive branch came to NWM on February 18, 2015, when the Vatican offered a group of forty-eight NWM pilgrims, including Gramick, VIP seating for a papal audience.[109] Gramick took the occasion as an opportunity to reflect on the new Vatican's new approach, saying,

> This Pope gives me hope….His desire to welcome the marginalized has begun to permeate church structures and is causing movement in our church….There is a new spirit in the Church, a spirit of bringing people from the outside closer to the inside, a spirit that all persons have value, even those whom some have labeled sinful or dissident.[110]

Later signs proved that Gramick's hope in Pope Francis was well founded. In April 2021, she and DeBernardo sent a note to the holy father and only two weeks later received a handwritten response that revealed the pope's "shepherd's heart" had "good feelings" toward them. The pair was elated and took his reply as an invitation to even more dialogue. After a second letter and reply, Gramick was "consoled and elated" upon reading Francis's description of her as "a valiant woman who has suffered courageously and makes decisions prayerfully."[111]

Gramick's cooperation with the Spirit and others is, without question, to be credited for many of the new ways that the Church under Francis understands, relates to, and cares for LGBTQ people. Perhaps more than any other minister to the LGBTQ community, she has embodied God's "closeness, compassion, and tenderness," words used by Pope Francis to describe her half century of service.[112] Decades of persistent leadership make Gramick the spiritual mother of LGBTQ Catholic ministry in the United States.

The importance of national organizations such as NWM and leaders such as Jeannine Gramick cannot be overstated. In recent years, it has also become clear that biological families have an important role to play in the movement for LGBTQ Catholic liberation. As Catholic families learn to affirm their LGBTQ children, they yearn for a Church that loves, welcomes, and accepts queer Catholics as much as they do. Their witness to God's love in LGBTQ lives and families has transformed the Church. Chapter 4 recounts the story of Fortunate Families (FF), a national ministry that began at a NWM symposium and today advocates for LGBTQ people in schools, parishes, and dioceses across the country. Unlike NWM, FF began as a support group for the families of LGBTQ people, not LGBTQ people themselves. Today, with NWM, it is one of the most effective grassroots ministries working for change through dialogue with the institutional church.

Chapter 4

SKIN IN THE GAME

Fortunate Families and a Ministry of Allies

> But the steadfast love of the LORD is from
> everlasting to everlasting
> on those who fear him
> and his righteousness to children's children.

—Psalm 103:17

A MINISTRY BY AND FOR FAMILIES

I learned much about Fortunate Families (FF) in an interview with Deb Word, FF president from 2013 to 2015. As a newcomer to FF's board of directors, I had heard about Deb's leadership, but never spoken with her in person.

My first question was simple and open: "What's your experience as an LGBTQ Catholic ally been like?" I asked. I was not prepared for her answer.

"I have a problem with the word *ally*," she countered.

I was taken aback. Had I said something wrong?

"The word *ally* describes my sisters or my friends," she explained. "I'm a mom, so I have skin in the game. The literal skin of my son is in the game. I'm *family*."[1]

Word's heartfelt answer reveals the high stakes for FF, whose mission is to "uphold and safeguard the dignity of LGBTQ+ daughters and sons of God."[2] To members of the organization, children are far more than the abstraction that church leaders, and even gay theologians, often make them out to be. LGBTQ people are known and loved by their families and known and loved by God. As Word reminded me, "If you're talking to a mom, you're talking to someone who wants the best for her child."[3]

For the most part, FF has avoided controversy in the Church by providing a supportive network and not openly criticizing Catholic teaching. Still, FF leaders are compelled to action when the Church excludes and harms their loved ones. Mary Ellen and Casey Lopata, the founders of FF, explain:

> When we experience discriminatory words and actions of those who lack understanding, strong feelings arise: frustration, anger and sometimes betrayal, especially if from our own Catholic leaders. Parents' understanding of our LGBT loved ones, our passionate commitment to justice for them, and the fact that parents are more likely to be listened to because we are the faithful heart and soul (and wallets) of our parishes, are precisely why Catholic parents are uniquely positioned to make a difference.[4]

Since 2004, FF has carried out its mission to facilitate "respectful conversation" and share its "personal stories within dioceses, parishes, and communities, especially with bishops, pastors and church leaders." It does so by building bridges with the institutional church and accompanying families that struggle with Catholic teaching and LGBTQ issues.[5]

The Lopatas

Over Thanksgiving weekend in 1983, a story familiar to many LGBTQ Catholics played out in Rochester, New York, when nineteen-year-old Jim Lopata tearfully confessed to his mother that he was "lonely.

I'm lonely for another man." His mother, Mary Ellen, immediately understood what her son was trying to communicate: he was gay. "I was shocked and confused," she later recounted. "I cried and cried."[6]

When Jim came out to Casey, his father, a short time later, Casey's first question was, "Can Jim be gay and Catholic?"[7] The Lopatas were faithful members of their parish and did not know any gay people besides their son, let alone other LGBTQ Catholics or parish allies. The couple's religious beliefs compounded their pain. Mary Ellen shared that "Catholic teaching only added to my confused and bewildered state."[8] The Lopata parents were hurting and felt alone, but as Catholics shaped by Vatican II's call for lay Catholics to engage their faith, they set out to grow in their understanding of the Church's teaching.

The process of coming to terms with Jim's gay identity took the Lopatas nearly a decade. Theology and doctrine were an important part of the couple's journey, but their son's experiences challenged what the Church held to be true. Mary Ellen and Casey knew Jim as a "good, deeply spiritual young man" full of love for those around him.[9] They knew he did not choose to be gay. They knew he was not disordered.

Balancing the Church's tradition with their own consciences and experiences, the Lopatas came to believe that it was the Church—*not* their son—that needed to change. Jim was created in the image of God and lived for others. "That's how I really know," Casey asserted, "that Jim can be gay and Catholic."[10]

The Rochester Springboard for a National Organization

As their theology evolved, the Lopatas entered into dialogue with others on the Church's relationship to LGBTQ issues. In 1987, they attended a workshop on homophobia and homosexuality hosted by their parish that became an opportunity for further conversion. Mary Ellen remembered,

> The most important thing that workshop did was to break the silence around homosexuality. I came away from that experience knowing that if I loved my son as I said I did, I could not remain silent. Somewhere along the way, I began

to realize what a special gift Jim (my son) is to me, to our family, and the whole Body of Christ not in spite of, but because he is gay.[11]

The Lopatas' changing perspectives led to action. Most of the Lopatas' early years in LGBTQ advocacy focused on creating change at the local level. In 1991, Casey joined Rochester's Interfaith Advocates for Lesbian, Gay, Bisexual, and Transgender People; by 1992, the Lopatas were ready to advocate within their faith community. As parents of a gay son, they knew "it can be critically important for parents, whose faith is so important, to find a sheltering place within a faith context."[12] With six other Rochester Catholic leaders, the Lopatas attended the NWM national symposium in Chicago. Afterward, the small group met to brainstorm and implement gay- and lesbian-affirming pastoral practices for the whole diocese. The budding community, which became known as the Catholic Gay and Lesbian Family Ministry (CGLFM), received tacit support from Rochester Bishop Matthew Clark, and after a few years he permitted the group to affiliate as an official diocesan ministry. With the Lopatas' help, CGLFM grew into a successful apostolate. In 1997, more than thirteen hundred LGBTQ Catholics, their friends, and allies attended a special Mass celebrated by the bishop in their honor.[13]

The Lopatas' work was just beginning. In 1994, Casey Lopata published the first issue of a CGLFM newsletter to stay in closer touch with local families. That was also the year the Lopatas helped found the National Association of Catholic Diocesan Lesbian & Gay Ministries (later the Catholic Association of Lesbian and Gay Ministries), a coalition of thirteen diocesan gay and lesbian ministries.[14] Initially conceived at the 1992 NWM national symposium, the now defunct group led by Rev. James Schexnayder, an Oakland priest who led his diocese's HIV/AIDS ministry and was active in the gay liberation movement, organized an annual national conference and provided sensitivity training and pastoral resources for Catholic leaders throughout the 1990s and early 2000s.[15]

In October 1994, the Lopatas attended NWM's first-ever national retreat for the parents of gay and lesbian Catholics.[16] At the time, NWM was seeking new members for the Catholic Parents Network (CPN), a discrete program to support parents "in various stages of facing the reality of having a gay son or lesbian daughter." CPN connected struggling families through a private mailing list, weekend retreats, support groups, and mentorship opportunities. The Lopatas eagerly joined to share their wisdom with others.[17] As Mary Ellen later reflected, "Isolation is one of the biggest impediments to understanding and peace faced by parents. Sharing one's story with another who can truly empathize is often the first step to healing."[18] Through their participation in various ministries, the couple laid a foundation for broader outreach.

REORIENTING CHURCH TEACHING WITH *ALWAYS OUR CHILDREN*

In the mid-nineties, the Lopatas directed their energies toward transforming the institutional church. One of the parents' proudest achievements came from participating in the dialogue that led to *Always Our Children: A Pastoral Message to Parents of Homosexual Children and Suggestions for Pastoral Ministers* (AOC).[19] During the document's drafting process, the Lopatas offered initial input and followed up with comments on a first draft. When AOC was released, Mary Ellen shared, "Many parents struggle with the conflict between loving their child and their understanding that church teaching condemns their child. For them to hear the bishop say to love their child first... can go a long way to help them resolve those conflicts and begin some healing."[20] Two decades after its publication, the Lopatas reflected that AOC was "arguably the most gay-friendly official document from the U.S. bishops or Vatican....An affirmative pastoral ministry tool for parents, church ministers and allies, AOC's welcoming pastoral focus continues to challenge the doctrinal severity of the institutional church."[21]

Spreading the Message and Founding Fortunate Families

Emboldened by AOC's success, the Lopatas turned to publishing as a way of spreading their message. In 2001, Casey edited *Seeds of Hope*, a practical resource manual for those interested in their experiences and work. Two years later, Casey and Mary Ellen oversaw the publication of *Fortunate Families: Catholic Families with Lesbian Daughters and Gay Sons*, which

> tells the stories of Catholic parents—striving to love and serve God by loving and nurturing their child. From the combined experience of over 200 Catholic parents,...we encounter the depth of their feelings for their lesbian and gay children, we learn how important their religion is to them, and we hear what they need from their church.[22]

To this day, the FF website continues the Lopatas' tradition of sharing stories through the dozens of testimonies from Catholic families and allies of LGBTQ people that it provides.[23]

By early 2004, the Lopatas perceived the need for a national organization to grow their ministry base. Dignity and NWM provided resources for LGBTQ Catholics, but what about families? The pair resigned from CGLFM and started Fortunate Families, named after their book published the year before. FF became a nonprofit organization and elected a board of directors with Mary Ellen Lopata at the helm as president.[24]

Changing Bishops' Hearts

One of the group's first projects was to launch a survey of Catholic parents of LGBT daughters and sons. Once the results of the survey were compiled and summarized, FF sent the report to each U.S. bishop with plans for action and accountability. Mary Ellen explained why FF initiatives were so important to advance LGBTQ ministry: "Parents are in a unique position to make a difference," she said. "Others may not agree with us, but no one, no institution can deny our experience. It is essential that parents...let those in authority know what it is like for parents of LGBT sons and daughters in the Church."[25]

The Lopatas' passion for dialogue included a partnership with NWM. In March 2007, the FF board of directors attended the NWM symposium in Minneapolis, where they planned a session for parents to speak with bishops. When word of the symposium reached the Vatican, church officials asked Catholic leaders to stay home. Two bishops attended FF's session anyway: retired Auxiliary Bishop Joseph Sullivan of Brooklyn and retired Archbishop Francis Hurley of Anchorage.

Both were celebrated for their commitment to pastoral care and social justice, and Sullivan regularly spoke up for LGBTQ Catholics.[26]

PARENT-TO-PARENT MENTORING AND DISCIPLESHIP

As FF expanded, the Lopatas continued to mentor other parents. One of FF's chief goals was to "connect parents to work for welcome and justice in the Church for their lesbian, gay, bisexual and transgender children."[27] The Lopatas' support for families flourished through telephone and email networks, a newsletter called *Voices for Justice*, and a bimonthly email update called *The Families Forum*. According to Deb Word, these publications reminded FF parents "of the need to reach out to our church fathers, to tell our stories, to 'put a face' on the issue that our church would sometimes like to sweep under the rug."[28]

In addition to communications and media ministries, in person gatherings brought FF leaders together for workshops, reflection, and strategizing. The first national meeting was held in October 2010, when more than fifty family members and allies traveled to Chicago for a weekend program.

To further equip parents for advocacy, Casey Lopata drew up "Talking Points for Catholic Parents with LGBT Daughters and Sons" in 2012. This brochure was augmented in 2015 when board members Jenny Naughton and Penny Smith-Bogart created a "parish toolkit" for parents interested in starting their own local ministries. The packet included advice for navigating institutional church structures, guidelines for small-group discussions and sharing, recommendations for implementing AOC in parish settings, and even a template for the parish bulletin announcements.[29]

In September 2012, FF sent letters to more than four hundred Catholic campus ministers alerting them to the plight of LGBTQ young people who, according to one 2012 survey, were "more than three times as likely to express symptoms of depression and more than twice as likely to have self-harmed than their heterosexual peers."[30] Reaching out to more parents, FF sponsored a series of five "Parent Gatherings" in Pleasanton, California, in April 2013. Around that time, a sizeable grant from the E. Rhodes and Leona B. Carpenter Foundation enabled FF to expand its programming across the country.

The foundation's investment paid off as FF-affiliated and FF-inspired ministries sprang up in parishes and dioceses from Atlanta to Detroit.

NEW STRATEGIES OF THE EQUALLY BLESSED COALITION

As with all LGBTQ Catholic ministries, FF has had a complex and at times conflicted relationship with Catholic teaching and hierarchy. Its foundational statement, for example, upholds traditional church teaching by encouraging "our children to live chaste sexual lives" but also concedes that children do not always follow the Church's teaching. Still, it claims, God calls the Church and families to love, acceptance, and dialogue. The FF statement contends that Catholics must carefully consider what conscience, the sciences, and LGBTQ experiences reveal about sexuality and appropriate pastoral care. It concludes by acknowledging that parents "earnestly pray for the development of church teaching on the topic of homosexuality and gender."[31] In this way, FF simultaneously affirms traditional Catholic teaching, emphasizes the importance of pastoral care, and signals parents' desire for an evolution in doctrine.

Tensions developed in FF's relationship with the institutional church after August 2010, when the former joined Equally Blessed (EB), a politically active, media-savvy coalition of LGBTQ-affirming Catholic organizations including Dignity, Call to Action, and NWM. According to its website, the coalition was

> devoted to informing, supporting, and giving voice to the growing majority within the Catholic Church in the United States that favors equality under law for LGBT people. We seek to educate, to inspire and to prompt Catholics to take action in the Church and in the wider culture on behalf of LGBT people, their families and friends.[32]

For several years, EB provided a unified, public, LGBTQ-affirming Catholic voice on a number of critical issues. Joining the coalition benefitted FF with generous funding from the Arcus Foundation, pooled administrative resources, and the opportunity to meet with federal lawmakers.[33]

One key trade-off, however, was that FF's membership with EB impeded the ministry's ability to build relationships within the institutional church. Up until 2010, individual FF members had pushed for changes to church teaching, but the organization itself had never publicly dissented. Deb Word explained, "Our hands were clean. We said, 'We love our children. Our children are Catholic. And there wasn't anything a bishop could say about that.'"[34]

The same could not be said about FF's coalition partners. Dignity, Call to Action, and NWM prophetically opposed church teaching. At one point or another, each group had been expelled, condemned, and/or censured by the hierarchy. FF's association with other members of EB meant that some church leaders refused to meet with FF leaders and, worse yet, prevented the ministry from parish- and diocese-sponsored outreach.

The hierarchy's reluctance to engage EB became most clear when FF applied for a booth at the 2015 World Meeting of Families (WMOF). As the most prominent national ministry for families of LGBTQ Catholics, FF was eager to participate in the international gathering to be held in Philadelphia. Deb Word, then board president, was chosen to be the intermediary between FF and WMOF organizers because she was a parent and her "hands were clean as far as the Church was concerned."[35]

In spite of Word's good standing vis-à-vis the institutional church, she could not save FF's reputation. Mary Beth Yount, the WMOF director of content and programming, rejected FF's application numerous times due to the ministry's strong condemnations of homophobia and transphobia. Yount explained,

> The FF website and associated links claim that the organization is meeting parents where they are at but then proceeds to indicate that if parents give any sense of disapproval of behavior at all (or even ambivalence), they are harming their children and even setting them up for greater risk of suicide.[36]

After a series of contentious email exchanges between Word, Yount, and then Philadelphia Archbishop Charles Chaput, FF decided to attend WMOF anyway.[37] FF leaders wore matching shirts and distributed literature to publicize the group's presence. At times their evangelization was a messy affair. Word remembered, "We were screamed at. We were yelled at. We had a mother stop us at breakfast and say, 'You are those people who are taking our son to hell with you.' Yeah—[WMOF] was a lovely couple of weeks in Philly."[38]

A NEW EXECUTIVE DIRECTOR

Following the WMOF, FF began to reassess its approach. In June 2014, Mary Ellen and Casey Lopata retired from the board of directors. With the Lopatas' retirement, the FF board of directors decided to hire an executive director to lead the group since ministry responsibilities had become too great for the committee to handle on a volunteer basis. And so, in 2017, they hired Stanley "JR" Zerkowski, an accomplished and effective lay minister, organizer, and leader.

Zerkowski grew up in a Polish Catholic enclave in Buffalo, New York. Homophobia was not apparent to Zerkowski in his childhood, and he came to love the Church. After earning a master's degree in church management and administration from Villanova University, he spent more than two decades serving as an openly gay, lay parish minister in the Dioceses of Palm Beach and Orlando.

One of Zerkowski's greatest strengths was leading social justice initiatives. During his time in Florida, he organized a mutual aid and prayer program that paired wealthy Orlando parishes with poor parishes in rural Kentucky. In the process of facilitating the program, Zerkowski developed a strong relationship with Bishop Ken Williams of Lexington and felt called to move there. In 2011, he joined the parish staff of Historic St. Paul Catholic Church downtown, a community "where ministry could evolve and I could have an impact during this season of my life."[39]

In Lexington, Zerkowski quickly became a distinguished leader in LGBTQ ministry and interfaith dialogue. He helped found diocesan ministries for LGBTQ Catholics and their families, brought together religious leaders for an annual Pride prayer service, and regularly wrote for LinQ, the Pride Community Services Organization of the Bluegrass LGBT magazine.[40] Zerkowski enjoyed the support of his parish community but also of the new bishop, John Stowe, OFM, who was appointed by Pope Francis on March 12, 2015.

When FF announced it was hiring an executive director, Zerkowski viewed it as "God opening a door that was bigger than Lexington."[41] He applied for the position, and FF's board of directors agreed with his vision for the future of the ministry. Zerkowski's long career in ministry with LGBTQ and other vulnerable people, his knack for relationship-building with church leaders, and his deep love for the Catholic Church prepared him to continue the Lopatas' work.

Zerkowski's gifts corresponded to a new vision that FF's board of directors intended to make a reality. Since its founding, FF had often wrestled with questions about its mission. The need for LGBTQ-affirming ministry was so great. Should FF focus only on serving the parents and families of LGBTQ people, or should it venture into related apostolates? Under the Lopatas' leadership, FF concentrated on the work it knew best: caring for families of LGBTQ people and sharing their stories with Catholic leaders.[42]

When Zerkowski became director, however, FF discerned that the time had come to expand its reach. The situation for LGBTQ people in society had drastically improved, and the struggle for many Catholic parents to accept their children was no longer as intense as it once was. At the start of Zerkowski's tenure as executive director, most of the telephone calls that FF received came from Catholics interested in his work in parish and diocesan LGBTQ ministry. They wanted to learn how parents and faith communities could "minister to, welcome, and embrace LGBTQ people without watering down Roman Catholicism."[43]

LEAVING EQUALLY BLESSED FOR A NEW FUTURE

There was still one major obstacle to growing FF's apostolate: the ministry remained part of EB. Zerkowski explained why that was a problem:

> It probably was not helpful for us to be part of the EB coalition if our ministry was one of dialogue and building bridges with pastors and bishops. Our mission was to accompany family and friends of LGBTQ people, and the best way we

could serve was to have their daughters and sons recognized as valuable, equal, and contributing members of the Church.[44]

To achieve this goal, the FF board of directors adopted a more conciliatory tone with the institutional church and amicably parted from EB in July 2018. FF made a clear choice to work within the structures of the institutional church to create welcoming spaces for LGBTQ people.

With Zerkowski at the helm, FF moved its headquarters to Lexington, Kentucky, where the LGBTQ ministries under his leadership affiliated with the group. Zerkowski soon implemented FF's plan for broader outreach to schools and parishes, beginning in his hometown, where he gave several talks to students and met with faculty at local Catholic schools. To generate even more conversation, FF sent copies of Fr. James Martin's, *Building a Bridge* to every theology teacher at a local Catholic high school in November 2019.[45]

Zerkowski also began traveling the country to provide "Days of Discernment and Visioning" for parishes and dioceses considering LGBTQ ministry. Since becoming director, he has led these workshop retreats for nearby parishes in Cincinnati, Louisville, and Covington, but also in more distant locations such as Chicago, Detroit, and San Diego. These days are grounded in worship and prayer but also foreground LGBTQ experience as part of the dialogue. When he travels, Zerkowski brings flair such as rainbow buttons, Our Lady of Fortunate Families prayer cards, and blueprints for church Pride banners. At St. Paul, Zerkowski's parish, FF partnered with the parish's Knights of Columbus to purchase a new banner in recognition of Pride month.

Today, Zerkowski's work is supported by members of the Catholic hierarchy and theological community. Bishop John Stowe serves as FF's episcopal adviser and is a source of both ministerial legitimacy and accountability. Other advisers include now retired Bishop Gumbleton of Detroit and Fr. James Martin, SJ. Friar Mario Serrano, OFM Conv, of Texas and Deacon Steve Hester of Rhode Island serve on the FF board of directors, and theological advisers include laypersons Andy Buechel, Arthur Fitzmaurice, Michel Iafrate, and Jason Steidl. In addition to these public relationships, Zerkowski regularly meets for private dialogue with Catholic leaders around the country.

In his capacity as executive director, JR Zerkowski sees FF as "a living Gospel. By telling stories and journeying together, we're revealing Jesus's presence in the Church." FF is a dynamic organization that is constantly discerning how it can better read and address the "signs of the times." Recently, the FF board of directors established subcommittees to focus on evangelization, education, Catholic schools, and trans issues. Zerkowski recognizes the last issue as an especially pressing need for the Catholic Church at this time.[46] While many Catholic parents may now be comfortable with the idea of having gay and lesbian children, transgender and genderqueer identities can be far more difficult to understand and accept. To address this lack of resources, FF welcomed Christine Zuba, a transgender Catholic, to the board of directors in January 2019.

REALIZING THE VISION

Mary Ellen and Casey's vision for ministry to the families of LGBTQ people has evolved since their son, Jim, first came out to them in 1983. Today, as FF grows around the country, the heart of its mission—the heart of parents—remains the same. In 2014, on the tenth anniversary of FF's founding, Mary Ellen remarked, "Catholics are taught that every child is a gift from God, a gift to their family, a gift to their community (especially their faith community) and a gift to the world." For that reason, FF exhorts the Church to "love each child as s/he is; encourage them to be who God created them to be."[47]

Thanks to advocates like the Lopatas and Zerkowski, FF's vision is already being realized in some Catholic communities across the United States. Although countless parishes and dioceses remain hostile to LGBTQ people, a few lead the way in their care for queer believers. One such parish is St. Paul the Apostle, a Catholic community in Manhattan. Chapters 5 and 6 will delve into the history and controversy surrounding the parish's LGBTQ ministries of the 1990s and 2000s. Lacking the support of their archdiocese, parishioners and priests at St. Paul the Apostle have modeled the creativity and resilience needed for pastoral care and LGBTQ Catholic ministry to thrive at the grassroots.

Chapter 5

DONALD MAHER AT ST. PAUL THE APOSTLE

A Controversial Figure

> So then you are no longer strangers and aliens,
> but you are citizens with the saints and also
> members of the household of God, built upon
> the foundation of the apostles and prophets,
> with Christ Jesus himself as the cornerstone. In
> him the whole structure is joined together and
> grows into a holy temple in the Lord.
>
> —Ephesians 2:19–21

A "MOST UNIQUE PARISH MINISTRY"

On March 15, 1993, more than three hundred people gathered for an interreligious St. Patrick's Day celebration sponsored by the Gay and Lesbian Catholic Ministry (GLCM) at the Church of St. Paul the Apostle in Manhattan.[1] Donald Maher, the driving force behind the ministry, had extended a special invitation to his friend

Brendan Fay of the Irish Lesbian and Gay Organization (ILGO), a group struggling for acceptance into New York City's St. Patrick's Day Parade. The parish's warm welcome was in stark contrast to ILGO's years-long conflict with parade organizers, who were the Catholic face of discrimination. That night at St. Paul, Irish music, dance, readings, and prayers shined a ray of hope for inclusivity in the Church.[2] Brendan Fay remarked, "One of the most significant stories to emerge out of [ILGO's] movement and encounter with exclusion, pain, and discrimination was the emergence of [GLCM's] ministry of welcome, this most unique parish ministry at St. Paul the Apostle Church."[3]

Since the late eighties, local ministries like GLCM have been catalysts for LGBTQ advocacy in the Catholic Church. Due to their uneasy relationship with many parts of the hierarchy, especially under the careful watch of John Paul II and Benedict XVI, these communities often developed in isolation from each other, tended to be highly localized, and depended on the support of pastors and parishes at the grassroots. This chapter will explore one such community at the Church of St. Paul the Apostle in Manhattan.

GLCM grew throughout the nineties as a prophetic community of hospitality for lesbian and gay Catholics amid the AIDS crisis. After a dormant half decade in the early 2000s, a new iteration took shape under Fr. Gil Martinez, who became pastor in 2006. Both epochs reflected the parish's openness to the Spirit's leading and compassion for those on the margins of society. Together with St. Paul pastors, laypeople and staff built an inclusive and affirming congregation that celebrates queer identities and fosters LGBTQ spiritualities.

AIDS Activism and Exclusion from the St. Patrick's Day Parade

The Gay and Lesbian Catholic Ministry emerged in 1991, a year when 29,850 U.S. residents died from AIDS.[4] Gay and lesbian Catholics such as Brendan Fay saw it as "a time of exile, mourning, discrimination, AIDS phobia, and violence against LGBT folks."[5] The LGBTQ community in New York City was reeling from the epidemic but had not been knocked to the ground. Community groups such as Gay Men's Health Crisis (GMHC) cared for the sick and dying.[6] Activist organizations such as ACT UP pressured the government to fund medical research.[7] In the city, New York Archbishop John Cardinal

O'Connor emerged as a target of protest for his stigmatization of gay relationships and condemnation of condoms to prevent the spread of HIV.[8] In the face of the HIV/AIDS crisis, the gay and lesbian community was still a political, social, and moral force to be reckoned with.

The spirit that animated GMHC and ACT UP to defend the dignity of people living with HIV/AIDS also led a group of gay and lesbian Irish to march in the New York City St. Patrick's Day Parade. For ILGO members, participation was a sign of their integrated Irish ethnicity and gay sexuality. Many were inspired by their Catholic faith to march.[9] The parade, however, was governed by the Ancient Order of the Hibernians (AOH), a fraternal organization known for its religious and social conservatism. It came as no surprise when the AOH rebuffed ILGO's petition to march in early 1991. Fay called the decision "one of the most painful moments for Irish gay and lesbian immigrants....We were told we did not belong."[10] ILGO's dispute with AOH turned into international news after New York City Mayor David Dinkins intervened in support of the gay and lesbian organization. Due to the mayor's public support for ILGO, AOH leaders reversed their decision on the condition that Dinkins accompany the group along the parade route.[11]

AOH's compromise for ILGO to join the parade did not translate into goodwill. As the 135 ILGO activists marched, they were subjected to a barrage of physical and verbal abuse. The *Washington Post* described how "insults and epithets, along with a few eggs and beer cans, were thrown at the group. Crude placards with anti-gay slogans were waved like oversized holy cards."[12] When ILGO passed the reviewing stand, Cardinal John O'Connor refused to greet the marchers, and officials from the Ancient Order of the Hibernians turned their backs on them.[13]

"There Is Nothing Timid about Donald Maher"

Among the ILGO marchers that day was Donald Maher, a lawyer in his early thirties. Brendan Fay described his fellow activist and friend as a "headstrong and passionate character, often over the top in his style and commitment. There is nothing timid about Donald Maher."[14]

Maher was born the third of five children to a socially conscious, middle-class Irish Catholic family in Brooklyn. His father was a well-known trade unionist and his mother was a homemaker. Maher recounted, "Life revolved around the parish....I was raised in a way that you took care of people."

As a youth, Maher carried the stigma of being gay even though he came of age at the height of Vatican II reforms and participated in the civil rights and anti-war movements. Decades later, Maher explained, "I was far better able to speak up for other people than I was able to speak up for myself on the gay issue." After graduating from Xaverian High School, he attended Brooklyn College and New York Law School to become a lawyer, believing that "it was attorneys who made the world a more just place."[15]

Maher fully came out to his family after he moved to Manhattan in 1985, but still he spurned what he described as the "gay ghetto"—those stereotypes, behaviors, and forms of community that separated gay men from heterosexual society. As the AIDS crisis unfolded, however, Maher became increasingly visible in the gay and lesbian movement due to his political organizing, fundraising, and even civil disobedience with groups like ACT UP and Queer Nation.

Around the same time, he experienced a spiritual conversion at a family member's funeral that beckoned him back to his Catholic faith. He began attending St. Paul the Apostle Church and soon became a lector, Sunday school teacher, and volunteer for Momentum, the parish's HIV/AIDS ministry. Paulist Fr. Eric Andrews was then a young priest assigned to the parish. He remembered Maher being "a part of every parish group. He'd be there. It was good for the parish, and the parish grew through his advocacy and presence."[16]

As a gay activist and parishioner, Maher intuited the need for an affirming ministry. After witnessing the homophobia that ILGO marchers faced, he set out to make his parish more hospitable to gays and lesbians. Maher believed that relationship-building with Catholic allies required openness and honesty. "I knew the value of coming out," he explained. "I thought that within the parish, like other spheres of life, I would put a face on the gay issue."[17] A few days following the march, Maher requested a meeting with Fr. Bill Dewan, the parish pastor.

A PARISH IN HELL'S KITCHEN

At other parishes, Maher's initiative may have been frowned upon. The Catholic Church has long struggled with pervasive homophobia, clericalism, and lack of lay leadership. In the early nineties, as today, many gay and lesbian Catholics were, in the words of Brendan Fay, "familiar with being told, 'You are not welcome.' Or, 'Here are the conditions under which you are welcome.'"[18] St. Paul the Apostle, however, was different from most parishes for a number of reasons.

First, the parish is located on the northern edge of Hell's Kitchen, one of New York City's most prominent "gayborhoods." Hell's Kitchen has been a center of gay life since the eighties, when rising real estate prices in the West Village and Chelsea, areas historically known for their LGBTQ presence, sent gays flocking north in search of cheaper rent. In 2018, one review described Hell's Kitchen as having the "highest concentration of LGBTQ services and resources,…largest clusters of LGBT-owned businesses," and, per the census, "highest rates of same-sex couples in the city."[19] The neighborhood, which stretches from West 42nd to West 60th Street between 8th Avenue and the Hudson River, has an array of clubs for dancing on Saturday night and restaurants for brunch on Sunday afternoon. It also is just south of Lincoln Center, one of the city's most prominent music and arts districts. A gay and lesbian ministry would be right at home in a gay and lesbian and arts-oriented neighborhood.

Second, St. Paul the Apostle is the motherhouse of the Paulist Fathers, a missionary order established in 1858 by Isaac Hecker, a U.S. philosopher, public theologian, and priest. Hecker was born a Protestant and tried out transcendentalism before becoming Roman Catholic in 1844 and a Redemptorist priest in 1849. He established the Paulist order as a society of missionaries dedicated to evangelizing the United States, which he believed was ripe for a Catholic revival.[20]

For more than 150 years, the brotherhood that Hecker founded has been at the forefront of innovative "mission preaching, media, campus ministries, parishes, downtown centers, the arts and more." According to their mission statement, Paulists strive to "discern the movement of the Holy Spirit within ourselves, within our ministries, within the Church and within the world."[21] They have a special gift for evangelization on the margins. Fr. Eric Andrews summarized the Paulist charism, saying, "We serve the Church by serving people outside the Church."[22] Paulist ministries include outreach to the divorced and remarried, lapsed Catholics, those questioning their faith, and LGBTQ people.

Third, the Paulists have a decades-long tradition of inclusivity within their own order. Their honesty about the reality of gay priests makes them far less defensive about LGBTQ issues than many other Catholic religious communities. The first Paulist to publicly come out was Fr. John Patrick Collins, CSP, who received his doctorate at the Institute for Advanced Study of Human Sexuality, was a DignityUSA board member, and helped organize the first AIDS hospice in San Francisco.[23] Fr. Thomas Stransky, CSP, then president of the Paulist Fathers, supported Collins and established a precedent for nondiscrimination in the order. Since then, a few Paulists have outed themselves from the pulpit without negative repercussions.[24] Many understand gay sexuality as a gift that enriches their priestly vocations, not a curse that inhibits them.

Fourth, the parish of St. Paul the Apostle Church has a long history of serving the local community through its promotion of progressive causes. Founded in 1858 on what was then the rural, northern edge of development in Manhattan, the parish has been home to successive waves of Irish, Italian, Puerto Rican, and other Latin American immigrant groups. As a faith community committed to the material welfare of its parishioners and surrounding neighborhoods, St. Paul carried out acts of mercy such as feeding the hungry through its soup kitchens, providing quality education in its now closed Catholic school, and caring for sick AIDS victims at the height of the epidemic. Parish leadership also focused on the need for systemic change by supporting social justice initiatives such as union organizing, access for people with disabilities, and Muslim-Christian dialogue.

Not a "Quiet Little Support Group"

After a fruitful meeting with Fr. Dewan, Maher initiated dialogue with other parish leaders in the summer of 1991. At the time, Paulist Fr. Marcos Zamora was offering "Second Look," a program for St. Paul parishioners and visitors to openly question and discuss Catholicism.[25] It was the perfect setting for Maher to sharpen his thinking. From the start, he wanted the gay and lesbian ministry to be part of the parish just like the St. Vincent de Paul Society, choir, and Sunday school. Maher found inspiration in Catholic ministries to ethnic communities, whose cultures were regularly celebrated in parish liturgies and festivals.[26] Why should the Church's relationship with gay and lesbian Catholics be any different? At St. Paul, he found support for his ideas from other parishioners and parish staff.

One of Maher's key allies was Fr. Steven Harris, a Paulist who had been a Broadway actor, director, and agent before joining the priesthood. The Paulist community gave him leeway to serve as a priest and continue working in theater. A 1996 review of a show he produced described how "Father Harris seems to have a hard time deciding where the Church begins and the theater ends."[27] In addition to incorporating Broadway lyrics into his sermons, Harris was also in charge of Momentum and later became chaplain to GLCM.

In the fall of 1991, Maher launched GLCM with a series of monthly meetings in the parish offices after the Sunday 5:15 p.m. Mass. He insisted the group's activities be listed in the bulletin alongside other groups, a provocative practice both then and now. Brendan Fay explained, "This ministry wasn't a hidden, marginal ministry within the wider parish, but it was up front and center, involving the whole parish. It was a ministry of conversation and conversion for all of us."[28]

GLCM's first year was full of unassuming events such as guest speakers, discussions, and socials. In December 1991, the ministry went Christmas caroling in the HIV ward at St. Luke's/Roosevelt hospital, located around the corner from the parish, and the following June, Maher organized GLCM's first liturgy, an ecumenical prayer service from the Liturgy of the Hours.[29] Observing GLCM's humble origins, the Paulists may not have realized what was in store. Maher explained, "Fr. Dewan thought I was coming to him for a quiet little support group—like an anonymous, 12-step program that would meet in the church basement. But that's not what I had in mind."[30] Maher was an organizer, after all, and brought his experience with trade unions, ACT UP, and Queer Nation to the nascent ministry. He knew how to use publicity to accomplish his goals. "I set about doing things in a very known, deliberative way," he said with a wry smile. "And I could attract a great deal of attention."[31] Priests, too, remember Maher as an instigator. Fr. Eric Andrews recalled, "The ministry was controversial not so much because of the outreach but because Donald was always pushing the envelope."[32] Although the Gay and Lesbian Catholic Ministry began quietly, within a couple of years it garnered press in outlets such as local TV news station WABC, the *National Catholic Reporter*, and even the *New York Times*.

Gay and Lesbian Liturgies

In its second year, GLCM began several years of innovative liturgies. Donald Maher was a thoughtful Catholic, creative showman, sensitive minister, and effective organizer. He knew that many LGBTQ people would never attend a Mass or set foot in the parish center because of their discomfort with the Church, so he organized high-profile, public celebrations of liturgical seasons, holidays, and saints' feast days. That way, LGBTQ folks could come and go as they pleased without drawing attention to themselves. The social element was front and center. As Brendan Fay recalled, "Donald Maher, the ministry, and the Paulists always put on the best show. I call it 'putting on the kettle.' The social ministry—the food, the coffee, the tea—was always there."[33] Years later, Maher himself admitted, "Everyone knew you'd get refreshments if you went to the gay ministry. I did refreshments well."[34]

GLCM's inaugural liturgy took place during Advent in 1992. It was the first time that many of the gay and lesbian attendees had returned to a Catholic parish since Dignity had been expelled from St. Francis Xavier in 1987.[35] Maher invited Sr. Jeannine Gramick of New Ways Ministry to speak for a program titled "Embracing the Exile." As an LGBTQ Catholic, Maher drew parallels between his experiences waiting for full inclusion in the Church and the Church's anticipation of Christ's birth before Christmas. He used the service to reinforce GLCM's ties to other parish groups. The *Coro Hispano*, St. Paul's Hispanic choir, sang, and the collection benefitted the parish's new ministry for the homebound and homeless. The night also built bridges to other New York City Catholic parishes with Daniel Coakley, the music director from St. Aloysius in Harlem, performing a rendition of "Precious Lord, Take Me Home."[36] Maher knew that GLCM's prophetic work was precarious, and he did everything he could to strengthen its standing in the local church.

A Pride Mass Fiasco

Maher's daring vision for full gay and lesbian inclusion became even more apparent the following June, when GLCM hosted St. Paul's first Pride Mass. It was a noteworthy moment for reasons no one could have expected.

Maher believed that celebrating a Pride Mass alone was too risky and would open the parish to criticism. He strategized by attracting allies. June 24 is the Feast Day of John the Baptist, Puerto Rico's patron saint, but it also corresponds to the conclusion of what was then known as Lesbian and Gay Pride and History Month. At the time, St. Paul was home to a sizeable Puerto Rican population, so Maher decided to bring the two communities together for a vigil Mass on the eve of the feast day.

Maher saw himself as a prophet who, like John the Baptist, upended the religious status quo, and he titled the bilingual and bicultural service, "A Voice in the Wilderness." As with the earlier Advent liturgy, Maher invited the *Coro Hispano* to participate. Maher's planning was so effective that he even convinced representatives from the archdiocese's Hispanic apostolate to attend. Paulist Fr. Steven Harris, then the parish's liaison to GLCM, planned to preside with Deacon Felipe Sin assisting the Mass.[37]

Before the 5:15 p.m. service even began, however, it was clear that something was amiss. A strange photographer took pictures of worshippers as they arrived, and unfamiliar faces were scattered among the pews. Soon, a crowd of eight strangers gathered around the altar. With a loud voice, one in the group read from a prepared statement that called the Paulist Fathers blasphemers for conducting a "Mass of Sodomites." Some of the protestors prayed the Rosary while others shouted, "Faggots and queers get out of the church!"[38]

When Brendan Fay saw that the protestors would not leave of their own accord, he intervened. "We are here to pray," he announced. "You have had your say. Let us carry on with what we came here for."[39] The unwelcomed visitors went quiet for a moment and returned to their seats. There were more fireworks to come.

At 5:30 p.m., Fr. Harris began the liturgy with protestors still present.[40] He had not forced them to leave because he did not want to further disrupt the Mass. Some semblances of normalcy returned to the service until Harris crossed the altar to proclaim the gospel. At that moment, the protestors began shouting again, and their leader rushed Fr. Harris in an ill-fated attempt to tear the lapel microphone from his vestments. Later, Harris described how, instead of coming off easily, the hook of the microphone "went through my hand like a fishhook."[41]

Harris began profusely bleeding on his vestments and the altar. Attendees called the police.

It was a notable moment for the Paulists to build solidarity with the LGBTQ community. Brendan Fay noted, "Fr. Steve and the others experienced, firsthand, what hate does."[42] When police officers arrived, they approached Maher with disbelief. Referring to recent ACT UP and Dignity/NY protests at the cathedral, they incredulously asked, "Ok—do we have this right, Mr. Maher? The gay people are in the pews behaving, and it's the *conservatives* who are on the altar acting up?" He shook his head, and the police asked him what they should do. Maher replied, "Do what you did to ACT UP and arrest them."[43] The tables had turned, and three traditionalists were arrested.

The aftermath of the Pride Mass was widely reported by Catholic and secular press. To his credit, Cardinal O'Connor quickly condemned the protestors' interruption of the Mass and all violence against "homosexuals."[44] Prosecutors subsequently charged two of the protestors with assault and disturbing a religious service.[45] As part of a plea bargain, the group's leader admitted his guilt and received community service. His codefendant, however, was convicted by a jury and sentenced to thirty days in jail.[46]

ORGANIZED OPPOSITION, FEAR OF RETRIBUTION, AND THE PAULIST RESPONSE

Maher later learned that the protestors were led by Paul Morrissey, the founder of the Morality Action Committee, a Queens-based organization that opposed same-sex marriage and frequently antagonized marchers at gay pride parades.[47] Morrissey singled out Donald Maher and the Paulist Fathers for special opprobrium. One Sunday morning, when Maher arrived at the parish to teach Sunday school, he found the building covered in leaflets condemning him as one who "OPPOSES CATHOLIC TEACHING...BUT TEACHES CATHOLIC KIDS." The flyers featured a large photo of Maher being arrested for civil disobedience at an ACT UP protest and provided contact information for the head pastor of St. Paul and the secretary to Cardinal O'Connor.[48]

For all that GLCM accomplished, it was still vulnerable to out-side agitators and criticism.

In January and February 1994, perhaps because of the ministry's explosive media coverage, representatives from the archdiocese met with the Paulist Fathers twice to discuss the group. It was an opportune moment for an intervention. The Paulists had recently replaced head pastor Fr. Dewan with Fr. Chuck Kullmann, who had never encoun-tered gay and lesbian ministry before.[49] Would he, like his predecessor, welcome the ministry, or would he cave to the archdiocese's demands?

Kullmann remembered that, when he arrived at St. Paul, "the parish was in a furor, and one piece of it was this gay and lesbian min-istry."[50] Some parishioners were concerned by how GLCM could affect the Paulists' relationship with the archdiocese. As a religious order, the Paulists report directly to the Vatican, which means they enjoy a measure of independence from local dioceses. Still, wherever they minister, Paulists depend on the local prelate's goodwill for their faculties. Throughout the early nineties, rumors swirled that Cardinal O'Connor might strip the Paulists of their mother church because of their support for gays and lesbians.[51]

Although this would be nearly impossible in reality, there was a rationale behind the fear. First, everyone knew about the animosity between the archbishop and LGBTQ activists. Just a few years ear-lier, Cardinal John O'Connor had expelled Dignity from St. Francis Xavier. Second, St. Paul was an influential and wealthy parish, the largest noncathedral parish in the United States at the time.[52] It would be a prize for the archdiocese if the Paulists had to leave.

GLCM was also controversial among the Paulists themselves. How much of the order's political and spiritual capital was the com-munity willing to sacrifice for a group of gays and lesbians? Many of the older Paulists had theological, ethical, and pastoral reasons for their opposition. Fr. James Lloyd, for example, had been instrumental in leading Courage, a 12-Step program for those struggling to remain celibate. Seeing openly gay and proud parishioners welcomed in the parish was an insult to Courage members who also met there. Accord-ing to Fr. Eric Andrews, prior to GLCM, the Paulists had welcomed gays and lesbians "individually, but not in groups, especially if they were not towing the [Catholic] party line 100%." GLCM "caused a group of Paulists to feel very uncomfortable with ministry that wel-comed people regardless of whether they were celibate or not."[53]

Fr. Kullmann also found Maher difficult to work with. The priest remembered, "Donald…could always be entertaining and charming, but he was always a noodge. He was never satisfied. He always wanted more. I could understand that. He was an advocate. But that didn't make him easy to work with."[54] Kullmann also grew tired of seemingly endless criticisms from the chancery office. "At one point," he shared, "it got to be so difficult with dealing with the chancery office on one side and Donald Maher and some of the more strident people on the other that I just wanted to shut the thing down."[55]

The parish council, however, reassured Fr. Kullmann of the ministry's importance to the parish's mission and identity. Rather than ending GLCM, Kullmann unsuccessfully tried to rein in the group. First, he appointed Carolyn Moorehead, a parishioner and professional therapist, to help moderate GLCM and share some of Maher's responsibilities. Her tenure lasted only months because gay and lesbian members of GLCM protested that she was a heterosexual who could not understand their needs. Second, Kullmann told Maher that another St. Patrick's Day service at the parish would not be allowed because the event was too controversial with the archdiocese. GLCM circumvented the restriction by holding the service at a nearby Protestant congregation, where Maher ensured that the ecumenical liturgy would be another spectacular, media-filled event. Brendan Fay preached; Mary Somoza, a disability rights activist, member of the New York City school board, and mother of children in the Sunday school program at St. Paul, shared a reading; and New York City public advocate Mark Green read from Scripture.[56]

Meeting the Cardinal

In December 1994, Maher, disappointed by what had transpired between St. Paul and the archdiocese in March, wrote to Cardinal O'Connor to request a meeting about the St. Patrick's Day Parade and GLCM.[57] The cardinal, who knew Maher's father, granted his request, and the pair met in the episcopal residence the following June. Maher recalled, "We had a polite, gracious first meeting." The archbishop who opposed gay and lesbian civil rights in public could be quite civil in private.

Maher's outreach to Cardinal O'Connor reflected his proclivity for building relationships. "Even if we have our differences," Maher said, "I show others mercy and grace."[58] Fr. Eric Andrews related how "even people who disagreed with Donald appreciated that he was always there."[59] Although many LGBTQ New Yorkers saw O'Connor as their nemesis, Maher built a friendly relationship with the prelate that lasted several years and included two more visits.[60]

Private meetings, however, did very little to change either side's stance on gay and lesbian issues. In fact, Maher built his public reputation as one of the cardinal's chief public critics. Throughout the nineties, he attended O'Connor's press conferences that touched on gay and lesbian matters. After the archbishop offered his remarks, Maher would step in to give the press pool an alternative Catholic perspective. The most noteworthy example of this came in May 1998 when Cardinal O'Connor held a press conference after Mass to publicize his opposition to a city council resolution legalizing same-sex domestic partnerships. A *New York Times* report of the story cited "Donald F. Maher, who leads the gay and lesbian ministry at St. Paul the Apostle Church on the Upper West Side," saying, "We heard lovely, beautiful words in the cathedral today. Regrettably, they were not in the homily. They were in the first reading, which was from the Acts of the Apostles."[61]

A Decade of Ministry

In spite of Maher's challenging relationship with Cardinal O'Connor and some of the Paulist priests, GLCM accomplished much within the parish. In 1994, to mark the twenty-fifth anniversary of the Stonewall riots, GLCM hosted a reception for the International Gay and Lesbian Catholic Conference, supported a full-page religious ad in that year's guide to Pride that encouraged gays and lesbians to "Seize the Spirit," and marched on the United Nations in support of gay and lesbian civil rights. That June, the group also hosted its first daylong retreat. In addition to these events, GLCM reorganized its leadership structure by creating an executive committee of Paulists and laypeople. Its growing importance in the parish was reflected by a new "hotline" voicemail box, ext. 303, at the parish office's telephone number.[62]

Over the next several years, GLCM repeated many of the traditions Maher had established. A 1997 "Proposal for the Ministry's 7th Year" listed events such as an Advent prayer service for December, Day of Recollection in June, and involvement in other parish ministries and activities throughout the year.[63] The calendar included a Sunday evening series titled "Absolutely Catholic," a program that welcomed a wide range of Catholics to share their stories. With guests such as Christine Quinn, a local gay Catholic politician, and a member of the parish's Courage group, Maher built bridges wherever he could, especially when it included people who opposed him. One of the most popular (and by far less provocative) activities that developed was a weekly Wednesday morning Mass, with breakfast to follow at The Flame Diner two blocks from the parish. For all the controversy it generated, GLCM was a community of Catholics like many others that gathered for worship and fellowship.

In the late nineties, GLCM and St. Paul the Apostle Parish hosted an annual St. Patrick's Day dinner and dance for the Lavender and Green Alliance, an organization founded by Brendan Fay in 1994 to represent gay Irish people. Many St. Paul parishioners attended these dances, including the elderly and homeless whom Maher was sure to invite. Volunteers from the Catholic Worker prepared meals of corned beef and cabbage, and the nights that followed were full of music and dancing. These celebrations meant the world to LGBTQ Catholics such as Brendan Fay, who recalled, "I can't tell you what it was like for us to be able to dance with one another. Sometimes we are only invited [into the church] to pray our rituals of forgiveness, to engage in theological defenses of our lives, or to plead for pastoral welcome, inclusion, and equality. At St. Paul the Apostle, we danced together in the parish hall. To me, that is as profound a theological statement as any that came from that parish."[64]

INTERPARISH AND ECUMENICAL PARTNERSHIPS

Maher was committed to expanding GLCM's reach beyond the parish. He regularly attended meetings of the New York Roundtable of Gay and Lesbian Ministries, a group of Catholics from the parishes St. Paul, St. Joseph, and St. Francis Xavier, which all had active ministries at the time. Maher surmised that the ministry would also be stronger by connecting with other religious traditions. GLCM events and liturgies often included representatives from multiple faiths, and Maher was a founding member of the Spiritual Rainbow, an interreligious coalition that hosted prayer services and provided gay-affirming resources for religious communities.

NAVIGATING CATHOLIC TEACHING

As a public, Catholic ministry, GLCM was accountable to both the archdiocese and the gay and lesbian community. This meant that Maher and others had to tread a careful line regarding Catholic doctrine. After the Morality Action Committee interrupted GLCM's 1993 Pride Mass, Maher responded with a strongly worded letter published by *Catholic New York*, the archdiocesan newspaper. GLCM, he clarified, was honest that Church teaching on sexuality was "problematic for most Catholics," whether gay or straight, and even "many of the clergy." Still, Maher did not believe it was GLCM's role to criticize Church teaching but only to "create a welcoming and hospitable place where the struggle involving human sexuality issues and the challenge to move all into the fullness of Catholic teaching can take place at its very best."[65]

Fr. Kullman, whose empathy for the ministry seems to have grown over time, echoed Maher's words in a 1996 profile piece for a local newspaper.[66] Kullman reflected that the parish did not focus on teaching celibacy but instead "on questions of spirituality, welcome, and fellowship." He confessed that the Church's teaching was "not an easy thing" for LGBTQ Catholics. "We don't question it," the priest explained, "but we don't harp on it either, in the sense that we recognize people as people first, and questions of [sexual] orientation second."[67]

GLCM'S END AND A NEW BEGINNING

Maher walked a tightrope as the leader of GLCM for more than a decade. His organizing created havoc for the Paulist priests and St. Paul community at times but also opportunities for deep transformation through compassionate ministry. Maher joked, "I brought myself to them [the Paulists], and they've been trying to cope with me ever since."[68] Nearly two decades after GLCM ended, he recognized it as a "time of grace for all of us. I realized then, and I realize now, that I've been given a very special grace to do this ministry. Grace begets grace."[69] Brendan Fay offered his own evaluation of the ministry's legacy: "What was going on at St. Paul the Apostle touches on Catholic ministry at its best. But let's be real as well and say that it was an experiment in listening to the Spirit. It was something courageous because there was no handbook or pastoral guide."[70]

Tragically, Maher had to face his own challenges when coping with the aftermath of the terrorist attacks on September 11, 2001. Recognizing his need for a change of scenery, Maher left the city to rebuild his life and well-being in rural Eastern Pennsylvania.[71]

After Maher left St. Paul, there was no leader able or willing to carry on the work he had started. Most of the ministry had stemmed from his own vision and initiative. After years of challenging the Church to grow in its care for gays and lesbians, GLCM began to fade from the parish's collective memory.

It would be several years before St. Paul the Apostle became home to another LGBTQ ministry. Once Out at St. Paul (OSP) got off the ground, however, its rise was meteoric. Today, depending on one's perspective, OSP is either one of the most famous or infamous LGBTQ Catholic ministries in the world. Although the OSP community is often a rope in the Church's tug of (culture) war, its own priorities, like those of Donald Maher's GLCM, are evangelization, hospitality, and fostering a culture of healing and reconciliation. Chapter 6 tells OSP's story.

Chapter 6

"OUR SEXUALITY LEADS US BACK TO GOD"

Out at St. Paul and Ministry Today

> Go therefore and make disciples of all nations, baptizing them in the name of the Father and of the Son and of the Holy Spirit.
>
> —Matthew 28:19

MEETING OSP

My first visit to Out at St. Paul (OSP) coincided with Pope Francis's 2015 trip to the United States. News broke that the holy father had met with Kim Davis, the notorious Kentucky Clerk of Courts who refused to marry same-sex couples, and I was heartbroken.[1] I thought Francis was trying to end the Church's futile engagement in culture wars. Wasn't he the one who once asked, "Who am I to judge?" I needed to sort through my feelings with other LGBTQ Catholics.

Happily, OSP's fall Mass was scheduled for that evening. In a side chapel of the church's cavernous sanctuary, I heard a message of love and acceptance from Fr. Gil Martinez, the parish pastor. New friends listened as I spoke of my disappointment with the pope. That night, OSP became my spiritual home.

For several years after joining OSP, I had no idea about the group's earlier iteration in Donald Maher's GLCM. And yet, for all their differences, the two epochs share much in common — inculturated ministry in Hell's Kitchen, a keen ability to listen and respond to the spiritual needs of LGBTQ Catholics, and a strong tradition of grassroots lay leadership.

FR. GIL MARTINEZ AND REVIVING PARISH LIFE

Out at St. Paul originated with the vision of Fr. Gil Martinez, who served as head pastor of St. Paul the Apostle from 2006 until 2018. Martinez was born in 1959 in El Paso, Texas, the son of an Apache mother and Mexican American father. He spent time working as a farmworker before studying conservation and natural resources at the University of California, Berkeley. There, he met the Paulist Fathers. "I remember being profoundly moved by the Paulists," he said. "The first time I went there was the first time I heard a homily that had anything to do with my life. I realized that faith isn't just going to church because I had to."[2]

After college, Martinez served as a park ranger at the Grand Canyon and Big Bend National Park for eight years. While working in the vast wilderness he had a persistent "awareness of being called out of myself" and an "experience of something that asked me to go deeper."[3] In 1986, a woman who had suffered a heart attack in the park told him he ought to become a priest.[4] Following the experience, he met with a priest to continue discerning his call and obtained a work transfer to be closer to parish life. In less than a decade, he joined the Paulists, moved to Washington, D.C., for seminary, and was ordained in 1995.

When Martinez arrived to serve as head pastor of St. Paul the Apostle in 2006, the parish attached to the Paulist motherhouse was in shambles. According to Fr. Eric Andrews, CSP, leadership "was in a spin."[5] The interim administrator who preceded Martinez could devote only part of his time to the task, the young adult ministry had collapsed, and GLCM was a distant memory. Martinez noted, "There was a lot of despair in the parish. People were just going through the motions."[6]

Martinez set about reviving the parish. One of his first initiatives was to involve the church in the New Sanctuary Movement, an inter-religious, "immigrant-led organization that creates support systems for and empowers those navigating the immigration system."[7] Martinez was the parish's first Latino pastor and had a heart for immigrant justice. His commitment was tested when, a few months into his assignment, a young gay man approached the church asking for sanctuary. The refugee from Indonesia was scheduled for deportation back to his home country where he would face violence, if not death, due to his sexual orientation. Martinez welcomed him to stay in the former convent attached to the parish.

The new priest's advocacy was controversial to the parish council. Was the church breaking the law? What if the young man was lying about the dangers of deportation to remain in the United States? Several parishioners left the parish over the incident, but Martinez turned the controversy into an opportunity for dialogue. Together, he and the remaining parish leaders interrogated the church's raison d'être. What is ministry? How could they more faithfully follow Jesus Christ? Because the young Indonesian man was gay, Martinez also raised issues related to LGBTQ outreach.

Principles for LGBTQ Outreach

Since his arrival, Fr. Martinez had noticed that there was "a fair amount of young gay men" at the 5:15 Mass.[8] One encounter with a gay parishioner particularly impressed him:

> This young man who was an actor always sat at the very back. He came up to me and said, "I'm gay and I've never felt welcomed to the Church before. This is my first time I realized that all are welcome. I'm part of this church…." That's when it occurred to me, and he told me, "There are other gays here, you know." And I said, "Oh yeah! I guess there are, I presume."[9]

When Martinez spoke to members of the parish council about welcoming the LGBTQ community, they were skeptical. Surely, the archdiocese would be hostile to the idea, and other parishes already had long-running groups.[10] Why couldn't gays and lesbians congregate in the West Village at St. Francis Xavier? Most of those who attended St. Paul, however, were local to Hell's Kitchen and younger than the members of other gay and lesbian ministries. Many St. Paul parishioners grew up in LGBTQ-affirming parishes and had a healthy relationship with the Church, a privilege not afforded to older generations. Fr. Martinez explained that "younger people felt they couldn't understand the experience of older folks and the pain of the past."[11] They needed a ministry to meet them where they were.

As part of Martinez's dialogue with parish leadership, the St. Paul community established five principles to guide its relationship with LGBTQ people. First, it was important to acknowledge that LGBTQ people were already part of the Church. Martinez stressed that the community needed to "be positive about [that fact]" by welcoming young people, being honest about LGBTQ issues in homilies, and providing opportunities for LGBTQ parishioners to contribute to church life. Second, forcing LGBTQ Catholics into the closet was out of the question. As Fr. Martinez described, "For this to be authentic Christian community, we had to have honesty. No one would ever have to lie or be discreet about who they were." Third, the parish would not hammer on the need for LGBTQ people to remain chaste. Why should LGBTQ parishioners be treated any differently than straight parishioners? Fourth, the parish "would trust the Holy Spirit to form people in their faith and conscience." Parish leaders resolved to listen and try to understand LGBTQ people rather than force on them a list of doctrines and ethical ideals. Fifth, the parish agreed that those parishioners who disagreed with LGBTQ outreach would take their opposition "down a notch." Fr. Martinez encouraged parishioners to understand that "God doesn't reject anyone."[12]

Servant Leadership and Building a Ministry Team

For his first two years at St. Paul, Martinez worked to build a good rapport with gay and lesbian attendees. According to parishioner Matthew Vidal, future members of OSP "were a second away from talking to each other and going to bars together and being great friends, but it needed a spark."[13] Fr. Martinez met with gay and lesbian parishioners after Mass, visited over dinner, and listened to their stories. Vidal recounted, "We would lament to Fr. Gil how there wasn't anything formal. And he said to us, 'We will! We will! There used to be something here, and there will be something again soon.'"[14]

Martinez tested the waters for the new ministry around Easter 2007, when he planned an event with Fr. James Alison, an openly gay theologian and friend of the Paulists. In addition to saying Mass, Alison asked a packed house of more than ninety attendees if it was possible to be gay and Catholic. Larry Holodak, a longtime St. Paul parishioner, described the evening as

> amazing at the time. I remember attending it but being so surprised and caught off guard about the feeling in the room. There was such a feeling. I've described it as damaged. People were just upset, they were dispirited, they were not in a good place....There was so much work that could be done.[15]

Martinez initially limited the ministry to relationship building with a small, discrete network of gays and lesbians.[16] Vidal recalled that Fr. Martinez "didn't even want it to be an official ministry. He was clear that he wanted to make it an event-based group that made LGBT presence very obvious and therefore very welcomed in the church."[17] That way, no one could claim that the ministry was forced on the parish by an ideological priest.

In the spring of 2009, Martinez became more intentional about discipling leaders. The first iteration of what became known as the ministry team included seven gay men who were active in parish life. Vidal said, "Gil picked people who already had strong faiths and theological backgrounds on why we accepted who we were and why what we were doing was right."[18] Nevertheless, it soon became clear that many had a complicated relationship with Catholic tradition. Attendees were eager to discuss programming and events but reluctant to commit to spiritual leadership and communal theological reflection. Channeling Pope Francis, Fr. Martinez explained, "That's fine if you're running an NGO, but we were doing something else."[19]

As the group forged ahead, one of OSP's first leaders came to understand that "Gil wanted to form people for ministry, not just a gay group."[20] After some time and considerable struggle, other members of the team caught on. Larry Holodak remembered,

> I had no experience at all about what a ministry was or what it did. When he told us when we first met that we were going to be evangelists I almost fell out of my chair. "I am not knocking on doors! I am not proselytizing!" And slowly there was this story of discovery of what did it really mean.[21]

Martinez focused on mentoring those who could carry out the ministry's mission. Fr. Mark-David Janus, CSP, who witnessed OSP's growth firsthand, remarked that Fr. Martinez "wasn't just developing events, he was developing souls—souls that were going to be in a position to be able to attend to other souls."[22]

Intentional discipleship was a practice that Martinez had picked up over years of campus and parish ministry. He remembered how, as a young priest, he "had all this energy and excitement, but I was organizing things and I was in charge. And I did this and I did that." That changed when he arrived at his assignment in campus ministry at Berkeley. Martinez learned about servant leadership from his mentor, Paulist Fr. Frank Sabatté, who told him, "'You know, it's not about you! The content of the ministry is people—the people who come in and the people who aren't there.' If you take that seriously, how do you design ministry where you're not the core and center of it?"[23]

To Martinez, servant leadership meant "creating spaces for people to do faith sharing, to support each other as Christian community, and to do faith formation with them—theological reflection on experience and ministry."[24] He began each ministry team meeting with faith sharing and reflection. "Everyone who was involved in this ministry was involved in their own spiritual formation and the spiritual formation of others," an early OSP member said.[25]

After nurturing the group's spirituality, Fr. Martinez's most difficult task was to step back and let the Holy Spirit do her work. When LGBTQ parishioners began to take the lead, Martinez said, "I bit my tongue so often….I found it very difficult, but it called leadership out of people, and it called the community to trust that the ministry belonged to, and came from, the community, and the Holy Spirit."[26]

Martinez's trust in the Holy Spirit stemmed from his reading of Isaac Hecker and his formation as a Paulist priest. For Paulists, discerning the Spirit's movement requires sensitivity to how God works in individuals and communities. The Paulist approach to pastoral care begins with the conviction that God is active in everyone's life. Martinez explained,

> [Ministry] begins with people's experience and truly honoring that. Not, "Let me listen to your experience as a gay man so I can find the right church teaching to beat you up with." That's an agenda and program like Courage. For Paulists, this means to trust what comes from the deepest level of one's conscience. But not by yourself. In the context of community.[27]

Going to Gay Bars

One of the firstfruits of the group's reflection came after Martinez shared an essay on pastoral leadership. The team was aware that many gays and lesbians were reluctant to enter a church because of the pain it had caused them in the past. How could OSP reach LGBTQ people outside the parish?

Someone suggested they hold an event in a gay bar. The idea was a lightning bolt. Imagine the press! Wouldn't the archdiocese object? Hosting theological discussions about gay Catholic experience was one thing, but visiting a local watering hole was another. To outsiders, gay bars evoke images of shirtless bartenders, late-night dancing, and cruising in the bathrooms. To many LGBTQ people, however, they are safe—even sacred—spaces for gathering without the fear of judgment from the outside world.[28] Why shouldn't a Catholic ministry be the first to communicate grace and reconciliation there?

Martinez was excited to watch the conversation unfold. Although he was determined not to intervene and make the decision himself, he did encourage the leaders to take a bold stand. Marie Smithgall, who joined the ministry team in 2016, remarked that "[Martinez] surprised me sometimes." Whenever there was division among the group because a proposal seemed too risky, "most often he would encourage us to do it."[29]

Based on its communal discernment, the ministry team decided to hold an event at a gay bar. Martinez was pleased with the groundbreaking decision. "We didn't go to the gay bar to be cool or to rub it in the face of the archdiocese," he said. "It really was organic. That was the exciting part of the early programs—it was organic to people's reflection as a team and community."[30]

OSP's first evangelical excursion took place at Vlada Lounge in Hell's Kitchen on Thursday, December 10, 2009. An email invitation welcomed newcomers to "a unique gay & lesbian fellowship event" that promised to "support and develop that important component of [the St. Paul] community."[31] Matthew Vidal, who cosponsored the event with his partner, Rick, described the event that put the ministry on the map: "The entire upstairs of Vlada was packed. We had a sign-up list and it was giant. We had a huge mailing list after that."[32] Martinez attended wearing his collar, a surprising act of witness that set a precedent for the barrier-breaking ministry to come.

After that, bar crawls became a staple of OSP's incarnational outreach. Their importance as a symbol and concrete means of evangelization cannot be overstated. Fr. Mark-David Janus observed, "Unique to OSP is the continual outreach—to be people of faith publicly reaching out to other LGBTQ people. The bar hops are huge. I don't know anybody else who does that."[33]

At these events, attendees receive a nametag to facilitate introductions and a bracelet to wear for drink specials. OSP provides food, usually mozzarella sticks and wings from the bar. Paulist priests are guests of honor at establishments such as Boxers, a sports bar, or Bottoms up/Vodka Soda, a two-level dance club. The priests return to the rectory after the first stop, but OSP members continue enjoying the night at other destinations. Several members of OSP first encountered the ministry through its bar crawls, surprised and delighted that a Catholic parish would sponsor such gatherings.

ONE PARISH MINISTRY AMONG MANY

In late 2009 the community discerned its name—Out at St. Paul—to expand its mission beyond gays and lesbians, announce its commitment to evangelization, and clarify that members had no intention of hiding in the closet.[34] LGBTQ parishioners were proud of their queer Catholic identity and unafraid to make their presence known in the parish, neighborhood, and archdiocese. It was a radical move that pushed the envelope for parish-based LGBTQ ministry. Edward Poliandro, a longtime parishioner of St. Francis Xavier and leader of its Gay Catholics community, acknowledged, "OSP was out in different ways than we were."[35]

What distinguished OSP from other parish-based ministries would become clearer with time, but the group was always one ministry among others at St. Paul. Fr. Eric Andrews emphasized that "Gil created the group with parity to other groups in the parish. They have an equal status with the other ministries."[36] From the start, the ministry received a spot in the weekly bulletin for its events. In December 2009, OSP members also began making announcements from the pulpit at the end of the 10 a.m. and 5:15 p.m. Masses. It was a big deal for the group to "come out" to fellow parishioners. Matthew Vidal, who was the first to stand in front of the congregation, shared, "I remember being really scared doing it. You could hear a pin drop at the 10 a.m. Mass when I said the word *gay*. I think they were shocked that [the announcement] was so blatantly said."[37]

Since then, the tradition of giving weekly announcements in front of the parish continues. Countless OSP members and visitors have noted how meaningful the practice is for LGBTQ visibility. Marie Smithgall took notice on her first visit. She reminisced: "I remember hearing OSP's announcement after church and thinking, 'Whoa! This is something special.' I don't remember who was preaching, but I got a good feel from the community and OSP was a big draw."[38]

With Fr. Martinez's encouragement, the ministry team adapted a tripartite mission statement that read, "Out @ St Paul (OSP) is the Lesbian, Gay, Bisexual & Transgender Ministry of our parish at St. Paul the Apostle in New York City, which seeks to engage our Catholic faith through service to our community, social activities and the exploration of Catholic spirituality."[39] The group's vision closely mirrored the mission statement formulated by the Apostolists, the parish's young adult ministry. OSP's mission statement gave the community a clear purpose, but it also made the group just like others in the parish.

"The Heart of St. Paul's"

OSP's inclusion in the parish may be most clear at the 5:15 p.m. Sunday Mass. The liturgy's late start time gives attendees a chance to enjoy Sunday brunch or a picnic in Central Park beforehand. At the

Mass, it is not difficult to spot LGBTQ parishioners. Lovers hold hands and friends share the sign of peace with hugs that last too long and double kisses on the cheek. Some attendees wear makeup, earrings, and nail polish to complement their flamboyant Sunday dress. Choral music incorporates traditional Catholic hymnody alongside more contemporary music that could be performed on Broadway.

LGBTQ representation at Mass and in parish leadership is central to OSP members' sense of belonging. At the 5:15 p.m. Mass, OSP members receive priority to serve as lectors and eucharistic ministers. It is not uncommon to find same-sex couples carrying up the gifts prior to their consecration. Santiago Rivera, a St. Paul parishioner and eucharistic minister who served on the OSP ministry team from 2012 until 2015, shared that "OSP is the heart of St. Paul's....It's really integrated with who the parish is and what it represents."[40] Michael Tomae found St. Paul in 2012 and joined the OSP ministry team in 2013. For him, OSP is the gateway to participation in the Church. "LGBTQ people," he explained, "are going to church because they want to—fully, as LGBTQ people. They like being part of that community."[41]

OSP members are not the only ones who appreciate St. Paul's welcome of LGBTQ Catholics. Young Catholics want their faith communities to champion justice for LGBTQ people. Families prefer to raise their children in LGBTQ-affirming spaces. Marianne Palacios, who served on the ministry team for four years, explained, "OSP makes Catholic allies feel comfortable in their own parish. It gives people a license to have their faith and progressive politics, too. It also opens the door for people who are interested in learning more."[42]

OSP regularly touches the lives of parish allies. Yasi Mahallaty began attending St. Paul in 2014 when she was new to the city. In 2016, she related,

> I really don't know what I would've done these past two years without OSP, because it was truly the first community that I had in New York, and moving here was really scary, so I'm very fortunate. The resilience and the amount of faith in the group and [their] openness to welcoming me into the community has meant so much to me. And I feel like I've grown as a young woman, as a person of faith, and as an ally to the community.[43]

OSP's participation at the 5:15 Mass and inclusion in parish life is a sign of hope for many. Marie Smithgall reflected, "The Church can be such a divisive and painful place for LGBTQ Catholics and other people. Seeing yourself represented and having that loving embrace from within the Church is really powerful....For many parishioners, OSP brings a sense of pride. They say, 'I want to be part of a parish that has programs like OSP!'"[44]

The sense of pride in OSP community continues after Mass, when OSP members loiter at the back of the building before security forces them out. Michael Roper, one of the group's senior members, is proud to be among the "gay men standing at the back of the church after Mass. You don't see the straight people doing that....We're always there. It's almost like we don't want to leave."[45]

When the church's gates are finally locked behind them, more intimate groups depart for dinner and drinks at nearby restaurants. An older group of gay men usually goes to Flame, a diner just a few blocks from the church, while younger gays may go to Bacon Bar or Mee Noodle Shop. Some inevitably show up for happy hour at Rise, a gay bar just a few blocks from the church that projects Madonna music videos onto its walls. Wherever these St. Paul parishioners end up after Mass, LGBTQ Catholic identity is a reason for celebration. A spirit of camaraderie, mutual care, and good humor permeates every opportunity for OSP members to gather.

High-Profile Events and the Annual Retreat

In 2010 and 2011, OSP held several high-profile events to bolster its public image and attract support from the surrounding neighborhood. Fred Negem, a New York socialite and member of the ministry team, led the way by creating connections between OSP and the arts and film community. "My idea of success," he said, "is to do really good events that people will notice. When you link yourself to that kind of fame, it gets you known and then you can do other things."[46]

One of the first events that Negem organized was a showing of *Forgiveness*, a 2006 film about an American Israeli haunted by his nation's violent past. Negem rented the Bruno Walter Auditorium at nearby Lincoln Center for the well-attended event, which concluded with a Q&A session with Udi Aloni, the film's director. Another gathering at the parish center welcomed furniture designer Mitchell Gold, whose 2008 book, *Crisis*, gave a platform for LGBTQ celebrities to share their personal stories about growing up queer.[47] The church was packed with Gold's fans but also OSP's first heckler, who stood up and called Martinez an "abomination for holding the event in the church."[48] Larry Holodak remembered the evening as

> very controversial to some people in the parish and the archdiocese. People could not believe that [Gold's book] was an appropriate topic. I thought people were there to watch what we were doing. People were trying to steal the narrative to claim that [Gold] was trying to contravene the Church's teaching.[49]

Of course, nothing that evening contradicted church teaching, but OSP's naysayers were never satisfied. As the ministry grew it became a lighthouse for its supporters and a lightning rod for its critics.

OSP built on its early publicity. In late winter 2012, Negem arranged for Alan Downs, a world-renowned psychologist, to speak at the group's first retreat in upstate New York. Downs was famous for his classic book, *The Velvet Rage*, which outlined the struggles that gay men face in pursuit of social and familial acceptance.[50] Although the popular author drew a large crowd when he came to St. Paul in 2011, only twenty attended the first retreat. Some who came were disappointed that Downs's message "wasn't as spiritual as we wanted it to be."[51] Future retreats would be more oriented toward LGBTQ Catholic spirituality and led by Paulist priests and theologians closer to the community.

Since 2015, OSP has met every year on the second weekend of February for fellowship, teaching, and prayer at San Alfonso, a Redemptorist retreat house on the Jersey shore. More than seventy attend what has become one of the ministry's most important annual events. One participant shared, "The retreat is a sacred time. You know it will be special. Things that only the Holy Spirit can show us happen there."[52]

The weekend is structured by daily prayer, meals, preaching, and small group sharing. Although OSP's retreat planning teams have welcomed world-renowned theologians such as Fr. Bryan Massingale and Dr. Mary Hunt to lead sessions, the weekend's highlight comes Saturday night, when three OSP members share their testimonials with the group. This sacred storytelling confirms God's work in the community and provides space for OSP members to support one another. Patrick Manning, a longtime OSP member, explained the retreat's impact on his life:

> I come back from that retreat, every time, just feeling so hopeful, and happy and excited and full of gratitude for this community that we have....In the Catholic Church, the word *kinship* is often floated a lot and I think that retreat is just the best example of kinship that exists. You see people from so many different walks of life: different ages, different diverse backgrounds, different ethnic backgrounds, different genders, coming together and meshing into this absolutely stunning community. It's just overwhelming for me.[53]

THE INTERPARISH COLLABORATIVE AND THE FIRST PRIDE MASS

In its early years, OSP sent representatives to meetings of the Interparish Collaborative (IC), a group of local LGBTQ Catholic ministries. The collaborative was established in 2005 with the help of Brooklyn Auxiliary Bishop Joseph Sullivan to "encourage dialogue to promote effective models of LGBT ministry."[54] When IC was five years old, controversy exploded around St. Francis Xavier's participation in the annual Pride parade. For many years, area LGBTQ Catholics had been openly marching, handing out literature, carrying a banner with the parish's name, and stopping for prayer in front of the cathedral. Their witness bothered traditionalist Catholics, and in June 2010, Archbishop Timothy Dolan asked them to stop marching.[55] Although the ministry eventually reached a compromise to march in the parade without its parish's name on the banner, the affair became a defining issue for the IC.[56]

After attending the IC meetings, OSP members realized that marching in the parade could imperil their relationship with the archdiocese. Was the risk worth the reward? They considered alternative ways that OSP could fulfill its mission during Pride Week. Santiago Rivera suggested that, instead of marching, they hold a Pride Mass in Sheridan Square, the West Village park where LGBTQ activists

launched the Stonewall Riots in 1969. Although OSP had been celebrating small, private Pride masses at St. Paul since 2009, a Stonewall Mass would "bring the Church out of the church building....We
were not trying to do anything political," Rivera said. "This was about
spirituality. The Mass aligned so well with our mission....Everyone was
excited about it, and it was a risk they were willing to take."[57]

The ministry team's intuition that the Mass would be a worth-
while risk proved correct. According to Martinez, the annual liturgy in
Sheridan Square became

> this experience where we could pray together, and other
> people—gay or not—could see that and come and join us.
> We would be out there declaring that the center of our lives
> and ministry is the Eucharist....And we prayed. We gath-
> ered to do what Christians do. What better place for gay and
> lesbian people than somewhere that has so much signifi-
> cance for our identification of who we are?[58]

OSP's public celebration of the Eucharist soon caught on with
LGBTQ Catholics from other local parishes, and the Pride Mass
became another hallmark of the ministry. Each June, organizers drape
a rainbow flag over a foldable table to serve as an altar in Sheridan
Square, which is itself festooned in rainbow string flags. More than one
hundred worshippers fill the small park for singing, prayer, a homily,
and Eucharist. The Mass is a time for reflection on the past, including
painful memories of homo/transphobia and the suffering caused by the
HIV/AIDS epidemic, but also thanksgiving for decades of activism and
the growing awareness of LGBTQ human rights. Passersby often stop
to join the communal prayer, and afterward, attendees walk across the
street for a social at a piano bar. According to Santiago Rivera, "Having
that Mass fosters a sense of belonging and a sense of hope. It's a really
important symbol for our community."[59]

Riding Out Tensions with the Archdiocese of New York

Despite OSP's best intentions, events like the Pride Mass have
led to a strained relationship with the archdiocese. The LGBTQ ministry, like others, bears the brunt of perennial criticism and mockery

from alt-right and traditionalist Catholic media such as Church Militant, First Things, and Lifesite News. Unfortunately, the archdiocese has acceded to these groups' complaints on numerous occasions.[60] Martinez believed that a fear of change motivated the archdiocese's responses. He shared, "The officials in the archdiocese were always threatened by anything that was working with the gays. They took it as a declaration of advocacy to change Church teaching."[61]

The archdiocese's first salvo came in 2015 with the death of Cardinal Edward Egan, the former archbishop of New York who had become OSP's unofficial patron after his retirement. On a few occasions, Egan presided at the Young People's Mass and, according to Fr. Mark-David Janus, "He wanted to lend his support to [OSP] by his presence. He wasn't going to make public statements, but he wanted to see it nurtured."[62]

Martinez, too, counted on Egan's support, recollecting, "Egan liked what we were doing very much. He supported what we were doing in the only way we could—in a church way, never explicitly saying 'gay' or 'lesbian,' but always lifting up 'the incredibly diverse mass at St. Pauls' and inviting Vatican people there."[63]

When Cardinal Egan died, the balance of power shifted. Within a few weeks of Egan's death, Martinez received an unexpected call from Mother Agnes Mary Donovan, the mother superior of the Sisters of Life. Martinez and Donovan were strangers, but the message she transmitted, Martinez recalled, was frank: "The archbishop wants you to know that he wants all this [OSP] stuff out of the bulletin and to get everyone to Courage."[64] The visit concluded with her warning that there would be severe consequences if he did not comply.

Fr. Martinez was concerned but not moved. His poise would prove crucial whenever chancery officials confronted him in the years to come. They came with three consistent demands from the archbishop. First, he wanted OSP's name changed. "Out" implied the Church's endorsement of gay identity, which caused a marketing and theological problem for Catholic leaders who still wanted to frame gays and lesbians as "homosexuals" or "same-sex attracted." Second, the parish needed to stop putting OSP announcements in the bulletin and giving OSP members a platform after the 5:15 p.m. Mass. The archdiocese did not want OSP to be, in Martinez's words, "as public. Essentially it was, 'Go back into the closet, don't talk about this stuff, ever.'" Third, the ministry needed to focus on teaching chastity, not

celebrating gay relationships. Didn't Martinez know that gay sex is ver-
boten for Catholics?[65]

Over the course of several visits, Martinez rebuffed the archbishop's demands. During each appointment, the St. Paul pastor talked
about OSP's commitment to Catholic spirituality, community, and service, challenging the men to find anything that was un-Catholic about
the ministry's activities. Chancery officials never answered him well,
and, in the end, the cardinal took no action.

OSP members were often unaware of the archdiocese's interventions. Matthew Vidal believed that Martinez "didn't want to worry
us" with what was happening behind the scenes.[66] Martinez fostered
a space where LGBTQ parishioners' gifts could flourish apart from
outside interference. "It's easy," Martinez explained, "to get caught up
in that external stuff, and it becomes internalized despair. That's what
the official Church teaching is trying to do—to make gay people feel
despair about who they are."[67]

Through these trials, Martinez found support among his brother
Paulists, but the archdiocese's criticism weighed heavily. "It cost me a
bit," he reflected. "I didn't know how tired I was."[68] Fred Negem remembered that "[Martinez] had the weight of the world on his shoulders.
But he came....Gil was always there. Thank God for that."[69] Other OSP
members believed that Martinez's labors were fundamental to the group's
success. Matthew Vidal remarked, "Without Gil, [OSP] wouldn't have
happened. Without a strong clergy member who was willing to stand
behind and champion the cause, it would've never taken off."[70]

Church-Changing Dialogue

OSP's relationship with church leaders outside of the archdiocese
was better than its relationship with Cardinal Dolan. One of Martinez's
objectives was to give OSP members opportunities to share their testimonies with ecclesiastical officials. Fr. Mark-David Janus, who helped
facilitate some of these meetings, disclosed, "The graced experiences
that people have with OSP members lead them to think again, to the-
ologize again."[71] These meetings, however, were not always easy. OSP's
attempts at dialogue yielded mixed results that highlighted tensions in
the Church's relationship with its LGBTQ members.

The first major opportunity for OSP members to share about
their lives and loves came in early spring 2009. At the time, the United

Nations was debating a resolution calling on the nations of the world to decriminalize homosexuality. To the chagrin of LGBTQ Catholics, Archbishop Celestino Migliore, then apostolic nuncio to the United Nations, vocally opposed the measure on the Vatican's behalf.[72] Sensing a need for dialogue, Martinez reached out to the nuncio and invited him to dinner with the ministry. To everyone's surprise, Migliore accepted the invitation. On April 30, 2009, more than a dozen OSP members, priests, and the nuncio's staff attended the gathering at the parish.

The evening was full of meaningful exchanges. After the apostolic delegate gave theological explanations for the Vatican's opposition to LGBTQ civil rights, several ministry team leaders shared how the Church's position hurt them. According to Matthew Vidal, the nuncio was so moved by their conversation that he rhetorically asked, "Do you think I or Pope Benedict would look at this room and say that God isn't here?"[73] The nuncio's final thought was that there were no easy answers, but he assured attendees that discussions about same-sex relationships and LGBTQ ministry were taking place at the highest levels of the Vatican.[74]

A second opportunity to meet with a high-ranking Vatican official came in May 2014 when Cardinal Walter Kasper, one of Pope Francis's closest advisors, visited the United States to promote his book *Mercy: The Essence of the Gospel and the Key to Christian Life*.[75] Cardinal Kasper was a rising star within the new pontifical regime and a friend of Fr. Mark-David Janus, who, in addition to being a mentor to OSP members, was also the president of Paulist Press, the publisher of Kasper's English-language works. Together, Janus and Martinez organized the May 3 meeting between the high-ranking cardinal and St. Paul parishioners. The gathering in the Paulist rectory was a who's who of lay leaders, Paulist priests, and Cardinals Kasper, Egan, and Dolan.

The night left an impression on Michael Tomae, who, at the age of twenty-four, was the youngest to attend. "Everyone knew Cardinal Kasper was Pope Francis's right-hand man. What you say to Kasper gets to Francis. I was just this kid, and Fr. Gil wanted me there." When Kasper had a free moment, Tomae approached him. The room grew silent and watched with anticipation.

After an initial introduction, the cardinal asked, "What do you get out of all of this? Why are young people in the United States still part of the Church when they're leaving the Church in Europe?" Tomae offered Kasper a simple, three-word answer: "Hope, community, and love." The young gay man then shared how much OSP meant to him as a sign of the Church's hospitality to LGBTQ people and how hopeful he was for change under Pope Francis's leadership.[76]

Those who watched the conversation unfold were moved by what transpired. Tomae later reflected,

> At the time, I felt that I had been given so much responsibility. My voice was representing millions of LGBTQ people around the world. I was honored, afraid, anxious, and proud. It wasn't just about faith—it was about creating a safer world for LGBTQ people.[77]

According to Fr. Mark-David Janus, the evening left an impression on the cardinal too.

> It was a new experience for him to see such a large and vibrant community of young gay people. And he enjoyed being with OSP. He enjoyed the spirit. When I would see him afterwards, he would always say to me, "Be sure to say hello to ze young people of St. Paul ze Apostle." It was an experience he remembered.[78]

Another chance to meet with Cardinal Kasper came in the fall of 2016 when a group of St. Paul parishioners made a pilgrimage to Rome. Encouraged by their earlier encounter, the pilgrims attended Mass with Cardinal Kasper before speaking with him in a small group setting. Once in private, a gay couple shared their testimony and asked why the Church opposed same-sex marriage. Kasper grew defensive. Martinez, who accompanied the pilgrimage, recalled how the cardinal "resorted to the old teaching. He sounded like [Cardinal] Ratzinger, using metaphysical language about intrinsic disorder, etc."[79] Everyone, including the Paulist priests, grew quiet. No one knew what to say.

The gay and lesbian pilgrims were hurt by what transpired. Cardinal Kasper was supposed to be one of their greatest allies, yet his lack of empathy was on full display. The experience upset Martinez as well. He later came to see the episode as a moment in his own process of conversion. "I regret not speaking up and defending this couple," he revealed.

It made me reflect on what OSP is all about. We demonstrate our faith as Christians by being open, honest, and clear, and I felt like I equivocated. I think it was harmful to both the gay and straight couples on that pilgrimage. It also made me realize that we're in the desert, and we're going to be there for a long time. I don't know when things are going to change. We can be a great Christian community, but it's the Holy Spirit who will save us, not what the Church teaches. I made a resolution to myself that I won't ever be quiet like that again.[80]

A Worldwide Audience for Owning Our Faith

As OSP tried to make inroads with Catholic leaders, the ministry team reflected on its mission outside the parish. One of the most persistent questions that OSP faced was whether it should expand beyond Hell's Kitchen. According to Santiago Rivera, the ministry team was especially concerned about its responsibility for young LGBTQ Catholics who suffered from spiritual abuse. "We always talked about the gay kid in Nebraska," Rivera explained. "What can he see in OSP? How can we really help them feel integrated in the Church?"[81]

In the twenty-first century, media and technology provided a way forward. OSP built a Facebook page and Twitter account to highlight the group's ministries and events. Around the same time, members of OSP began discerning even bolder ways of sharing their stories with the world. They decided to launch a media campaign called Owning Our Faith.

The project was inspired by the ministry's relationship with Covenant House, a New York City organization that provides housing and social services to young people experiencing homelessness. For several years, OSP members had served Covenant House by planning social events for the young people who lived there. Through these opportunities to meet and mentor Covenant House residents, OSP members learned that many of the young people had been kicked out of their homes for their sexual orientation or gender identity. Worse yet, many were on the streets because they came from religious families that rejected them.

Seeking to challenge the parts of Catholic tradition that added to the young people's suffering, Michael Tomae organized a team to produce a short documentary with the testimonies of LGBTQ Catholics and their families.[82] Many of those who contributed to Owning Our Faith were members of St. Paul. Patrick Manning, for example, is a professional journalist and eucharistic minister who described his participation in the project "as the most proud I've ever been of the thousands of stories I've published."[83] The video included several personal stories and theological perspectives. Some who spoke were in long-term same-sex partnerships while others were single or celibate. Interviewees struck a careful balance between their love for Catholic tradition and honesty about the discrimination they faced. Matthew Purtorti, for example, was a member of the ministry team who shared:

> The Catholic Church probably thinks it is accepting of gay people because its message is that gay people exist and we should love them and not discriminate against them. But because the Church also tells gay people, essentially, that they need to be celibate, what the Church is saying is that you cannot live fully. You can be gay, but you can't live that life. That inherently is discriminatory.[84]

The team behind Owning Our Faith incorporated as a nonprofit organization, translated the video into six languages, and created a website where people from all around the world could share their own experiences.[85] Nearly ninety thousand people from 150 countries watched the mini documentary online, and Tomae, Putorti, Martinez, and others were featured on news outlets from Fox News to CBS *Sunday Morning*. Several OSP members visited parishes around the country to show the film, host discussion sessions, and spread the message of LGBTQ-affirming faith.

Emails poured in with praise. Parents wrote about how Owning Our Faith helped them reconcile their children's LGBTQ identity with their Catholic faith. LGBTQ people returned to church after hearing the documentary's inclusive message. In September 2015, Martinez gave the pope a Spanish-language copy of the film while on a visit to Rome.[86] In the end, Michael Tomae said, Owning Our Faith showed members of OSP that they "were capable of so much more. It took us to that next level."[87]

RECONCILING FAITH, SEXUALITY, AND GENDER IDENTITY

OSP's high-profile events, dialogue with bishops, and participation in campaigns such as Owning Our Faith may give the impression that the community is more concerned about publicity than the details of everyday life. Nothing could be further from the truth. "For a lot of us," Marianne Palacios shared, "OSP is our friend group, our support group, our spiritual lives, our social lives, and it's home for people. It's a comforting thing providing the support and love that parishes and churches are supposed to provide."[88]

The OSP community welcomes people from a wide variety of backgrounds. According to Marie Smithgall,

> OSP meets people where they are and becomes what they need at different points in their life. New York City is a transient place and the face of OSP changes as people move in and out. We try to offer what people are looking for at any given time in their spiritual or personal journey.[89]

Spiritual diversity is a ministry hallmark. Fr. Mark-David Janus, reflecting on OSP's pastoral orientation, praised the group's "sensitivity that people are at different phases of the journey....People don't have to sign on the dotted line. That vision of accompaniment is enormously important."[90]

As part of its mission to accompany LGBTQ Catholics, OSP plays a pivotal role helping its members reconcile their sexuality, gender identity, and spirituality. New parishioners come with questions. Is it possible to be gay and Catholic? Can I be honest about who I am and be a follower of Jesus Christ?

Larry Holodak's testimony reveals the impact that OSP had on his life. Prior to joining the ministry, Holodak was not public about his sexuality. "As I was going through my sexual identity journey," he reflected, "I was in conflict with my own feelings, thinking about what we [Catholics] considered right and wrong and about how I felt as a gay person and a person of faith." Through OSP he learned about the Church's traditional teaching on homosexuality, but he also heard LGBTQ-affirming theologies for the first time. With time and the support of other OSP members, Holodak came to believe that his Catholic faith was compatible with being gay. He said, "Each time I went to an OSP event it was the next step of my own coming out. I thought, 'I'm going to Vlada. I'm going to that gay bar, and I don't care who sees me.' Those events were so consequential as I dealt with all the conflicting feelings I had at the time." Today, Holodak is a mentor to many in the group and sees OSP as a gift "that I hadn't expected when I first started attending St. Paul."[91]

OSP was also instrumental in Michael Roper's return to active Catholic faith. The youngest child of a large Irish Catholic family, he spent the early years of his life as a Holy Cross brother. In 1972, Roper left the order to explore his sexuality and came to the realization that the institutional "Church hadn't made room for me." He left religious life and found a vocation in education, teaching for several decades in Catholic and secular schools. During that time, Roper did not attend Mass outside of weddings, funerals, and school functions. Then, when he was in his early seventies, a coworker invited him to the 5:15 p.m. Mass at St. Paul. Roper agreed to go and was so moved by the service that he started to cry. "I'm sure the people around me thought that somebody died," he remembered. "After Mass, Gil was greeting people out on the porch of the church, and I thanked him for giving me a home. I remember I kissed his hand. I just felt this was a home for me....OSP was the community that I was always looking for but had never found."

Being part of OSP reconfigured how Roper imagined his place in the Church. He no longer needs the institutional Church to affirm him but knows that he belongs whether others acknowledge it or not. "I can't expect the institutional Church to make room for me," he declared. "I am the Church. I make the room for me."[92]

OSP AS CHOSEN FAMILY

Several OSP members describe the ministry as a family. Most New Yorkers move to the city for school or work, and the Big Apple can feel lonely for those without local connections. Being LGBTQ and Catholic often augments feelings of alienation. Many LGBTQ Catholics express how difficult it is for them to be queer among fellow Catholics and how difficult it is for them to be Catholic among fellow queer people. OSP is a liminal space that fills their longing to belong to both groups. Michael Tomae related, "The community means a lot to OSPers because they accept each other. They've formed a New York City family."[93]

Such was the case for Marianne Palacios, who arrived in New York in 2014. She shared, "Having just gone through my own process of coming to terms with being queer, having a difficult relationship with my ex-girlfriend who had broken my heart, and having been rejected by my Catholic school community and my very Catholic family in Florida, I was furious with the Catholic Church."

At one of the most challenging moments of her life, a lesbian friend invited her to OSP. Palacios began attending, and the ministry soon became her chosen family. Since 2015, she has been an integral part of the ministry and parish. "We're really good at caring for one another," Palacios said. "I know when I need something, I have a parachute because OSP is there. I know my OSP friends would help me no matter what. Someone would step up. We care about each other."[94]

The community's care spans life and death. In OSP's early years, one of the group's most respected members was Ned O'Gorman, a poet, educator, two-time winner of the Guggenheim Fellowship, contributor to *Commonweal Magazine*, and founder of the Children's Storefront, a tuition-free school in Harlem. One of O'Gorman's friends described him as the "elder statesman of gay Catholics" who constantly encouraged his fellow Catholics to "be more and better as the Church."[95]

O'Gorman ran the OSP book club in his Upper West Side apartment until he was diagnosed with pancreatic cancer in late 2014. When it became clear that death was approaching, family and friends surrounded him with love. "OSP's mission was realized in the compassion and support that we gave to him and his family," Larry Holodak said with tears in his eyes. "A number of people who knew him well as he became sick and began to die at home were part of his dying process." The community signed up for shifts to visit each day and trained to become eucharistic ministers so they could bring Communion. Finally, Holodak recounted, "We were there the day he died. We did a prayer service in his room. It was clear he was at the end of his life. We were there for him and for his family. That was huge."[96]

Balancing Community and Hospitality

Maintaining a ministry that is simultaneously close-knit and hospitable to newcomers is a perennial challenge. How can OSP welcome visitors while at the same time fostering the deeper relationships that come through time spent with the community's shared joys and struggles?

Opinions on whether OSP is a hospitable community or not are mixed. Santiago Rivera remarked, "As the group grows, figuring out what community means is something that we struggle with. You start seeing pockets of who speaks with whom. We can still work toward a more inclusive group. How do you really integrate a group and create a comfortable space?"[97] Rivera's question is especially crucial for ministries that serve Catholics with painful memories of exclusion. The emotional wounds that LGBTQ people carry can reinforce feelings of being left out, even when ministries do their best to offer hospitality.

At St. Paul, OSP ministry team members seek out those who appear lonely or lost after the 5:15 p.m. Mass. According to Michael Tomae, "If you're on the ministry team and you're in the back of the church, you're expected to go up and introduce yourself to people who look like they don't know anyone. It was very important that everyone felt welcome, and it was our responsibility to make sure that that was happening."[98]

Still, cliques are a temptation. Attractive and charismatic parishioners often congregate together, leaving the shy and awkward aside. Friends who have known each other for years embrace and catch up while those new to the parish have little to discuss. Hospitality, a key part of OSP's work, does not always come easily.

Intergenerational Ministry and Service

Closely related to the theme of welcome is OSP's struggle to develop intergenerational relationships. In the New York City LGBTQ community, ageism is a serious problem and social circles tend to be segregated by age. Gay bars and other LGBTQ social spaces privilege youth by reinforcing hierarchies that render older generations invisible.

OSP strives to provide a counterwitness to these hurtful cultural mores. The ministry has a sizable number of parishioners in their sixties, seventies, and eighties, an inestimable treasure given the large number of gay men their age who died during the AIDS epidemic. Community, spirituality, and service offer a framework for inclusion.

Although older OSP members may eschew bar nights, they feel welcome at Supper Club, a communal meal that takes place every month after the 5:15 p.m. Mass. Michael Tomae shared how the tradition

> allowed the young and old members to get together, sit at a table, and take over a whole restaurant. Everyone looked forward to it. Some of the wealthier OSPers would buy appetizers and the first round of drinks. It was a big family dinner.[99]

Other monthly events such as faith sharing/Bible study and book club also bring together a wide age range of participants. Patrick Manning, who started the faith sharing group, reflected, "This was a space where we could be very personal but also get some education about the readings for the upcoming Sunday."[100] Several who attend faith sharing left seminary or a religious order several decades ago, while others are recent graduates of Catholic schools like Fordham and Notre Dame. Conversations often veer away from interpretations and applications of the Bible to sharing about complicated relationships with faith and the institutional church. In this way the group provides, in Manning's words, a "community atmosphere for people who are like minded and had similar experiences [to] come in and explore their faith."[101]

Service, finally, is another way for OSP to build intergenerational community. Many volunteer with the Gay Men's Health Crisis (GMHC), an organization founded in the eighties to provide meals, medication, and housing resources for people living with HIV/AIDS. OSP members go to serve dinner for GMHC's clients, who are often much older, once a month. Chip Davy, a member of the ministry team who has served with GMHC for several years, disclosed, "Many OSP volunteers feel a sense of duty to assist those in the LGBTQ community who have seen such very difficult times and ended up paving the way to the greater acceptance the same volunteers enjoy today."[102] Some of GMHC's clients also belong to OSP, a fact that strengthens the bonds between the two communities.

LGBTQ LITURGY, SPIRITUALITY, AND THEOLOGY

Sacraments and liturgies include rituals for new life and death. At least three same-sex couples who were members of OSP have had their babies baptized at St. Paul, a sign of their, and the ministry's, fruitfulness. In 2018, OSP members gathered at the Easter Vigil to celebrate the baptism of one of their own who decided to become a Christian. After the vigil, the group departed for the aptly named Rise Bar to toast the resurrection and their companion's rebirth in Christ.

In addition to these joyful occasions, OSP gathers to mourn. The most moving example of this may have come in June 2016 when OSP held a service to mourn the Orlando Pulse Night Club shooting. Organizers covered the head altar with icons of canonized and uncanonized saints beloved by the queer community: Sebastian, Perpetua, and Felicity; Harvey Milk, Matthew Shepard, and Marsha P. Johnson. The prayer service was patterned after a Mass and included Scripture readings, a homily, choral music, hymns, a litany of the names of the dead, and a candle lighting "communion" service. More than two hundred people from the parish and surrounding community attended.

OSP's liturgical and communal life has been a rich resource for theological reflection. LGBTQ Catholics are often adept apologists, able to articulate and defend God's work in their lives. This is the fruit of countless years wrestling with Catholic traditions and institutions. According to Fr. Mark-David Janus,

> LGBTQ people have a very particular lesson to teach the whole Church, which has tried to drive them out more than any other group. And yet they don't go. They have a way of believing, a core of believing, that's enormously strong. There's a richness there and that makes OSP potentially a gift to all believers.[103]

Part of OSP's contribution to the Church's faith arrives during Advent, when the community offers a series of personal reflections on the season's lectionary readings. Marie Smithgall coordinated the effort for several years. "We hope," Smithgall wrote for the first day of Advent 2019, "that these thoughtful and personal words will facilitate reflection and prayer to strengthen our faith and sense of community."[104]

Today, more than six hundred people from around the world receive the devotional.

CHANGES AND TRANSFORMATIONS

OSP, like any ministry, is constantly evolving. When Fr. Martinez started mentoring OSP ministry team members, he envisioned them serving two or three years before "rolling off" to make room for newcomers. Martinez understood the dangers of clinging to power and fostered an environment of detachment. "How do you participate," he asked, "in a way that your ownership of [ministry] is only complete after you give it away?"[105] When a member discerns that it is time for them to "give it away," the team considers who would make a good replacement. Most often, those invited to join the ministry team are already heavily involved in planning events and welcoming newcomers.

Over the years, dozens of St. Paul parishioners have served on the ministry team. This means that the OSP community is now saturated with disciples who are better equipped to care for one another. Such a rapid turnover also means that the group has a short institutional memory, and much effort must go into planning leadership transitions and training. This is less of a problem when there is a steady head pastor such as Martinez to guide the group, but it becomes more of a challenge when parish leadership is in flux.

Such was the case in July 2018 when the Paulists assigned Martinez to a new parish in Los Angeles. OSP members wondered what the change would mean for them. Did their standing in the parish and archdiocese depend on Martinez? Would his replacement be willing to stand up for them as he had?

Due to unforeseen circumstances, the year that followed Martinez's departure was trying for both the parish and OSP. In November 2018, the new head pastor fell ill and had to resign from his responsibilities. Over the next eight months, St. Paul had three temporary administrators before Fr. Rick Walsh was appointed in July 2019.

Since Martinez left, OSP has continued to discern its way forward with the help of other Paulist priests such as Fr. Rospond, the ministry's new chaplain. Still, important questions remain. What is OSP without Martinez's animating leadership? How do old and new personalities affect the way that ministry functions? These types of questions are not unique to OSP, but LGBTQ ministry is uniquely vulnerable to changes in local church leadership.

Growing Edges

With all the evidence of God's work, members of OSP are keenly aware of the group's growing edges. When considering OSP's future, Marie Smithgall noted, "It's important for OSP to look at ourselves as a group and push a little bit to consider where our weaknesses are and where we need to spend more time."[106] Each September, the ministry team meets for a daylong retreat to discern which of the community's needs it will address in the year to come.

From 2017 to 2020, the ministry team prioritized political and prophetic issues. Donald Trump's election in 2016 was a catalyst for introspection that caused the ministry team to interrogate OSP's relationship to social justice issues. OSP's demographics reflect Hell's Kitchen and the Upper West Side: the vast majority of participants are white, middle or upper middle class, and cisgender. Marie Smithgall described how easy it is for the community to unknowingly conform to the sins of the society around it: "Diversity is something that OSP needs to come to terms with. The fallacy that people fall into is that just because we're gay, we're part of the LGBTQ group, doesn't mean that we don't have problems with racism, or sexism, or transphobia."[107]

For all the privileges that most OSP members enjoy, inequalities are painfully apparent within the community itself. This is especially true regarding experiences of patriarchy and misogyny. Marianne Palacios, one of only three lesbians who consistently attends OSP, said,

> People ask me all the time why there aren't more women in OSP, and I say OSP isn't a feminist community. The Paulists aren't feminists. They are so willing to stand up to Church teaching on queer issues. Why aren't they willing to stand up for women's rights issues? The biggest issue for me in the Church is leadership for women. I think the Paulists would be more supportive of my right to marry a woman than of my right to be ordained.[108]

Compounding these issues, the men in OSP tend to be unaware of the struggles their sisters face. Gay Catholic men see themselves represented in positions of spiritual authority, making it easy for them to bond with priests. Catholic women, on the other hand, can never become priests, a lack of representation that stifles their gifts and impedes their ability to build meaningful relationships with parish leadership. Without women in prominent pastoral and teaching roles, women's spiritual needs often go unmet. "Where are the women my age?" Palacios rhetorically asked. "The Church isn't serving them."[109]

"It's Our Sexuality That Leads Us Back to God"

"There are two groups who pray the Rosary consistently at St. Paul," Fr. Mark-David Janus likes to say. "It's the Polish ladies at the end of the 7:30 a.m. Mass and it's the gays at the end of the 5:15 p.m. Mass."[110]

Since 2007, OSP has welcomed scores of LGBTQ Catholics back to the heart of faith and community by daring to claim that Catholic spirituality and queer sexuality and gender can be reconciled. As Michael Roper, a respected member of OSP, beamed, "It's our sexuality that leads us back to God."[111] The ministry stands as a powerful critique of those in the hierarchy who would try to force LGBTQ Catholics into hiding. While OSP members remain out and proud members of Christ's Body, those who want to shame them into hiding are powerless.

Groups like OSP have become visible in the Roman Catholic Church thanks to lay leadership and grassroots initiative, but also thanks to priests like Martinez and Janus who have provided institutional connections and support. The next chapter highlights the role that one of OSP's most prominent supporters, Fr. James Martin, SJ, has played in building bridges between queer believers and the institutional church. Martin's apostolate, grounded in fidelity to Catholic teaching and his priestly vows of obedience, exploded in influence during Pope Francis's pontificate. Today, his ministry focuses on amplifying queer voices and bringing communities like OSP into the mainstream of the Catholic Church.

Chapter 7

FINDING ALLIES IN THE INSTITUTION

One Jesuit's Approach to LGBTQ Catholic Ministry

> Then he said to his disciples, "The harvest is plentiful, but the laborers are few; therefore ask the Lord of the harvest to send out laborers into his harvest."
>
> —Matthew 9:37–38

MEETING THE POPE

"Pope Shows 'Care for LGBT People' in Meeting with Ally Rev. James Martin," read an October 1, 2019, headline in *The Advocate*, a prominent U.S. LGBTQ publication.[1] Six years prior, the magazine jumped to name Pope Francis its Man of the Year after the pontiff famously asked, "Who am I to judge?"[2] Now, editors linked Francis and Martin as allies. They were right to do so.

The day before the *Advocate* story appeared, the pope received Fr. Martin, author of *Building a Bridge* and a well-known advocate for LGBTQ Catholics, in a thirty-minute private audience in the Apostolic

Palace. According to America Media, where Martin was editor at large, details of the visit signaled the pope's favor.

> It took place not as a private encounter in Santa Marta, the Vatican guesthouse where he lives, but in the pope's private library where he meets heads of states and international organizations, cardinals and bishops conferences, leaders of the other Christian denominations and of the world's major religions, as well as distinguished persons. By choosing to meet him in this place, Pope Francis was making a public statement.[3]

Although their conversation was off-limits to the public, Martin quickly interpreted it as "a real sign for his pastoral care and concern for LGBT Catholics and LGBT people worldwide."[4]

The visit prompted a firestorm of praise and criticism, highlighting the deep divisions between those who supported Francis's papacy and those who opposed it. Francis DeBernardo of New Ways Ministry hailed the occasion as a "day of celebration for LGBTQ Catholics who have longed for an outstretched hand of welcome from the Church that they love."[5] Damian Thompson, a traditionalist Catholic and editor of *The Spectator*, a British newspaper, sulked that the pope's audience was "intended to taunt the U.S. conservatives that he demonizes."[6] Martin, well acquainted with fame and controversy, took it in as "one of the highlights of my life."[7]

Fr. Martin's rise to prominence as an advocate for LGBTQ people coincided with, and was made possible by, a number of factors, not the least of which was the papacy of Pope Francis, his brother priest in the Society of Jesus. For several decades, Francis's predecessors had maintained overtly hostile relationships with LGBTQ Catholics and their allies. The new pontiff ushered in a new era. Francis's concern for people on the margins invigorated ministries outside the Church and in the streets. Allies to LGBTQ Catholics could finally work with the holy father's blessing.

Notwithstanding Pope Francis's mission to those on the fringes of the Church, Fr. Martin has been careful to guard his vocation against accusations of disobedience or dissent. Visions for pastoral reform challenge the status quo but remaining within the institutional church requires restraint and careful attention to the changing currents of church leadership and politics. This is especially true for leaders in LGBTQ ministry, which is replete with cautionary tales of those who pushed too hard or too quickly against Church mores.

Martin is a faithful and prudent priest. His ministry is a long-term calling, not a kamikaze mission. He has pursued and continues to receive all the necessary permissions from his Jesuit superiors, both at the local level and in Rome. At times, this includes accepting the limitations of his office.

While Fr. Martin's careful integration of Catholic tradition and LGBTQ ministry has opened doors for him in many church circles, it has created frustrations for LGBTQ Catholics and allies who do not believe that his message goes far enough. Pushback also comes from traditionalists and the Catholic alt-right who view his support for LGBTQ people as an affront to the Church's longstanding tradition.

Whatever the response, Martin's writing and advocacy have set waves of change into motion with remarkable force. This chapter will trace how his compassionate and often controversial message developed. Fr. Martin's criticism of the Church's pastoral failures and reimaging of its teaching have enabled his outreach to thrive within a constantly evolving ecclesial milieu.

BECOMING A SPIRITUAL AND MEDIA GIANT

James Martin's background as a Jesuit priest and media personality prepared him well for the press and polemics of his apostolate to LGBTQ people. Born and raised in the suburbs of Philadelphia, he attended the University of Pennsylvania's Wharton School of Business before spending a few years working for General Electric in the greater New York City area. In 1986, Martin began to discern a religious vocation and, in 1988, entered the Society of Jesus.

His early years in the order confirmed his calling to the priesthood and helped him come "to know God—and myself—better."[8] This knowledge transformed his relationships with others. Martin's heart for the poor and marginalized grew as he worked in a hospice for the sick and dying in Jamaica, served the homeless in Boston, worked with gang members in Chicago, and cofounded the Mikono Centre, a shop in Nairobi, Kenya, where refugees could sell their crafts.

Ministry to LGBTQ people was not a frequent topic of conversation among his Jesuit cohort. Martin recalled, "Sometimes we would talk about LGBTQ discrimination but, frankly, we were more concerned with our overall formation: our studies, work with the poor, and our prayer. We talked much more about the materially poor than about LGBTQ people." Although there were LGBTQ people among the groups that Martin served, it was not until many years later that he really began to accompany openly LGBTQ people through his ministry as a priest, spiritual director, and confessor in New York City.[9]

Fr. Martin developed his gifts as an author and spiritual leader while still in his thirties. Before his ordination to the priesthood on June 12, 1999, he had already written *In Good Company*, a personal memoir recounting his experiences with the Jesuits; published *This Our Exile: A Spiritual Journey with the Refugees of East Africa*; and edited *How Can I Find God?*, a collection of essays on the search for God in the modern world. In 1998, he also began working at America Media, where he is now editor at large. By the time he published the bestselling *The Jesuit Guide to (Almost) Everything* in 2010, he had appeared on CNN and Fox News, written for the *New York Times* and *Wall Street Journal*, and could count Stephen Colbert and Philip Seymour Hoffman among his famous friends.[10]

Much of Martin's success in building a following came from his use of social media. His first post as a public figure on Facebook, where he now has close to six hundred thousand "likes," came in 2010; his first tweet on Twitter, where he now has three hundred thousand followers, debuted the following year. In a religious discourse often dominated by shrill, traditionalist voices, Fr. Martin's socially conscious advocacy highlighted Christian justice and political issues neglected elsewhere.

Social, print, and other media made Fr. Martin's ministry accessible to a worldwide audience while also putting him on the Vatican's radar. In April 2017, Pope Francis appointed Martin to a five-year term as a consultor to the Dicastery for Communication, which oversees the curia's communications and media apparatus.[11] With such a powerful media, social, and ecclesial presence, Martin is a certifiable A-list celebrity priest.

Lessons from the Past

Due to his larger-than-life persona, people took notice when Martin began speaking up in defense of LGBTQ people. For many years he had used his platform to highlight issues such as racism, poverty, and immigration, but LGBTQ topics could be far more dangerous. Whereas Catholic Social Teaching clearly condemns racism, economic inequality, and the abuse of immigrants, homophobia is much more a part of the warp and woof of Catholic tradition. How could he begin to address it?

There were clear warnings to tread carefully. Martin was aware of what had transpired with Fr. John McNeill, a former Jesuit from New York City whose LGBTQ-affirming theology and ministry led to his dismissal from the Society of Jesus.[12] According to Martin, Jesuits still have ambivalent feelings about McNeill's legacy. On the one hand, some see him as "a courageous pioneer" in LGBTQ ministry who "put himself on the line for what he believed." On the other hand, McNeill was well known for breaking his vow of chastity by living in an open relationship with another man before he left the order. McNeill's infidelity to his vocation, Martin said, "mitigated people's admiration for him."[13]

Although Martin shared many of McNeill's concerns about the Church's mistreatment of LGBTQ Catholics, he did not share McNeill's disregard for obedience and chastity. Martin was eager to maintain a healthy relationship with his community and the hierarchy by working within the bounds of church teaching and structures to bring change.

1990s Catholic Media Spotlight on Gays and Lesbians

Fr. Martin cemented his reputation for LGBTQ ministry in the wake of his 2017 book, *Building a Bridge*, but his record on LGBTQ issues long preceded its publication. Prior to 2000, gays and lesbians occasionally appeared in his writing. At the time, Martin saw them as an underrepresented group with "few advocates in the Church."[14] His writing highlighted their experiences. In 1994, he interviewed Camille Paglia, an iconoclastic lesbian whom he described as "America's premier intellectual renegade." The piece was a humanizing exploration of Paglia's thought and relationship to Catholicism, a rare spotlight on a lesbian in the male-dominated world of Catholic media.[15]

Later, gays and lesbians were a part of his frequent column, "Of Many Things," which explored hot-button issues through a cosmopolitan Catholic lens. In 1998, for example, Martin commented on the debut of *Corpus Christi*, a controversial Terrance McNally play that portrayed Christ as a modern gay man. At a protest of the play's opening, the Catholic League's William Donohue described the work as "hate speech dressed up in artistic robes."[16] Martin's response was far more measured. He compared the play to other popular depictions of Christ as a woman or person of color and encouraged Catholics to be "open-minded" about it. The Catholic League's protests of the play before its debut were overblown, Martin suggested, and made the Church look bad.[17]

A few weeks after the op-ed on *Corpus Christi*, Martin again criticized the Catholic League for its constant complaints about the persecution of U.S. Catholics. The group's perpetual peevishness, he warned, could "lead to an under appreciation of true persecution, as well as to embarrassing public statements." Recalling the murder of young gay man Matthew Shepard the month before, Martin concluded that the persecution of Catholics in the United States was nothing like the persecution faced by African Americans, Jews, and gays.[18] Even at this early point in his writing career, Martin attended to the real suffering faced by sexual minorities.

HOMOSEXUALITY AND THE PRIESTHOOD

Occasional op-eds that touched on gay and lesbian issues were small matters compared to his explosive November 2000 article, "The Church and the Homosexual Priest," which appeared in *America*. Three years before the U.S. Supreme Court struck down anti-sodomy laws and five years before the Vatican banned gay seminarians with its "Criteria for the Discernment of Vocations with regard to Persons with Homosexual Tendencies," Martin offered an incisive piece intended to correct "misunderstanding about what it meant to be a gay priest." According to Martin, "There were very few people who understood anything about them, and most of what was written about them was usually ignorant. There are so many issues to understand: chastity, celibacy, homosexuality, religious orders, the priesthood, clericalism, and so on."[19]

"The Church and the Homosexual Priest" was noteworthy for several reasons. First, it was honest about the number of homosexual priests. According to one study that Martin cited, homosexuals comprise anywhere from 23 to 58 percent of the clergy.[20] Martin argued that the Church needs to acknowledge their existence in its ranks. Second, he elucidated the struggles that homosexual priests face reconciling their spiritual and sexual identities. The faith tradition that describes homosexual acts as "intrinsically disordered" leaves many priests conflicted about their ability to minister and isolated within a community that does not accept their sexual orientation. Despite the *Catechism*'s call for homosexuals to be treated with "respect, compassion, and sensitivity," Martin explained that priests who come out face "the possibility of strongly negative reactions" and even "hatred and rejection" from their parishioners and superiors.[21]

In addition to outlining the struggles of homosexual priests, Martin expounded on the gifts they bring to the Body of Christ. Recalling the *Catechism*, he affirmed that God calls homosexuals, like straight men, to the "responsibility and right" of shepherding the Church. In this pastoral role, the suffering they experience as members of a sexual minority makes them more empathetic to those who experience similar "stigma and frustration."[22] According to Fr. Martin, a homosexual priest's sexual orientation can also help conform him to Christ. Growing up with experiences of isolation and loneliness helps many develop "deep inner lives" and a strong relationship with God, which bear fruit in creative enterprises such as liturgy, art, and music.[23] Homosexual priests, Martin made clear, are a gift, not a liability, to the Church.

The theme of homosexuality and the priesthood became an even greater topic of debate in the years that followed. In 2002, the *Boston Globe* published its extensive investigations into the Church's systematic cover-up of child sexual abuse.[24] Catholics searched for answers, and some blamed homosexual priests.[25] The libelous link between pederasty and homosexuality had long been used to malign gays and lesbians in the public square.[26] Now it provided homophobic Catholics with a convenient scapegoat for the scandal.

Martin spoke out against the unjust accusation. In his December 16, 2002, column, he pondered a Vatican document then under consideration that some feared would ban gay men from ordination. Martin took a bold stand. Keeping gay men out of the priesthood, he stressed, would "represent little more than codified scapegoating." The sex abuse crisis called for the interrogation of ecclesial culture and initiation of far-reaching reforms, not demonizing an already vulnerable group. In addition to obfuscating the crisis's true causes, a ban on gay priests would destroy the vocations of seminarians already in formation, hinder those called to ministry in the future, confuse Catholics who were encouraged by the *Catechism* to accept gays and lesbians with "respect, compassion and sensitivity," and raise doubts about the ordination of celibate gay priests who faithfully served the Church.[27]

Tragically, the Vatican proceeded with its ill-considered plans. In late 2005, the Congregation for Catholic Education (CCE) issued its instruction on the admission of "men with homosexual tendencies" into seminaries. Basing its exclusionary policy on unjustified claims that homosexuality hinders healthy relationships, the instruction advised against admitting to "the seminary or to holy orders those who practice homosexuality, present deep-seated homosexual tendencies, or support the so-called 'gay culture.'"[28]

A VATICAN CRACKDOWN HITS CLOSE TO HOME

The CCE directive called for a response, but *America* was undergoing a challenging transition. Under the leadership of Fr. Thomas Reese, who started as editor in chief in 1998, the publication had become more open in its criticism and questioning of the institutional church. This atmosphere of candor created problems with the Vatican. In the early 2000s, the CDF, then led by Cardinal Joseph Ratzinger, warned the magazine's editors about its "treatment of sensitive church issues," including Martin's article on homosexual priests.[29] Fearful that the CDF might fire Reese or assign a board of censors, *America* adopted a more conciliatory tone.[30]

The magazine's new direction did little to shake Vatican suspicions. A few weeks prior to his election as Pope Benedict XVI, Cardinal Ratzinger directed the Jesuit superior general, Peter-Hans Kolvenbach, SJ, to remove Reese from his post. Reese, faithful to his vows of obedience, formally resigned in early May 2005.[31]

The Vatican decision to fire *America*'s top editor demoralized the magazine's staff, but Martin was determined to continue his writing, even as an occasional critic of the Church.[32] If *America* could not provide a forum for some of his more controversial op-eds, he would go elsewhere. In early 2006, he published his reply to the Vatican directive banning gay seminarians in *Commonweal*, a lay Catholic magazine. Martin's strategy safeguarded *America* from further censure while also ensuring his voice would be heard in the public debate.

Fr. Martin's retort to the CCE reiterated themes that appeared in his earlier work. After covering the wide variety of responses to the Vatican directive, he invited readers to empathize with "gay seminarians, gay priests, and, in particular, gay men discerning a vocation....It's difficult," he acknowledged, "to imagine a gay man (or a man struggling to understand his orientation) feeling more encouraged to pursue a vocation after reading it. The result will be a diminution in future vocations to the priesthood."[33]

The vocations of those already in formation were also at risk. Martin had counseled some young gay men who remained confident in their calling, but others believed that the prohibition excluded them from future ministry. Finally, he again wondered how the CCE instruction would affect already ordained priests who were celibate and faithful to their vows. "At best," Martin wrote, "these men will grit their teeth in anger and get on with their work; at worst, they will feel demoralized and, ultimately, consider leaving the priesthood."[34]

Time would tell how bishops and leaders of religious communities would interpret the instruction. No matter the eventual outcome, Martin lamented the statement's intended and unintended consequences. At a moment when the Church was already suffering from a lack of religious vocations, the CCE added a cruel impediment to the priesthood.

SAME-SEX MARRIAGE, A TRADITIONALIST POPE, AND THE CULTURE WARS

In the late 2000s, same-sex marriage became a hot topic in U.S. political discourse. With Benedict XVI as pope, many American bishops were eager to prove their fidelity to traditional church teaching through their opposition to LGBTQ civil rights. Martin condemned those unwilling to empathize with LGBTQ people, yet he did so without supporting same-sex marriage initiatives, either. His public ministry remained within the bounds of established church teaching.

One of Martin's earliest interventions came in November 2009, when the Archdiocese of Washington, D.C., threatened to withdraw from its social services contracts with the city rather than cooperate with a local measure that would legalize same-sex marriage.[35] In an op-ed poignantly titled "What Should a Gay Catholic Do?," Martin avoided the political questions at play and instead reflected on how the Church's posturing affected gay people.

He noted the tradition's opposition to same-sex love, marriage, and adoption, in addition to policies that excluded openly gay seminarians and led to the firing of gay and lesbian employees. These troubling realities, Martin pointed out, hindered the flourishing of gay and lesbian Catholics. "Officially at least, the gay Catholic seems set up to lead a lonely, loveless, secretive life. Is this what God desires for the gay person?"[36] With time, his answer to the rhetorical question was becoming more obvious.

Fr. Martin tracked the collateral damage caused by the Church's offensive against same-sex marriage. In 2010, he shared the story of an eight-year-old boy from Hingham, Massachusetts, who was denied admission to a Catholic school because his parents were lesbians.[37] A similar report had recently emerged in Boulder, Colorado, where Archbishop Charles Chaput demanded that parents submit to church teaching before enrolling their children in parochial schools.[38] Close to Boston, however, Cardinal Sean O'Malley stood with the LGBTQ family. Martin praised the cardinal for his "pastoral, but sensible — even practical" decision.[39] The Church, he wrote, needed to reconcile with the fact that not all Catholics accept church teaching, and children should not be excluded from religious community because of their parents' convictions. Furthermore, given the welcome that many divorced and remarried Catholics received in parishes and Catholic schools, targeting same-sex couples for their rejection of church teaching appeared to be a form of unjust discrimination.

Indeed, Martin elucidated, homophobia was a problem throughout the hierarchy. The op-ed ended with a critique of a comment by Pope Benedict XVI, who had recently named same-sex marriage and abortion as the most "dangerous and insidious threats" to humankind.[40] Martin pointed out the logical fallacy in the holy father's claim, going so far as to call the pope's words "bizarre." How could same-sex marriage compare to the devastation wrought by war, the death penalty, and systemic poverty? Between the stories of children being rejected from Catholic schools because of their parents' sexuality and the pope's claim that same-sex marriage was as serious a moral issue as abortion, Martin concluded that the Church seemed to exhibit a "simple dislike, or even hatred, of gays and lesbians."[41]

LAYING THE GROUNDWORK FOR FUTURE LGBTQ MINISTRY

While Fr. Martin denounced the ways he saw the institutional church hurting LGBTQ people and their families, he also highlighted more pastoral and affirming approaches. In a June 2011 opinion piece, Martin complimented Brooklyn Bishop Joseph Sullivan, who appealed for the Church to love and welcome LGBTQ Catholics.

In his writing, Sullivan used the acronym "LGBT," a moniker that was growing in popularity at the time. Martin encouraged his readers to do the same. "Many Catholic leaders," he explained, "still use 'homosexual,' a word that the gay community has moved away from." Why, Martin asked, "shouldn't a group of people be free to call themselves what they want?"[42] To justify the change in nomenclature, which carried important theological and anthropological ramifications, he again cited the *Catechism's* appeal for Catholics to treat homosexuals with "respect, compassion, and sensitivity." The phrase was quickly becoming a mantra for his ministry. For Martin, Catholic tradition already held the seeds for more affirming pastoral practices. They just needed the right soil and conditions to grow.

The following year, in a piece titled "Respect, Compassion, and Sensitivity," Martin coaxed out the meaning of the *Catechism's* positive words. In that reflection, he began by naming the anti-LGBTQ elements of church teaching: "Homosexual activity is 'intrinsically disordered,' that is, 'always and everywhere wrong'" (*Catechism of the Catholic Church* §2358). For better or worse, Martin was never dishonest about what the *Catechism* says. After clarifying that he had no intention of contradicting church teaching, he turned the reader's attention "to *another* part of the Church's official teaching, something equally as valid," and proceeded to unpack *Catechism* §2358.[43]

The rest of the article laid out many of the themes that are now familiar to his readers: the struggles that LGBTQ people face, the need for the Church to listen to marginalized people, the meaning of solidarity and compassion, and Jesus's interaction with Zacchaeus, the chief tax collector of Jericho, as a model for ministry. More than a year before Pope Francis's pontificate began, Fr. Martin was already practicing the hospitality, empathy, and spiritual care that the future pope would embrace. More importantly, however, was his use of Catholic tradition. Rather than wielding faith as a weapon in the culture war, he emphasized that "treating gays and lesbians with 'respect, compassion, and sensitivity' *is* Catholic teaching."[44] Martin was setting an example for affirmation that set him apart from most priests and bishops.

One of the first tests to Martin's pastoral approach came after the Supreme Court decision *Obergefell v. Hodges* legalized marriage equality in 2015. Many Catholic commentators lamented the outcome, including then USCCB president Archbishop Joseph E. Kurtz, who called it "a tragic error that harms the common good and most vulnerable among us."[45]

Martin took a different tack. His response to the decision came via a Facebook post that soon went viral. To start, he called attention to the homophobia stirred up by the court case: "No issue brings out so much hatred from so many Catholics as homosexuality. Even after over twenty-five years as a Jesuit, the level of hatred around homosexuality is nearly unbelievable to me, especially when I think of all of the wonderful LGBT friends I have." The Church, Martin chided, consistently failed to meet its own standards of "respect, compassion, and sensitivity." Still, he believed that God was inviting believers to the even higher ideal of love.

In this context, Martin described love as "getting to know LGBT men and women, spending time with them, listening to them, being challenged by them, hoping the best for them, and wanting them to be a part of your lives, every bit as much as straight friends are part of your lives." His final words on the matter echoed both 1 Corinthians 13:1–13 and "Love is love," the slogan then popular with advocates of marriage equality: "Love first. Everything else later. In fact, everything else is meaningless without love."[46]

A Catholic Voice for LGBTQ People

Throughout the 2010s, Martin's public advocacy for the LGBTQ community blossomed on several fronts. At the start of the decade, he highlighted the tragedy of LGBTQ youth suicide. "The recent rash of suicides among young gay youth," he argued, "cannot fail to move the Christian heart, or indeed any heart capable of compassion." Admitting that many young people felt wounded by their faith communities, he placed himself in the shoes of a gay teen. His pastor's heart beats through the moving words of "A Prayer When I Feel Hated":

> Loving God, you made me who I am. I praise you and I love you, for I am wonderfully made, in your own image. But when people make fun of me, I feel hurt and embarrassed and even ashamed. So please God, help me remember my own goodness, which lies in you. Help me remember my dignity, which you gave me when I was conceived. Help me remember that I can live a life of love....Help me remember that nothing is impossible with you, that you have a way of making things better, that you can find a way of love for me, even if I can't see it right now. Help me remember all these things in the heart you created, loving God. Amen.[17]

The following year, Martin invited his followers on social media to wear purple for Spirit Day, an annual demonstration of solidarity with those who are bullied for their sexuality and/or gender expression. For Martin, there was no question about the need for Christ's followers to stand up against anti-LGBTQ violence. Catholics, he said, are "called by Christ to support those who suffer or struggle in any way." Wearing purple would be an unambiguous sign of compassion for young people who felt alienated within the Church and serve as a penitential "sign of remorse over any LGBT hate speech." Confessing that the Catholic Church had been a "source of great spiritual pain" for gay and lesbian people, Fr. Martin modeled steps for reconciliation and healing.[48]

Around that same time, Martin began framing the stigma that LGBTQ people face as one of many pro-life issues, capitalizing on the political and ethical rhetoric that has dominated the U.S. Catholic Church since *Roe v. Wade* legalized abortion in 1973. Martin's pro-life language set him in the tradition of Cardinal Joseph Bernardin, archbishop of Chicago from 1982 until 1996, who called Catholics to defend a "seamless garment of life." This interpretation of Catholic social ethics contends that Christians must repudiate all forms of violence against human life, not just those committed against the unborn.[49]

According to the Trevor Project, an organization dedicated to suicide prevention, LGBTQ youth are five times more likely to attempt suicide than their heterosexual peers, a statistic that Fr. Martin has often cited to raise awareness.[50] In a piece in 2018, Martin made the link between his pro-life stance and LGBTQ issues explicit: incidents of "prejudice, violence, and murder" against LGBTQ people are matters of life and death. If the Church stands up for immigrants and refugees, and for people who are poor, unborn, and elderly, why not for LGBTQ people too?[51]

Opposing Catholic Discrimination

Martin's defense of the LGBTQ community extended beyond the pro-life cause to other social and economic spheres. Although he relied on Catholic teaching to ground his public witness, his positions often set him at odds with the Vatican and U.S. bishops. A clear example of this can be seen in his criticisms of anti-LGBTQ employment discrimination.

In July 2011, U.S. President Barack Obama rescinded "Don't Ask, Don't Tell" (DADT), the government policy from the early nineties that forced gay, lesbian, and transgender members of the military into the closet. Martin lauded the president's decision, which he saw as an affirmation of "simple human dignity." Gays and lesbians, he reminded readers, are created in the image of God and worthy of "respect, compassion, and sensitivity" in all areas of life, including employment. Martin explained that excluding openly gay and lesbian people from the military was a "sign of unjust discrimination," something explicitly condemned by *Catechism* §2358.[52] Since the repeal of DADT had nothing to do with affirming same-sex marriage, a much more challenging doctrinal hill for Catholics to overcome, Martin argued that Catholics could celebrate the new policy in good conscience.

Although by today's standards Martin's post-DADT op-ed may seem unremarkable, his stand was courageous at the time. In 1992, the CDF, then headed by Cardinal Joseph Ratzinger, issued "Some Considerations Concerning the Response to Legislative Proposals on the Nondiscrimination of Homosexual Persons." The decree opposed legislation "in various places which would make discrimination on the basis of sexual orientation illegal."[53]

Like other CDF pronouncements under Ratzinger, the 1992 directive condemned any government plan that could be interpreted as pro-LGBTQ. Such "initiatives," it underscored, "even where they seem more directed toward support of basic civil rights than condonement of homosexual activity or a homosexual lifestyle, may in fact have a negative impact on the family and society." The CDF argued that governments must preserve the right to discriminate against gays and lesbians in areas such as "the placement of children for adoption or foster care, in employment of teachers or athletic coaches, and *in military recruitment*."[54] Denying homosexuals civil rights, Ratzinger believed, was necessary to maintaining a healthy society.

The CDF's 1992 directive set the Vatican as one of the chief opponents to LGBTQ liberation around the world, and Ratzinger's anti-gay tone would go on to dominate the Vatican for two more decades. As that era drew to an end, but before Benedict XVI announced his resignation, Martin's op-ed in support of DADT's repeal came as a not-so-veiled rebuke of the CDF leader who had become pope.

With time, Martin also condemned employment discrimination in the Church itself. As the 2010s progressed, advancing LGBTQ civil rights presented an increasingly serious threat to church leaders enmeshed in the culture wars. In 2013, the U.S. Supreme Court overturned the federal Defense of Marriage Act, and in 2015 same-sex marriage became the law of the land. Traditionalist Catholic perspectives were losing ground in popular culture, and fear gripped the U.S. episcopacy. Many bishops saw LGBTQ people as a threat to their authority and so began to purge Catholic institutions of anyone who dissented from traditional Catholic teaching on homosexuality. Dozens of faithful LGBTQ and allied employees across the country lost their livelihoods, the tragic consequence of an insecure hierarchy incapable of reconciling with the world around it.[55]

Fr. Martin was a light during this dark time, often expressing his solidarity with LGBTQ people who lost their jobs. In 2017, he tweeted about Mary Kate Curry, a lesbian forced to resign from her position as a theology teacher in Florida when school administrators learned of her engagement to another woman.[56] In 2018, he came to the defense of a campus minister in Cleveland who was fired for liking a Facebook post that celebrated a gay wedding.[57] The following year, he lamented the dismissal of a married gay music minister in Georgia.[58] In each case, Martin built up his reputation as a sign of contradiction to institutionalized homophobia.

Defending LGBTQ people fired for marrying their partners required a new turn in Martin's rhetoric. As a Catholic priest in good standing, he would not express support for same-sex marriage, a state of life still at odds with Catholic teaching. Instead, he argued that firing LGBTQ people was a symptom of "unjust discrimination." Martin pointed out, as he would in future articles and commentary, the glaring disparities between the hierarchy's treatment of its straight and LGBTQ workers. Heterosexual employees of Catholic institutions regularly deviated from traditional Catholic sexual ethics by using birth control, having sex outside of marriage, and divorcing, yet the bishops rarely protested. Why did they fire only LGBTQ employees for not living up to the tradition's standards?[59] In a 2019 tweet, Martin concluded that the hierarchy had turned LGBTQ workers who married outside of the Church into targets for discrimination.[60]

Chapter 8

ADVOCACY FROM WITHIN

James Martin's Bridge

> Do your best to present yourself to God as one approved by him, a worker who has no need to be ashamed, rightly explaining the word of truth.
>
> —2 Timothy 2:15

THE PULSE NIGHTCLUB MASSACRE AND NEW LGBTQ MINISTRY

By the mid-2010s, a great gulf separated the institutional church from LGBTQ people. The LGBTQ civil rights movement had effectively transformed society, yet most Catholic leaders held onto prejudices from the past. It took a national tragedy for a new wave of advocacy to challenge their obstinacy.

In the early hours of June 12, 2016, a gunman opened fire at Pulse, a gay nightclub in Orlando. By the time the rampage ended, forty-nine were dead and fifty-three more were wounded. Most were Latine and a large number were Catholic. At the time it was the deadliest terror attack in the United States since September 11, 2001, and to this day it remains the largest massacre of LGBTQ people in U.S. history.[1]

While some Catholic bishops condemned the violence, most, including New York City's Cardinal Timothy Dolan, refused to acknowledge that homophobia and transphobia were at the root of the killing. In a city with the largest population of LGBTQ people in the United States, the archbishop could not bring himself to use the word *gay*. It was a pastoral failure of epic proportions.

Fr. Martin took note. "I found this revelatory. The fact that only a few Catholic bishops acknowledged the LGBT community or even used the word *gay* during such a critical time showed that the LGBT community is still invisible in many quarters of the Church. Even in tragedy, its members are invisible."[2] Later, Martin described his response to the shooting as a "kairos moment": "The lack of any real response from most U.S. bishops," he shared, "made me think that it was time to do something more public."[3]

The day after the terror attack, Martin addressed his audience in a Facebook video. Staring into the camera from his office at America Media, he named homophobia as one of the most probable causes for the massacre. Over and over, he also used the terms *gay* and *LGBT*, identifiers that most bishops could not articulate.[4]

The video was a moving gesture. Fr. Martin's naming of a community in so much pain doubled as a criticism for Catholic leaders whose compassion fell so short. The Church needed to do better. "For too long," he decried, "Catholics have treated the LGBT community as 'other,' but for the Christian, there is no 'other.' There is no 'them.' There is only an 'us.'" Reflecting on Christ's example, Martin reminded fellow believers of how

> Jesus consistently reaches out to people on the margins to bring all people in. Those who are invisible to the community are seen by Jesus. He makes everyone an "us." Catholics have a responsibility, I think, to make everyone feel visible and valuable, especially in times of loss. The Church, then, needs to stand in strong and public solidarity with all of "us" in Orlando.[5]

The video spread like wildfire on social media, and within a few days it had nearly two million views.[6] Martin's simple yet compassionate message was a consolation for LGBTQ people around the world. His role in providing spiritual care for the community would only grow from there.

BUILDING A BRIDGE

A few weeks later, New Ways Ministry reached out to Martin to see if he would accept its Building a Bridge Award, an accolade that honors "individuals who by their scholarship, leadership, or witness have promoted discussion, understanding, and reconciliation between LGBT people and the Catholic Church."[7] It was not clear at first if Martin would be willing, or able, to receive the prize. The CDF had never rescinded its 1999 condemnation of NWM, which meant that affiliating with the group could jeopardize Martin's own ties to the institutional church.[8]

Martin sought the support of his religious community before committing. In an interview with the *National Catholic Register*, a traditionalist media outlet, he explained,

> Before I went to New Ways Ministry for the talk, I asked my local Jesuit superior, the provincial of the Jesuits in the Northeast Province, and asked for permission, and he said Yes. Next, I asked the provincial of the Maryland Province, and he said Yes. I asked my editor-in-chief, who said Yes. He then sent the talk to an outside theologian for vetting.[9]

The theologian also gave his approval.

Martin's desire to follow ecclesiastical protocol sprang from his vow of obedience. Practically, it also helped him maintain the trust and goodwill of his religious superiors and community. In the same *National Catholic Register* interview, he revealed, "I've never been asked by my superiors to stay away from the topic [of LGBTQ ministry], but everything I say and write reflects on the Society of Jesus and the Church, so I'm very careful and they know that. They assume, rightly, that I would never contradict Church teaching."[10]

His care paid off. Having gone through the proper channels, Martin received permission to attend NWM's award ceremony, and *America* even agreed to print his acceptance speech in its May 29, 2017, issue.[11] He gave the talk, titled "We Need to Build a Bridge between the LGBT Community and the Catholic Church," in a hotel ballroom outside of Baltimore on October 30, 2016.

The image of "building a bridge" was nothing new. Around that time, Pope Francis had repeatedly used the image in response to nationalism and xenophobia around the world.[12] Fr. Robert Nugent and Sr. Jeannine Gramick, the founders of NWM, had also published a book with nearly the same title in 1992.[13] Whereas Nugent and Gramick's work offered a comprehensive introduction to contemporary scientific perspectives on sexuality, gay and lesbian theologies, and a history of gays and lesbians in the Church (along with a healthy dose of criticism for the hierarchy!), Martin's message was simpler:

> The relationship between the LGBT Catholic community and the Catholic Church in the United States has been at times contentious and combative, and at times warm and welcoming. Much of the tension characterizing this complicated relationship results from a lack of communication, and, sadly, a good deal of mistrust, between LGBT Catholics and the hierarchy. What is needed is a bridge between the community and the Church.[14]

Rather than blaming one group or the other for their contentious relationship, Martin directed his remarks to both sides of the divide. Reconciliation, he believed, required a bridge with two lanes of traffic guided by respect, compassion, and sensitivity.

Speaking to church leaders, Martin offered advice for engaging the LGBTQ community and building that bridge: priests and bishops ought to use language that LGBTQ people prefer, not their own terminology; the Church must recognize that LGBTQ Catholics are already part of the Church and bring a multitude of gifts to the Body of Christ; Catholic leaders need to listen to and act in solidarity with persecuted LGBTQ folks around the world. For Martin, Jesus was the model for ministry. Rather than judging and excluding outsiders, Christ accompanied and befriended them. Martin exhorted church leaders to do the same.

Addressing the LGBTQ community, Martin described many of the barriers that he saw preventing a stronger relationship with the institutional church. It was important, he said, for LGBTQ Catholics to recognize and respect the spiritual authority of "popes and councils, archbishops and bishops." Even when they disagree, all Catholics should take the magisterium seriously. Martin was troubled by the way he heard many LGBTQ people mock priests and bishops. Productive dialogue requires communication founded on mutual respect and trust, not cruelty and sarcasm. Martin also stressed that church leaders are human beings with their own faults and struggles. Ministry can be challenging, and the hierarchy deserves compassion. Finally, Martin encouraged LGBTQ Catholics to acknowledge the complexity of "the Church" and its teaching. The hierarchy is comprised of multitudes of ministries that address countless cultural contexts. Not all would please LGBTQ people from the West.[15]

Martin concluded his talk with a reflection on the nature of bridge-building. He admitted that there may be many challenges to establishing dialogue, but God keeps the bridge standing. Trust in God and solidarity with one another are key for success. "We are all on the bridge together," he insisted. "Because, of course, the bridge is the Church. And, ultimately, on the other side of the bridge for each group is welcome, community, and love."[16]

From an Explosive Talk to an Explosive Book

Martin's speech was in no way revolutionary, but it touched a nerve. After *America* published the talk online, the Catholic web exploded with commentary. His publisher, HarperOne, suggested turning the lecture into a book, and Martin agreed. He secured his provincial's *imprimi potest* authorization to print, and the first edition of *Building a Bridge* appeared in June 2017.[17]

The book expanded on Martin's original talk with a new introduction and section titled "Biblical Passages for Reflection and Meditation." Fresh material showed that his understanding of the issues was evolving and that he was prepared to take on an even greater role in pastoral leadership. The second half, described by Martin as the "more important part of the book," offered biblical stories and paradigms that he found helpful in his own reflection.[18] This section was an extension of his Ignatian spirituality, which invites practitioners to creative prayer and discernment as they imagine themselves within the biblical narrative.[19]

Martin provided his readers with the same spiritual tools that helped him in his own journey.

Endorsements for the book brought together an unlikely coalition of Catholic leaders from inside and outside of the institutional church. The bishops and cardinals who provided a blurb were allies of Pope Francis: Cardinal Kevin Farrell, prefect for the Vatican Dicastery for Laity, Family, and Life; Cardinal Joseph Tobin, archbishop of Newark; Bishop Robert McElroy of San Diego. More surprising than these, however, were public endorsements from ecclesial outsiders. Martin welcomed support from Sr. Jeannine Gramick, who still stood condemned by the CDF, and Fr. James Alison, a priest then in questionable standing and longtime critic of the Church's teaching on homosexuality. By obtaining endorsements from disparate locations in the Church, Martin modeled the bridge-building he prescribed.

A Roller Coaster of Publicity and Criticism

With the publication of *Building a Bridge*, Martin set out on a publicity and ministry tour. Most of his talks were given to grassroots Catholic communities in parishes, universities, conferences, and retreats. The crowds that followed him were starved for words of hope and affirmation. Martin recalled how "young LGBT people hugged me, parents and grandparents of LGBT children wept, and people told me, in stronger terms than I could ever have anticipated, how grateful they were."[20] At St. Cecilia's Church in Boston, more than seven hundred people filled the church on a weeknight to hear him speak with the parish's Rainbow Ministry.[21]

Fr. Martin typically lingered afterward to meet his audience, turning his ministry of speaking into a ministry of listening. Some sessions lasted hours. Lauren Markoe, a reporter for Religion News Service who attended one of Martin's events, described how "the moment after Father Martin ended his presentation with a brief, fervent prayer, the stage began filling with men and women of every age. They all had stories to tell, and they needed a priest to hear them."[22]

Media coverage in newspapers, magazines, and TV programs was extensive. In the secular press, Martin became the face of the struggle for LGBTQ liberation in the Catholic Church. A 2017 *New York Times* profile, titled "Jesuit Priest Stands Up for Gay Catholics, Then Faces

Backlash," framed him as an indomitable hero battling institutionalized homophobia. In 2018, a *Mother Jones* headline praised Martin as "The Outspoken Priest Who's Revolutionizing the Catholic Church's Approach to Queer Rights." Although other LGBTQ Catholic and allied leaders had been pressing for change since the early seventies, secular reporters portrayed the newcomer as a provocateur boldly leading the charge.

Some LGBTQ Catholic commentators were not so easily impressed. Jamie Manson, a longtime member of Dignity and then a reporter for *National Catholic Reporter*, asked, "Can Fr. James Martin's Bridge Hold Up?"[23] She was not optimistic. Catholic leaders, Manson argued, were not as eager to dialogue with the LGBTQ community as Martin supposed. To prove her point, she gave a long list of injustices that the hierarchy had committed against LGBTQ people in recent years. The institutional church had done great harm, Manson showed, and many priests and bishops still needed to reckon with their own internalized homophobia. She concluded that dialogue between LGBTQ Catholics and their bishops would be impossible without acknowledging clericalism and the "lack of mutuality" between them.[24]

Like Manson, members of my own spiritual community expressed skepticism. Fr. Martin first came to speak with Out at St. Paul in Manhattan months before his book was released. Many who attended his talk did not think that "respect, compassion, and sensitivity" went far enough. Some OSP members were in long-term, committed relationships and had families of their own. They wanted their relationships to be recognized as holy and part of God's plan for their lives. At the end of the talk, one OSP member asked Martin if he thought Catholic teaching on same-sex marriage would ever change. The young man left in anger and tears when he answered with a blunt but gentle "no."

Still other OSP members saw Martin's two-way bridge as a fantasy that reflected his own clerical privilege. Dialogue might seem easy for him because he was a priest, but it was nearly impossible for lay Catholics, especially women, who lacked institutional access. OSP members knew this from experience. Several had attempted to reach out to Cardinal Timothy Dolan, but it seemed as if their lane on the bridge was blocked by the other side. Xorje Olivares, a member of the OSP ministry team at the time, felt as if Martin placed "the onus on queer folks to lay the foundation for the bridge, only to have the Catholic Church walk all over our labor to tell us what they've told us for centuries—that somehow we weren't worthy."[25] New approaches to ministry required clearing a path through the clericalism and homophobia that hindered LGBTQ Catholics in the first place.

Other criticisms for *Building a Bridge* emerged from more conservative camps. Eve Tushnet, a lesbian Catholic and proponent of LGBTQ celibacy, asked why Martin's book did not address the Church's traditional teaching on chastity.[26] Her review in the *Washington Post* revealed sexual ethics as the "book's embarrassing secret. It's never mentioned, and so the difficulties the teaching itself poses for gay Catholics in our culture are never addressed."[27] Tushnet was not alone in her assessment. David Cloutier, an ethicist at the Catholic University of America, contended that no amount of bridge-building could fix "a clash of fundamental moral visions that must be engaged."[28]

PUNCHES FROM ABOVE AND THE (ALT-)RIGHT

As *Building a Bridge* gained more and more traction, bishops and archbishops published their own criticisms. Charles Chaput, then archbishop of Philadelphia, encouraged Catholics to reject Martin's style of pastoral ministry. Affirming LGBTQ people, he argued, is a sign of worldliness, not faith. Chaput condemned *Building a Bridge* for its failure to acknowledge the "*substance* of what divides faithful Christians from those who see no sin in active same-sex relationships. The Church is not simply about unity—as valuable as that is—but about unity in God's love rooted in truth." That truth, Chaput's column explained, could be found in Romans 1:21–27: homosexuality is a consequence of rebellion against God. For that reason, LGBTQ people "need conversion, not merely affirmation."[29]

A month after Chaput's critical essay, another salvo came from Cardinal Robert Sarah, the prefect of the Congregation for Divine Worship, well known for his hostility toward the LGBTQ community. In a piece for the *Wall Street Journal*, Sarah rejected Martin's criticisms of the Catholic hierarchy for not being sufficiently attentive to the needs of LGBTQ people. The Church's vocation, Sarah wrote, is to bear witness to God's truth revealed in Jesus Christ, and part of that revelation includes chastity. Since homosexual intimacy is (per Catholic teaching) immoral, the Church must strive "to protect her children from the harm of sin, as an expression of her pastoral charity." According to Sarah, Martin's book failed in this regard because it did not explicitly condemn homosexual activity. Genuine pastoral ministry required a bold and countercultural witness rooted in the "wisdom and goodness of Christ."[30]

In addition to the reproach he received from episcopal detractors, Martin became a punching bag for self-proclaimed defenders of Catholic orthodoxy. From 2017 to 2021, for example, no fewer than two dozen articles about Fr. Martin appeared in *Crisis Magazine*, a publication calling itself "A Voice for the Faithful Catholic Laity." Article titles previewed the aspersions to be cast: "The Perfidious James Martin, SJ"; "The (Evil) Genius of Father Martin"; "Fr. Martin among the Libertines." Joseph Sciambra, a leader in the anti-LGBTQ Catholic movement, repeatedly accused Martin of grooming young people for sexual abuse. Michael Voris, head of the alt-right group Church Militant, called him a "facile, worm-tongued deceiver and false teacher."[31] Austin Ruse, an ultra-traditionalist provocateur, described the Jesuit as "pansified," "effeminate," and "out of the closet."[32] Incivility ruled the alt-right's denunciations.

Amid the controversy, Church Militant urged its followers to "spam" Martin's social media accounts and goad him into blocking them. His Facebook, Twitter, and Instagram feeds were inundated by thousands of hateful and homophobic attacks. Death threats arrived at his office at *America*, most likely incited by alt-right religious media outlets.

At times, online attacks morphed into real-world confrontations. Around the country, groups of traditionalist Catholics protested Martin's talks. Some picketed venues where he was scheduled to speak, including parish talks, retreats, and commencement exercises at Catholic colleges and universities, while others disrupted the talks themselves. Thousands signed online petitions and flooded parishes and dioceses with angry phone calls.[33]

Protestors succeeded in creating an atmosphere of fear and intimidation. A few event planners, unwilling to risk the danger, discomfort, and controversy of hosting Martin, canceled his speaking engagements altogether. This included a highly publicized appearance at the Theological College, a seminary connected to the Catholic University of America, where Martin was scheduled to give a talk titled "Encountering Jesus."[34]

Fr. Martin Responds

Martin's responses to his critics were as wide ranging as their criticisms. Most of the time, he demonstrated a generosity of spirit and what his biographer described as "a remarkable calmness."[35] A few instances, however, revealed his frustration and anger with those who slandered his ministry.

Martin's thoughtful reply to LGBTQ Catholics came in the second edition of *Building a Bridge*, which was published in March 2018. His interactions with LGBTQ Catholics, allies, and others after the first edition caused him to reframe several of his perspectives. One clarification addressed LGBTQ Catholics who felt powerless to confront homophobia in the Church. After the first edition of the book, some readers felt that Martin made it seem as if church leaders and lay Catholics bore equal responsibility for bridge-building. In the second edition, he clarified that the primary obligation lay with the hierarchy, not LGBTQ Catholics, "because it is the institutional church that has made LGBT Catholics feel marginalized, not the other way around."[36] In a similar vein, Martin admitted that the institutional access he enjoyed as a priest was a form of privilege not afforded to everyone. Martin's acceptance of protest and open dissent as necessary forms of dialogue showed his growing appreciation for the ways that even the most disenfranchised believers could help transform the Church.[37]

Responding to critics such as Eve Tushnet and David Cloutier, Martin explained why he had left sexual ethics out of the original discussion. His chief aim, he said, was to build a path for reconciliation and dialogue, not to lay out an ethical framework. He knew that Catholic leaders and LGBTQ Catholics often stood a world apart in their understandings of homosexuality, and each group had important reasons for what they believed. What good would rehashing long-standing disagreements accomplish? Martin preferred to "focus on areas of possible commonality."[38]

Fr. Martin also answered his episcopal critics. In September 2019, he gave a lecture at St. Joseph's University, a Jesuit institution in Philadelphia, that prompted Archbishop Chaput to issue yet another warning against his pastoral message. This time, Chaput attacked Martin by claiming that he did "not speak with authority on behalf of the Church."[39]

Martin took Chaput's criticism of the university talk seriously, particularly since it was so public. In his rejoinder to the archdiocesan paper, he thanked Chaput for the opportunity to dialogue, then defended his ministry. Martin reminded the archbishop of his support for traditional Catholic doctrine, which he had made explicit in an April 2018 *America* piece explaining the Church's teaching on homosexuality.[40] Martin also reminded Chaput of the ecclesiastical approval that his ministry enjoyed. The speech he gave at St. Joseph's was the same one he had given to the World Meeting of Families the prior year, and the latter had been fully "vetted and approved beforehand by the Vatican."[41] If Chaput took issue with Martin's teaching, it was because Chaput had a problem with Catholic tradition and authority.

Martin addressed Cardinal Sarah's concerns in an *America* piece written by Michael O'Loughlin. A chief fault with Sarah's approach, Martin said in an interview, was its refusal to take LGBTQ suffering seriously. If churchmen such as Sarah would spend more time listening and learning, they too would begin to empathize with the pain that LGBTQ people feel. Martin then took another opportunity to correct a mistake that the Vatican official, along with many of his other critics, continued to make. "Cardinal Sarah's op-ed," he said, "inaccurately states that my book is critical of church teaching, which it is not. Nor am I....*Building a Bridge* is not a book of moral theology nor a book on the sexual morality of LGBT people. It is an invitation to dialogue and to prayer, and I'm sure that Cardinal Sarah would agree on the importance of both."[42]

If Fr. Martin's response to Chaput and Sarah strengthened his identification with the Church's traditional teaching and authority structures, his response to alt-right Catholics strengthened his identification with marginalized sexual and gender communities. On several occasions Martin turned the opprobrium he received into expressions of solidarity. After Austin Ruse described him as "pansified," for example, Martin shared on his Facebook page: "Insults and slurs like 'pansy' are what LGBT people face every day, even from Catholics. But hatred and contempt, like this public example posted today on Twitter, only strengthen my desire to advocate for LGBT people, especially within our church."[43]

Later, Martin shared how his interactions with LGBTQ people helped him overcome internet vitriol. "Sometimes," he wrote, "it was hard to keep up with the attacks online, but the hateful comments and personal attacks were always put in perspective after just a few minutes with LGBT Catholics and their family members. Just a few tears from an LGBT Catholic more than made up for an ocean of hateful attacks."[44] Rather than wallowing in self-pity, Martin redoubled his efforts to defend LGBTQ people by making their struggles his own.

Finding Encouragement in Community and Spirituality

In a way, Martin's advocacy functioned as a spiritual emetic that forced up the bile of Catholic hatred for sexual and gender minorities. Slurs, usually whispered about LGBTQ people in secret, became public when critics applied them to him. The Church, his ministry revealed, was sick and needed a cure.

Some of Martin's supporters responded with remedies in hand. Damian Torres-Botello, a gay Jesuit writing for the *Jesuit Post*, lambasted opponents who wanted to "tear down, to shame, and to reject the truth of Gospel love." *Building a Bridge*, he said, enabled people with differences to "meet each other as human persons," something its caustic critics refused to do.[45] Emily Reimer-Barry, an ethics professor at the University of San Diego, condemned the "shaming discourse" of groups such as Church Militant that contributed to feelings of "worthlessness, humiliation, and self-loathing" in the LGBTQ community. *Building a Bridge*, she argued, offered a much needed path toward dialogue, mutuality, and pastoral accompaniment.[46]

More prominent church officials came to his defense as well. San Diego Bishop Robert McElroy wrote an op-ed in *America* expressing his own concern over the dangerous "cancer of vilification" in the Church. "The coordinated attack on *Building a Bridge*," he warned, "must be a wake-up call for the Catholic community to look inward and purge itself of bigotry against the LGBT community."[47] In these and many other interventions, defenses of *Building a Bridge* served as defenses of LGBTQ people. Publicity generated by Martin's ordeal transformed into momentum advancing the broader movement for LGBTQ affirmation.

Throughout the controversy over *Building a Bridge*, Martin took consolation in his faith, especially his relationship with Jesus. In prayer, Martin speaks with Christ as a close friend who knows and empathizes with his deepest struggles.[48] Once, for example, when he was grappling with feelings of rejection from a fellow Jesuit, Martin meditated on Luke 4, the story of Jesus's unhappy return to his hometown. Martin's encounter with Christ that day would have a profound effect on his future ministries. Reflecting on his experience in light of the Messiah's, Martin asked Jesus in prayer how he dealt with feelings of rejection from family and friends.

The priest heard an unexpected question in reply: "Must everyone like you?" He took Christ's words as "an invitation to move away from the need for everyone to love you, like you, or even approve you." A few years later, when Fr. Martin was experiencing "pushback from various quarters in the Church, including a few cardinals and bishops, I remembered that invitation."[49] Jesus's probing question reinforced his dedication to LGBTQ ministry.

Meditating on the crucified Christ also provided reassurance. Martin is loath to compare his sufferings to Christ's, but as a Jesuit he also sees Jesus as his "model in all things," including how to face challenges in ministry. When reflecting on the crucifixion, Martin took note of Jesus's response to his abusers:

> It's something that we tend to pass over, but even after they have arrested, harassed, beaten, brutalized and crucified Jesus, people taunt him. As he's hanging on the cross. It's shocking to think about. And what is his response? He says nothing. He prays for those who have crucified him and to those who taunt him, he says nothing at all.

Christ's response to humiliation gave Martin a pattern to follow in his own ministry. "I'm not comparing myself to Jesus," he explained, "but we need to learn from him. So to most of these taunts and to this hate I say nothing at all."[50]

In addition to his relationship with Christ, Martin found encouragement in friendship. Although some media portrayed him as a solitary figurehead for the LGBTQ Catholic movement, Martin was never a lone ranger. Many of his strongest champions were fellow Jesuits. He shared,

> I've had many Jesuits ask me to talk with their students or parishioners or parents, or have invited me to give talks at their schools or parishes or retreat houses. Often even Jesuits I don't know well will say to me, "Thanks for what you're doing." My close friends have been with me every step along

the way and get me to see things in perspective and even laugh about things.[51]

Lay friends were at his side as well. Kevin Ahern, a theology professor in New York City, whisked him out of the city for day trips exploring old convents in the Hudson Valley. Sr. Janice Farnham, a mentor from his time at Weston Jesuit School of Theology, accompanied him and nurtured his vocation. Ivan Briggeler, a parishioner at St. Ignatius of Loyola in Manhattan, drove three hours to Baltimore for Martin's 2016 NWM ministry talk.[52] As the storm over *Building a Bridge* raged, Martin's friends and communities were a source of comfort and strength.

Affirmation and Resistance from the Hierarchy

Within a couple of years, Fr. Martin had earned his reputation as one of the leading voices in LGBTQ Catholic ministry. During that time, he fine-tuned his messages to address more specialized audiences. Sometimes, he wrote to LGBTQ people, encouraging them to remain steadfast in their faith.[53] In other cases, he gave the broader Church strategies to be more welcoming.[54] Many of these resources came via print media, but some were created for the internet. Especially popular were YouTube videos that carried his message around the world.

Martin's apostolate also grew through invitations to speak at Catholic conferences. Years of defending his work proved his unshakable fidelity to his vows of obedience and church teaching. This meant that more and more Catholic leaders were willing to entertain his message.

Some invitations to speak came from expected places. From 2017 to 2020, for example, he attended the Ignatian Family Teach-In for Justice, an annual gathering of students from Jesuit institutions. Starting in 2018, he also brought his LGBTQ-positive message to the Los Angeles Religious Education Congress, one of the largest annual gatherings of Catholics in the United States. He spoke regularly at Jesuit and other Catholic colleges and universities, not simply to LGBTQ groups but to faculty and student groups as well. Invitations to speak at parishes and retreat houses also continued, and they increasingly focused on ministry to LGBTQ people.

These events, however, paled in comparison to the Vatican's World Meeting of Families where, in August 2018, Pope Francis was to be the keynote speaker in front of more than 130,000 Catholics gathered in Dublin, Ireland.[55] Martin received his invitation to speak at the urging of Cardinal Kevin Ferrell, one of his most vocal supporters and a lead organizer of the meeting. On the day of the event, more than one thousand people gathered in a standing-room-only auditorium to hear Martin's speech, titled "A Good Measure: Showing Welcome and Respect in Our Parishes for LGBT People and Their Families."[56] Martin's speech was the first time the Vatican sanctioned use of the term *LGBT*. According to Jon Sweeney, Martin's biographer, the opportunity to speak was also "an unmistakable sign of Vatican approval of his book."[57]

A MEETING WITH THE POPE

The clearest sign of Pope Francis's approval, however, was yet to come. In late September 2019, Martin was in Rome for a plenary meeting of the Dicastery for Communication when he learned that Pope Francis wanted a one-to-one meeting with him. According to Martin, "Some mutual friends had alerted him that I would be in town, and when I saw him during the audience for the Dicastery of Communications, he said to me, 'I want to have an audience with you.'"[58]

In a few days Martin received a formal invitation at the Jesuit curia, where he had been staying. On the morning of September 30, the Vatican released Pope Francis's schedule for the day, and it included a half-hour meeting with "Padre James Martin, SJ."

At 11:30 a.m., Martin was escorted into the pope's personal library in the Apostolic Palace. Francis was waiting to greet him with a smile. Per protocol, Martin asked what the pope wanted to discuss. When Francis gave him the floor, Martin shared about LGBTQ ministry and the people he had met. In a later interview with Michael Vasquez of the Human Rights Campaign, Martin recollected, "I can't share many of the details, [but it was] very encouraging. I left walking on air.... LGBT people don't have a lot of advocates in the Vatican. I was just bringing the voices of LGBT people into that room with me, and that's what I felt like my mission was."[59]

Photos from the event showed both Pope Francis and James Martin smiling. In a September 30 tweet released shortly afterward, Martin wrote, "I felt encouraged, consoled, and inspired by the Holy Father today. And his time with me, in the middle of a busy day and a busy life, seems a clear sign of his deep pastoral care for LGBT Catholics."[60] Others saw the meeting in a similar light. Francis DeBernardo, executive director of New Ways Ministry, wrote,

> This meeting with the pope refutes the unjustified barrage of criticism he has received from a minority of church leaders and other anti-LGBTQ sectors of the Church. Even more so, it recognizes that Fr. Martin's approach to LGBTQ pastoral ministry, already praised by bishops, archbishops, and cardinals, has won the approval of the highest levels of the Church. It is a clear signal that Pope Francis is calling the Church to conversion away from the negative messages it has sent in the past about LGBTQ people.[61]

Pope Francis's public meeting was great news for Martin's ministry, but it was a triumph for LGBTQ Catholics. At long last they knew the pope heard and cared about their struggle.

VINDICATION AFTER DEFAMATION

As with many benchmarks in Martin's ministry, meeting with the pope stirred up consternation and then fierce resistance from anti-LGBTQ forces in the Church. The most significant challenge came after Francis received bishops from New Mexico, Arizona, Colorado, Utah, and Wyoming on February 10, 2020. The American bishops were in Rome for their *ad limina* visit, a quinquennial meeting that gives the pope a chance to reiterate his pastoral priorities and counsel his brother bishops on local issues. Officially, the content of these meetings is off the record, but afterward bishops often share what the pope communicates to them.

Ten days after Francis met with bishops from the American West, the Catholic News Agency (CNA), a traditionalist media source, reported on their gathering. Supposedly, the pope had expressed his frustration about the way his September 30 meeting with Fr. Martin had been interpreted in public. According to an unnamed source attributed to one of the bishops in the meeting, "The Holy Father's disposition was very clear, he was most displeased about the whole subject of Fr. Martin and how their encounter had been used. He was very expressive, both his words and his face—his anger was very clear, he felt he'd been used." A second anonymous source backed up the story, claiming that the pope met with Martin not to encourage him but to give him a "talking to."[62] These were highly irregular statements from bishops, not only because they were anonymous, but because *ad limina* visits are intended to be private, pastoral, and not politicized. The claims also seemed outlandish, given the pope's clear welcome of Martin's ministry.

And yet, the story spread like wildfire in some Catholic media. Had Martin lied about the nature of his meeting with the pope? If so, it could discredit his entire ministry.

The Jesuit's response to the bishops' claim was cool and collected. "I can't comment on what the Holy Father told me," Martin told CNA, "since he asked me not to share the details with the media, other than to say that I felt profoundly inspired, consoled, and encouraged by our half-hour audience in the Apostolic Palace, which came at his invitation."[63]

It did not take long for cracks to appear in CNA's reporting and highly unethical reliance on unnamed sources. On February 21, Archbishop John Wester of Santa Fe, New Mexico, went on the record to deny key claims of the anonymous report. "The general tone of the pope's responses to issues raised with him," Wester assured, "was never angry, nor do I remember the pope saying or implying that he was unhappy with Father Martin or his ministry."[64] On February 22, Bishop Steven Biegler of Cheyenne, Wyoming, seconded Wester's claims. The meeting, Biegler said, "was a cordial, forthright, and encouraging conversation."[65]

More than a year after the controversy, Martin shared something that he kept private at the time but felt comfortable disclosing "now that the controversy has died down." The day after the libelous CNA report was released, a friend of both Fr. Martin and Pope Francis happened to be visiting the holy father. He lamented to the pope about how the anonymous bishops had attacked Martin. Pope Francis was so upset that he would be portrayed as angry with Martin that he immediately left a message, facilitated by their mutual friend, on Martin's cell phone, saying how much he enjoyed their audience and again expressing support for his ministry. "I kept the recording," Martin said, "and listen to it whenever I get discouraged."[66]

The escapade was a self-inflicted wound for Martin's detractors. *National Catholic Reporter*, a progressive Catholic media outlet, made hay out of the affair. Michael Sean Winters, an op-ed writer, opined, "Perhaps someone should let our friends at CNA know that in the journalism business, comments made on the record are intrinsically more reliable than anonymous comments. Indeed, while we may not deem anonymous comments intrinsically evil, they are intrinsically suspect."[67]

CNA editors defended their original reporting and the anonymous bishops never came forward, but their loss of credibility and moral authority could not be denied. A February 27 editorial by *National Catholic Reporter* staff remarked, "It is enough to say here that websites labeling themselves Catholic have engaged in absolutely unhinged homophobia and made Martin a primary target. That bishops—dare we point out that they are fellow priests—should provide even the slightest legitimacy to such dangerous thinking is horrifying."[68]

NEW MINISTRIES

In recent years Martin's advocacy has continued to grow, in both its scope and its influence. One of the new issues Martin has begun addressing is the plight of trans people. After the U.S. hierarchy lost its fight against same-sex marriage, many bishops turned their attention to opposing the movement for trans liberation. On several occasions, Martin has challenged bishops' willful ignorance with stories of trans perseverance and faith in the face of persecution.[69]

The day after his audience with Pope Francis, Martin was invited to a meeting with the Vatican's Congregation for Education to talk about trans issues. This second meeting did not receive as much attention as the first but, according to Martin, may have been equally significant. He spoke with Cardinal Giuseppe Versaldi, the prefect of the Congregation for Education, and Fr. Friedrich Bechina, the congregation's undersecretary, about the congregation's 2019 document "Male and Female He Created Them," which was widely interpreted as an ignorant and transphobic attack on trans people. Martin took the opportunity to read letters from trans people and allies, who expressed their frustration and hurt with the Church. After Martin shared the experiences of trans people, the cardinal and priest offered some context for the document, expressed "sorrow if people thought the Congregation was accusing people of being ideologically distorted," communicated their "care for transgender people," and spoke of their desire to "continue dialogue to reflect on [trans and allied] experiences."[70]

Martin has also become a lead organizer for the LGBTQ Catholic movement. In late 2019, he announced plans for Outreach 2020, a national meeting of LGBTQ Catholics and allies to strategize and reflect on pastoral ministry. The gathering, slated to be held at Fordham University in June 2020, welcomed an all-star lineup of Catholic theologians, ministers, and church leaders. Unfortunately, it had to be postponed due to the COVID-19 pandemic. In lieu of the in-person meeting, he organized forty of the speakers to record greetings and reflections for LGBTQ Catholics around the world, which were posted on YouTube.[71]

Even amid the worldwide crisis, Martin did not flag. In late 2020 and early 2021, he partnered with the Tyler Clementi Foundation, a nonprofit whose mission is "to end online and offline bullying in schools, workplaces, and faith communities," to publicize "God Is on Your Side: A Statement from Catholic Bishops on Protecting LGBT Youth." With Martin's help, the foundation brought together more than a dozen Catholic bishops along with numerous communities of men and women religious who were willing to "say to our LGBT friends, especially young people, that we stand with you and oppose any form of violence, bullying, or harassment directed at you."[72] Even as the United States Conference of Catholic Bishops continued to protest same-sex marriage and LGBTQ civil rights, Martin fostered opportunities for bishop-advocates to take a different path.

A JESUIT APPROACH TO LGBTQ MINISTRY

In September 2017, Fordham University ethicist Charles Camosy interviewed Fr. James Martin about *Building a Bridge*. In his final question, Camosy asked, "As someone who cares very deeply about the Church's unity in the midst of its diversity: How do you gauge the level of polarization in the Church at the moment?"

Fr. Martin's response reflected his recent experience. "The level of polarization is the worst I've ever seen in my thirty years as a Jesuit," he sighed. Martin suggested that much of the blame for Catholic dis-unity fell on opponents of Pope Francis, whose "emphasis on mercy, on accompaniment, on encounter and, especially, as in [his apostolic exhortation] 'Amoris Laetitia,' on discernment, has driven some peo-ple into near hysterics."[73]

Indeed, ecclesial renewal did not come easily for the pope or Martin, who understood his apostolate as an extension of Francis's ministry. In the same interview with Camosy, Martin shared how a bishop friend who worked at the Vatican once told him, "It's not sur-prising that you're getting so much criticism. They can't attack the pope all the time, so they'll attack you."[74]

Throughout decades of public ministry and three pontificates, Martin has been faithful to his vow of obedience and submission to church teaching. This has become much easier during Francis's pon-tificate, when a member of his own religious community ascended the Chair of Peter. The pair shares a vision for the Church's mission to the margins. For Martin, outreach takes the form of advocacy on behalf of LGBTQ Catholics. As he helps build a bridge of reconcili-ation between the Church and LGBTQ people, he welcomes new allies to join the cause. Clerical rank may have helped Martin become an effective organizer, but his amplification of LGBTQ voices ensures that their experiences are driving the movement. In the process, Martin has secured support from unlikely quarters and helped forge a fresh coalition in the struggle for LGBTQ affirmation.

As Martin and his allies press ahead, a new wave of LGBTQ Catholic ministries is building momentum for the future. The next and final chapter will explore the frontiers of ministry through the lens of queer ecclesiology and the experiences of three recently founded organizations. Their stories expand on one of the themes that has become increasingly clear thus far: when change comes to the Cath-olic Church, it begins at the grassroots and margins. Salvation from homophobia and transphobia will not come from the hierarchy but from the peripheries, where God is active among those who suffer, are excluded, and need God's help the most.

Chapter 9

AN APOLOGY FOR HOPE

Queer Ecclesiology and the Future of LGBTQ Ministry

> Always be ready to make your defense to anyone who demands from you an accounting for the hope that is in you.
>
> —1 Peter 3:15b

THE SILENCE OF DIOCESAN LEADERS

A few years ago, I had coffee with a bishop from outside my diocese. The meeting was arranged by the parents of a gay friend. He had left the Church, but they stuck around to advocate for LGBTQ people. They thought my conversation with the bishop could help bring much-needed change to their diocese.

It was my first meeting with a prelate, and I was pleasantly surprised by the encounter. He respected my learning and experiences. After I shared my conversion story (I grew up an evangelical Protestant), coming out story, and a little about ministry, he even affirmed God's work in my life. I walked away encouraged.

Since then, I have stayed in touch with my friend's parents and others in the diocese. Regrettably, little has changed. While pastoral in person, the bishop and his staff have made few, if any, public gestures of support for LGBTQ people. Young people continue to walk away from their faith while diocesan leaders watch in silence.

This experience, I believe, is emblematic of LGBTQ Catholic advocacy. For decades, grassroots believers have tried to dialogue with the institutional church. We have written letters, showed up for in-person meetings, shared our hearts, and even protested. Sometimes we face outright rejection, but more often we find bishops, priests, ministers, and administrators who are nice in person but unwilling to follow up with any meaningful action. Doctrine is doctrine, they say. The Church's position cannot change.

For these and countless other reasons, LGBTQ Catholics and allies are perennially disappointed. It is no wonder why so many leave the Church. Being LGBTQ and Catholic can feel like one letdown after another. There must be a better way.

This final chapter is an apology for hope. Turning to the hierarchy for affirmation may be a fool's errand, but there is a different story unfolding at the Catholic grassroots. To see God's work in action, we must reorient our framing of "the Church." If the bishops are our standard for Catholicism, we are lost. When we turn to the people of God on the Church's margins, we find a way forward.

ECCLESIASTICAL INTRANSIGENCE

The moral and pastoral failings of Christian leaders are familiar, if tiring, storylines. Throughout the twentieth century, civil rights and social justice luminaries lambasted pastors, priests, and bishops who refused to support movements for justice and equity. In his magisterial "Letter from Birmingham Jail," Martin Luther King Jr. decried white moderates who preferred a "negative peace which is the absence of tension to a positive peace which is the presence of justice."[1] During the farmworkers movement of the late sixties, Cesar Chavez criticized Catholic priests who were unwilling to accompany organizers: "Why do the Protestants come out here and help the people, demand nothing, and give all their time to serving farm workers, while our own parish priests stay in their churches, where only a few people come, and usually feel uncomfortable?"[2] Even Servant of God Dorothy Day pilloried the hierarchy. "As a convert, I never expected much of the bishops," she explained. "In all history, popes and bishops and abbots seem to have been blind and power-loving and greedy. I never expected leadership from them."[3]

Today, there are several reasons why the Catholic hierarchy may be reluctant to come out in support of LGBTQ ministry.

First, some priests and bishops undoubtedly follow their con-sciences, believing that Catholic tradition keeps them from affirming theologies and pastoral practices. Ordained as ministers of Christ, their vocation is to safeguard Catholic teaching, and they take this responsi-bility seriously. Most believe that Jesus taught marriage belongs between a man and woman.[4] Many interpret the creation story in Genesis to mean that transgender folks are mistaken about their gender identity.[5] Even if priests and bishops wanted to change church teaching, they would never presume to alter what they have received as God's plan.

Here, we might be tempted to empathize with the hierarchy's plight since it claims to be bound by a fixed tradition. Problems arise, however, when Catholic leaders confuse culture wars with their respon-sibility to safeguard the Gospel. The hierarchy's recent opposition to LGBTQ civil rights (along with most of the magisterium's teaching on homosexuality and transgender identity) is, at most, only a few decades old, a modern attempt to counter social change with ahistorical cul-tural and theological ideologies.[6] In Scripture, Jesus never condemned gay relationships or genderqueer people. The author of Genesis did not spell out guidelines for modern understandings of gender. Stoking culture wars is not the same thing as preserving Christian kerygma.

Second, the Catholic Church's anti-LGBTQ posturing may be a bid to preserve its authority, which has drastically declined in the United States over the last several decades. There are many reasons why this is so, but increasing secularization, religious disaffiliation, and rapidly falling attendance mean that Catholic leaders do not possess the social, spiritual, or moral capital they once did. The sex abuse crisis has accelerated this decline, and the hierarchy is sensitive to the loss.[7] Countless priests and bishops have staked their positions in culture wars as a way of remaining relevant, and many would prefer to die on lonely hills rather than dialogue with those who disagree.

Third, many in the hierarchy react against change that springs from the Church itself. Vatican II empowered lay believers to embrace their roles as priest, prophet, and king. Some grassroots Catholics, relying on their consciences, dissented from church teaching on issues such as contraception.[8] This dynamic became even more acute with feminist critiques of Catholic patriarchy. In the second half of the twentieth century, women seeking ordination posed an unprecedented threat to the authority of the all-male priesthood and episcopacy.[9] With so many challenges to their moral and spiritual leadership, what were Catholic leaders to do?

Regrettably, many priests and bishops doubled down on the issues that separated them from their coreligionists: contraception, abortion, and women in ordained ministry. The problem was exacerbated by John Paul II, who interpreted Vatican II to centralize papal power and, over several decades, appointed churchmen known for their submission to his leadership and hardline stances on disputed issues.[10] From the eighties on, holding firm to homophobia and transphobia—like the exclusion of women from ministry—became a litmus test for orthodoxy in church circles. Most bishops, priests, and administrators were eager to follow the program since their livelihoods depended on it.

Fourth, ecclesiastical opposition to LGBTQ-affirming ministry sometimes stems from the personal insecurities that Catholic leaders face due to their own sexual orientation and/or gender identity. We should never underestimate the effects of internalized homophobia and transphobia on the clerical class. Although definite statistics are hard to come by, the lowest estimates claim that around 15 percent of the clergy is homosexual, while higher estimates claim that the number is closer to 75 to 80 percent.[11]

The ecclesiastical closet fosters secrecy, shame, and self-loathing that priests, bishops, and popes channel into crusades against LGBTQ people.[12] Rather than learning from dialogue with healthy, openly queer folks, many church leaders are familiar only with the dysfunctional and often abusive personalities and relationships cultivated within their own institutions. For decades, these unhealthy church environments, closed off from the rest of the world, have yielded the rotten fruits of teaching that dehumanizes queer people and political engagement that opposes LGTBQ civil rights.

Although Pope Francis has signaled a limited openness to change from his predecessor's policies, the barque of Peter does not turn on a dime. Many bishops appointed by John Paul II and Benedict XVI still hold office. In the United States, culture war bishops dominate the USCCB.[13] The Supreme Court legalized same-sex marriage in 2015, but Catholic leaders continue to obsess over questions of "religious freedom" and preserving their right to discriminate.[14] In a society that now accepts same-sex couples, many church officials have turned trans folks into new targets for discrimination.[15] The hierarchy is as committed to death-dealing policies as it ever was, and there is little reason to believe that it has the power or will to change on its own.

There Is No Salvation Outside the Poor

The situation for LGBTQ people in the Roman Catholic Church is dire and begs the question: If LGBTQ liberation will not come from the hierarchy, whence will it come?

The history of the Roman Catholic Church in Latin America illustrates that queer Catholics and their allies are not the first to wrestle with this type of question. In the mid- to late twentieth century, Latin American believers struggled with an institutional church whose fortunes were often tied to colonialist and authoritarian governments. For generations, many bishops and priests had sided with the rich and powerful at the expense of the poor and powerless. Religious leaders who were supposed to be agents of liberation served the forces of death, and Christ's good news for the poor was obscured by ecclesiastical wealth and greed.[16] Who could break the Church's collusion with systems of oppression?

Latin American theologians found the answer among the poor. In the sixties, a movement of base communities arose to serve and organize the poor in rural areas where clergy were sparse. These grassroots groups fostered solidarity through social, political, and spiritual action, setting a powerful example of Christian faith at work. The mutual aid networks that developed throughout Latin America addressed people's material needs while also resisting the dehumanizing social structures that oppressed them. Base communities opened a new way of being Church that modeled the Christian preferential option for the poor, the belief that Christians, following the God of Hebrew and Christian tradition, ought to side with those who suffer from oppression and injustice.[17]

Jon Sobrino, a Spanish Jesuit and theologian who was ministering and teaching in El Salvador at that time, reflected on the revolution happening around him. Paying attention to life at the grassroots, he saw that God was working among the poor to bring salvation into the world. Unless the institutional church learned from the poor and other victims of human history, it could never be a source of hope within a "gravely ill civilization."[18]

To build his case, Sobrino cited the work of José Comblin, a Belgian priest and theologian from Brazil. In his ministry, Comblin had observed a wide gap between how the poor were conceived by outsiders and how they lived. He wrote,

> The mass media speak of the poor always in negative terms, as those who don't have property, those who don't have culture, those who have nothing to eat. Seen from outside, the world of the poor is pure negativity. Seen from within, however, the world of the poor has vitality; they struggle to survive, they invent an informal economy and they build a different civilization, one of solidarity among people who recognize each other as equals—a civilization with its own forms of expression, including art and poetry.[19]

Comblin's insight into the lives of the poor helped Sobrino reimagine the role of the poor—and the Church—in salvation history. Traditionally, Catholics had imagined the Church as the sine non qua of salvation, a conviction expressed over the course of many centuries in the maxim *Extra Ecclesiam nulla salus* (Outside the Church there is no salvation).[20] Sobrino, however, inverted the traditional formulation by asserting *Extra pauperem nulla salus* (Outside the *poor* there is no salvation). The experience of the poor, he wrote, "is salvific, for it generates hope for a more human world. And it is an experience of grace, for it arises where we least expect it."[21]

Although the poor may have few material goods, Sobrino explained that they "possess something that makes them truly live and that they offer to others."[22] In a world consumed by greed and injustice, the poor are a prophetic sign of God's inbreaking reign. Hope springs from their lives on the margins, where justice, compassion, and empathy are powerful proofs of grace. For this reason, it is the poor and excluded—not the rich and powerful—who reveal God's unfolding plan for humanity. "By starting from [the civilization of] poverty, and opposing [the civilization of] wealth," Sobrino concluded, "the world can be turned around."[23]

The Church and a Culture of Death

So, what does all of this have to do with LGBTQ people in the Catholic Church?

Queer folks, like the poor in Latin America, have long suffered from social and ecclesial injustices. According to the Human Rights Campaign (HRC), LGBTQ youth are twice as likely to be physically assaulted, kicked, or shoved than their straight peers.[24] Bullying and ostracization take a heavy toll on young lives. According to a 2015 study, LGB youth were nearly five times more likely to attempt suicide in the prior year than their heterosexual peers.[25] Neither are adults exempt from violence. The FBI reported that 17 percent of hate crimes in 2019 were based on sexual orientation and 2.7 percent of hate crimes were based on gender identity.[26] That same year, at least forty-four trans or gender nonconforming people were murdered in the United States.[27]

Tragically, religion often augments the suffering of LGBTQ people. Queer youth raised in religious communities are more than twice as likely than their nonreligious peers to attempt suicide.[28] According to Carl Siciliano, the founder and executive director of the Ali Forney Center, a New York City shelter for homeless LGBTQ youth, at least 90 percent of homeless LGBTQ youth in New York City were kicked out of their homes by their parents for "religious reasons."[29]

LGBTQ adults are also victimized by the Church. Many Catholic leaders make it impossible for LGBTQ people to flourish in Catholic spaces. Alana Chen, for example, was a young woman from Colorado who died by suicide after a priest encouraged her to hide her lesbian identity.[30] In many parishes, dioceses, and schools, Church workers who marry their same-sex partners lose their livelihoods.[31] In some places, Catholic bishops even deny LGBTQ Catholics a church funeral, a final humiliation after so much spiritual abuse in life.[32]

Beyond the tragic stories that make the news, queer folks are subjected to other indignities daily. Fr. James Martin, SJ, describes LGBTQ people in the Church as modern-day lepers who have been "mocked, insulted, excluded, condemned or singled out for critique, either privately or from the pulpit."[33] Rather than promoting a culture of life, the Church fosters a culture of shame and suffering. Who will rescue the Church from this body of death?

Turning to the Queer for Salvation

Following the thought of Comblin and Sobrino, a queer ecclesiology posits that salvation can be found among the Church's queer members—that is, where most Catholics least expect it. Magisterial teaching, after all, describes LGBTQ people as "intrinsically disordered," and Courage, the only church-endorsed ministry for those who "suffer from same-sex attraction," treats queer Catholics like addicts in need of a 12-step program. At various times, queer folks in the Church are pitied as if they are sick, counseled as if they are confused, and despised as if they are depraved.

These judgments can have deadly effects on queer people, but most often they are ecclesiastical projections that have little to do with LGBTQ lives or self-understanding. If church leaders would get to know queer people, they would discover an abyss between how church teaching characterizes the LGBTQ community how LGBTQ people live and experience God. To put a queer spin on Comblin's writing:

> The Church speaks of queer people always in negative terms, as those who are intrinsically disordered, those who suffer from a "condition," those who reject God's plan for human sexuality and gender identity. Seen from outside, the world of LGBTQ people is pure negativity. Seen from within, however, the world of queer folks has vitality; they struggle to build a world where everyone can flourish, they create their own families and communities, and they grow in intimate relationships not based on ideological theories of sexual and gender complementarity, but on genuine affection, self-sacrifice, and mutual care. They create a joyful culture of solidarity and affirmation—one grounded in Pride and the celebration of God-given desires and gifts.

Countless queer Christians and theologians have written on the joy and gifts that queer people bring to the Church, but perhaps none so eloquently as Elizabeth Edman, an Episcopalian priest, lesbian, and political organizer. In her autobiographical work, *Queer Virtue: What*

LGBTQ People Know about Life and Love and How It Can Revitalize Christianity, Edman argues that the "queer moral center...is not only *not* at odds with core tenets of Judeo-Christian belief, but it is resonant with and in fact points to the most important, challenging, and vivifying aspects of the Judeo-Christian tradition." She finds queer habits of "spiritual discernment, rigorous self-assessment, honesty, courage, material risk, dedication to community life, and care for the marginalized and oppressed" to be especially prevalent—and prophetic—ways of life.[34]

According to Edman, these practices are demanding expressions of Christianity, not compromises with sinful culture or fallen human nature. Rather than undermining the gospel, queer folks embody the heart of Christian faith and challenge others to do the same. Like Sobrino, Edman finds hope for Christian liberation (in her case, from queerphobia) among the people of God who have been relegated to the Church's peripheries. To find salvation, church leaders must learn from *them*.

Indeed, queer believers know the way out of queerphobia because many of them have escaped it themselves. The prayer, discernment, and struggle needed to reconcile LGBTQ sexualities and/or gender identities with Catholicism builds strong faiths and resilient communities. Queer Christians are passionate evangelists committed to sharing the good news of affirmation. LGBTQ Catholics reimagine Catholic theology in light of their own experiences of God, create kinship groups to welcome those rejected by parishes and biological families, and drive local and global social movements that save LGBTQ lives. Queer spirituality draws strength from the God of Christian revelation who lovingly creates each person in the *imago Dei* and wills for the emotional, relational, and spiritual well-being of all God's creatures.

In the Catholic Church, LGBTQ believers have embodied the liberating gifts that Edman describes. They show pride in God's work in their lives and relationships, empowering other Catholics, queer or straight, to embrace their callings and gifts as well. Queer openness, honesty, and vulnerability are potent antidotes to the hiding, hypocrisy, and insecurity that dominate the hierarchy's response to LGBTQ issues. In countless times and places, LGBTQ Catholic ministries have provided life-giving alternatives to ecclesiastical ignorance, cruelty, and abuse. This allows us to say with certainty, *Extra queer nulla salus* (Outside the queer there is no salvation).

Queer faith is good news for the Church because it opens space for personal growth and collective transformation. With LGBTQ Catholics active in the Church, the Body of Christ is not doomed to repeat the mistakes of its past. The love, acceptance, and pastoral care that LGBTQ ministries offer help break the institutional church out of its shame, oppression, and fear. As the Body of Christ searches for new, healthy ways of relating to LGBTQ people, it will succeed only if it watches and learns from those who have been instruments of God's work for generations.

REVOLUTION AT THE GRASSROOTS

The good news is that decades of advocacy from LGBTQ Catholics and their allies have yielded substantial fruit at the grassroots level. In recent years, there has been a worldwide revolution of tenderness and compassion toward LGBTQ people, and an overwhelming majority of U.S. Catholics have been transformed by it. From 1996 to 2020, the number of Americans who supported same-sex marriage rose from 27 percent to 70 percent.[35] According to Gallup, U.S. Catholic support for gay marriage has been five or more percentage points higher than the national average for several years.[36] Among Christians, grassroots Roman Catholics routinely rank among the most affirming.[37] These encouraging statistics extend to Catholic views on LGBTQ civil rights. In 2020, the Public Religion Research Initiative (PRRI) found that 74 percent of Catholics "supported legal protections for LGBTQ persons in the areas of employment, public accommodations, and housing."[38]

Even as parts of the Catholic hierarchy double down on homophobia and transphobia, ordinary believers propel broader social trends of acceptance and affirmation. Families, friends, and allies recognize that their queer loved ones are not disordered but created in the image of God. In many Catholic communities, there is no question about whether Christian discipleship is compatible with LGBTQ self-understanding. Most Catholics believe that same-sex relationships can be holy and that sexual and gender justice should be part of the Church's mission. The Holy Spirit is moving the people of God toward a hopeful future.

In order to find where God is at work in the Church today, we now turn to the stories of three recently established ministries: LGBT

Catholics and Friends at St. Ignatius of Loyola in Manhattan, Affirmed in the Archdiocese of Chicago, and Vine & Fig, an online ministry that reaches LGBTQ Catholics around the world. Each is a sign of hope for a Church that desperately needs it. LGBTQ Catholic ministry is alive and well and it is vivifying the Body of Christ.

LGBT Catholics and Friends

On October 30, 2016, Ivan Briggiler, a Catholic father of three, was traveling back to New York City from Baltimore with his fifteen-year-old son, Marcos. Also in the car was Fr. James Martin, SJ, their friend who had just received New Ways Ministry's Building a Bridge Award. Ivan and Marcos attended the ceremony to support Fr. Jim. Marcos had come out to his family the year before, and Ivan wanted to do everything he could to affirm his son's faith.

As they drove, Fr. Jim scrolled through his social media, deleting the hateful messages he had received during the ceremony. Ivan thought of Sr. Jeannine Gramick, the indomitable founder of New Ways Ministry who had been on the front lines of ministry for several decades. He knew the challenges that ministers to LGBTQ people faced but still wondered about starting a group at his own parish. "Why can't the Church help me raise a gay Catholic kid within the community?" he asked. "The Church is missing the opportunity to bring up these kids within the Catholic faith."[39]

After their trip, Ivan spoke more with Fr. Jim, then with Fr. William Bergen, SJ, then with other parishioners at St. Ignatius of Loyola, his parish on Manhattan's Upper East Side, and finally with Fr. Dennis Yesalonia, SJ, who had become the head pastor six months earlier. Each was enthusiastic about his idea for a new parish ministry. According to Briggiler, Fr. Yesalonia's major concern was the need for a safe and affirming environment. Otherwise, everything was primed to go.

Over several months, a parish committee brought together staff and parishioners to plan the group's launch. John Vernon, a lay minister who became the group's co-leader, shared how their discernment process boiled down to two questions they asked of Jesus: "What is it that you want me to do for you? What is it that you want this ministry to do for you?"[40]

To answer these questions, organizers consulted with local and national LGBT ministries. They wrestled with the type of community they wanted to become. Would they focus on the needs of the LGBT community or work more closely with the parish? According to John Vernon, Fr. Yesalonia encouraged them to "always go outward," so they chose the latter option.[41]

Unlike other New York City LGBTQ Catholic communities, the St. Ignatius of Loyola group welcomed adults, youth, family members, and allies.[42] Before going public, they named themselves LGBT Catholics & Friends (C&F), created a logo (an image of a church with their name inscribed over rainbow steps), and wrote a mission statement: "We are a group of LGBT parishioners and family and friends and parents of LGBT persons. We are a parish ministry of, by and for our lesbian, gay, bisexual, and transgender sisters and brothers in Christ and those who love and support them. Our ministry extends to, and embraces, the mission of the entire parish, our home."[43]

In a June 2017 letter to the parish, Fr. Yesalonia explained why the ministry was needed:

> I believe that the strength of our faith, the pervasiveness of the desire to be part of this community, and the depth of our love for one another as friends in the Lord propel us to acknowledge, accept, affirm, and nourish in their faith those members of our parish who identify as lesbian, gay, bisexual, transgender, and questioning (LGBTQ). To that end, I have authorized the creation of a Parish LGBTQ Ministry whose mission will be to nurture the faith life of the entire parish through the unique perspective these sisters and brothers bring to being Catholic in an environment which in significant ways has banished them to second class status. The LGBTQ members of our parish have waited patiently for this day to come. We can delay no longer. Justice demands it; compassion and mercy accompany it.[44]

Lay-led subcommittees emerged within the ministry to nurture a tripartite Ignatian mission of community, spirituality, and service. C&F's first event, held in a member's home, was an October 26, 2017, discussion of Fr. Martin's book *Building a Bridge*. The gathering was a useful step to test the waters. A month and a half later, the new ministry hosted "Our Stories: Being LGBT and Catholic" as part of its outreach to the broader parish community. The evening was headlined by Francis

DeBernardo, executive director of New Ways Ministry, but it also gave several members of the new ministry, including Ivan, the opportunity to share testimonies of God's work in their lives.[45]

Similar events followed in the years ahead, with nights dedicated to transgender Catholics, Black Catholics, and families of LGBT Catholics. These education campaigns carried an activist edge. By sharing stories of struggle and marginalization, C&F members came out to the parish with a call for social and ecclesial transformation.

A Mass of Welcome on December 7, 2018, gave straight parishioners the opportunity to answer C&F's call for affirmation. C&F members made announcements about the special event for weeks ahead of time. Rose DiMartino, who co-led the ministry with John Vernon, shared how the group told allies, "You have to come [to the Mass]. If you really want to walk the walk here, instead of just saying in your heart, 'I'm not homophobic,' you need to show up."[46] The parish community did not disappoint, and more than four hundred people attended the Mass presided over by Fr. Yesalonia.

Since that successful event, C&F has collaborated with other parish ministries to strengthen bonds of faith and integrate LGBT parishioners into the broader community. In a few short years, C&F has hosted a spaghetti dinner with the Family Ministry, sponsored a discussion on refugee justice with the Music Ministry and Ignatian Social Justice group, and organized well-attended scavenger hunts around the city. John Vernon explained how C&F's programming bolsters its profile in the parish:

> It isn't like the LGBT guys are over here, doing this and that by themselves. We're actually doing [these activities] for the greater service of the parish and the greater service of the community....And as we do this, together, you'll come to know who we are. And that way you'll become aware of our concerns. And hopefully, you'll appreciate us and support us, and we'll achieve acceptance.[47]

As C&F looks to the future, it is hopeful for opportunities to attract young people. Most of the current leaders are in their forties, fifties, and sixties. While some LGBT youth attend events with their families, there is a gap between their experiences and those of older members who still struggle with decades-old spiritual trauma. LGBT young people also struggle in Catholic spaces that are not fully affirming. According to Rose DiMartino, most queer youth want to be part of religious communities that are "more welcoming of their entire selves."[48]

Despite the challenges, those who helped start C&F are hopeful and ambitious. Ivan Briggiler, whose relationship with his gay son first moved him to ministry, disclosed, "If my son had the courage to come out, I need to have the courage to come out, too, as a parent of a gay kid….It's a hard road, but it's not a road that I'm willing to leave. I'm not going to give up any ground. They will have to kick me out, but I'll be there. I'll be there talking to a future generation of—hopefully—gay teenagers or whomever wants to come to St. Ignatius."[49]

Affirmed

Chicago's Affirmed ministry originated among allies from the Young Adult Community (YAC) at St. Clement, a progressive Catholic parish in the affluent Lincoln Park neighborhood. With groups dedicated to moms and dads, couples, youth, social justice, and more, the parish has long been a hub for innovative ministry.[50] In the eighties and nineties, St. Clement served people suffering from HIV/AIDS, and in the early 2000s it even sponsored a group called the Gay and Lesbian Network "to support our gay and lesbian parishioners, their families and their friends."[51]

According to Michael Bayer, a lay minister who joined parish staff in January 2018, St. Clement "saw itself as being a welcoming sort of place," but there were signs of trouble. In 2018, not a single person on the YAC's 2,000+ member LISTSERV was openly LGBTQ.[52] This bothered some YAC members. Katherine Abel, a young adult leader, wondered why LGBTQ attendees did not feel comfortable coming out. She and others wanted everyone to know they were welcome and loved.[53]

In mid-2018, Bayer and YAC leaders approached Fr. Paul Seaman, St. Clement's head pastor from 2017 until 2019, to ask for visible signs of support for LGBTQ people. They suggested reading an affirming statement after every Sunday Mass and hanging a rainbow banner in front of the church. Fr. Seaman, however, was not satisfied with their proposal. Announcements and rainbow banners were flashy, but the parish lacked a foundation for sustained, intentional ministry. He encouraged them to go back to the drawing board.[54]

After discerning several more months, YAC proposed a new ministry dedicated to LGBTQ inclusion. This time, Fr. Seaman, with the archdiocese's backing, approved. Bayer explained that the new group was not "designed to challenge doctrine or take on any kind of advocacy around the Church's teaching. This is a ministry of pastoral care and support that begins with our higher theological truth that every individual is made in the image and likeness of God."[55]

Given the great need for pastoral care in Chicago, Bayer and Abel decided to welcome people of "all generations and even all parishes and all faiths."[56] Leaders chose the name "Affirmed" to reflect their belief that all people are created *imago Dei*. Psalm 139:14 inspired their message: "I praise you, for I am fearfully and wonderfully made. Wonderful are your works; that I know very well." On August 6, 2019, a Facebook page launched describing Affirmed as

> a ministry of fellowship and support for LGBTQ+, gender minorities, and allies seeking to cultivate a space in which every person is affirmed as made in the image of God, called to a deeper relationship with Jesus Christ, and invited to share their gifts with the broader parish community. This ministry is sponsored by Saint Clement Catholic Church in Lincoln Park, Chicago, but all are welcome to join, regardless of religious beliefs.[57]

The group's first formal event was a discussion around *Building a Bridge*. Bayer and Abel prepared for a dozen participants, but more than three times that number showed up. One man drove more than two hours each way to attend. Another, a recent college graduate, never believed it was possible to integrate his faith and sexuality until he met others like him at Affirmed.[58]

Within a few months, people from around the world were contacting Bayer and Abel to ask them how they too could start a group. Bayer reflected, "This ministry, even if we're not marching in the streets demanding change but just having a space where people can have these conversations, is so desperately needed. Why doesn't this exist everywhere? Why is this such an island?"[59]

The ministry partnered with Holy Name Cathedral and St. Vincent de Paul, other LGBTQ-friendly parishes, and hosted events in bars, giving Affirmed a reputation that it "was not only ground up, but was truly collaborative, where parishes were not competing with one another."[60] Bayer believed cooperative ministry would be a pragmatic way to conserve limited financial and staff resources, safeguard against future archdiocesan consolidations, and foster lay leadership outside of traditional parochial structures.

Less than a year after Affirmed began meeting, the coronavirus pandemic interrupted its plans for in-person gatherings. Like other ministries, the group adapted to a new digital format. Bayer and Abel embraced Zoom as a medium for large-group conversations. During the pandemic they welcomed activists, ministry leaders, and scholars such as Juan Carlos Cruz, Rabbi Megan Goldmarche, Dr. Patrick Hornbeck, and Fr. James Martin, SJ, who, in August 2019, wrote a piece for *America* that highlighted Affirmed as an example of the Church's openness to LGBTQ Catholics.[61]

Another activity that flourished during the pandemic was Book Club. Organized by Rebecca MacMaster, a master of divinity student who became involved with St. Clement as a pastoral intern, the club met weekly to discuss theology, spirituality, and ethics. In addition to offering faith formation, the Book Club was described by MacMaster as a space "where once a week you could express your anger, your hopes, your worries, your joys, week in and week out, in a time that was really hard and difficult. It felt life-giving." Although MacMaster said the ministry could be "really hard" and even "sad at times," there was also "profound love and joy" to be found in fostering community.[62]

As Affirmed grew, Bayer and Abel welcomed new LGBTQ+ leadership. Since both were straight allies, they were sensitive to the need for queer perspectives. According to Bayer, 75 to 80 percent of participants identified as LGBTQ+, a reality that affected how Bayer and Abel ministered.[63] The latter, who has a lesbian sister, shared,

> It was much more our place to listen and to really hear, because we don't know as much. I love my sister and I know about her faith, but there are so many different journeys that are a part of having the LGBTQ Catholic identity that I didn't understand and still don't understand....As long as we are in charge of certain things, we are listening the whole time. And it's never driven by what we want something to be. Eventually we'd like for the programming to be headed by an LGBTQ person who really feels like they can.[64]

The fledgling ministry also had to navigate changes in parish leadership. Less than a year after Affirmed began, Fr. Peter Wojcik was appointed to replace Fr. Seaman as head pastor of St. Clement. A couple of months later, Bayer's position at the parish was eliminated. Although Bayer remained involved with Affirmed a few months after his departure and Wojcik signaled his support for the ministry, such dramatic transitions in parish leadership could have wreaked havoc on the lay-led group.

Today, the outreach soldiers on. Abel explained, "This is definitely an opportunity to change minds, change hearts, and bring people closer to what Jesus would want—that is, accepting people regardless of their situation."[65] With such committed allies, a friendly archdiocese, and increasing LGBTQ representation, Affirmed is a sign of hope for Chicago and beyond.

Vine & Fig

While groups like Affirmed and LGBT Catholics and Friends flourish within parish structures, others are establishing new ministries online. Such is the case with Vine & Fig (V&F), "An Affirming Space for Queer Catholics" that "seeks to elevate the lives of queer Catholics as we find beauty and power at the intersection of our faith, gender, and sexuality."[66]

V&F sprouted in 2018 from collaboration between Patrick Weston, a web developer living in Columbus, Ohio; Pat Flores (né Gothman), a "former seminarian, former theology teacher, and former religious brother" from Dallas, Texas; and Michael Vasquez, an activist leader and then master of divinity student at Duke University.[67] Together, the three men, committed to their Catholic faith as much as their queer identities, brainstormed ways to help others integrate their spirituality and sexuality.

As the trio explored resources for LGBTQ ministry, they found a lack of affirming theology, spirituality, and community for young queer folks. In places like Dallas and Columbus, there were no supportive parishes or ministries. National groups such as DignityUSA and New Ways Ministry seemed more oriented toward activism and organizing than discipleship and mentoring. While there were plenty of internet resources for LGBTQ evangelicals and ex-evangelicals, they found precious little for queer Catholics. "What do gay people of faith do?" Pat Gothman asked himself. "Where do you go?"[68]

They turned to the internet for a solution. Why not build a website? Pat, Patrick, and Michael named their project after the eschatological word picture painted by Micah 4:4: "but they shall all sit under their own vines and under their own fig trees, and no one shall make them afraid." In an early podcast, Pat shared why the image was meaningful. First, it envisioned a "safe, sacred space where we could just be how God made us, unafraid and fully ourselves." Second, it illustrated the fruitfulness of queer folks in the Church. A key part of V&F's mission would be communicating the gifts that LGBTQ Catholics bring to the Body of Christ.[69]

At the time, Pat was dating Jacob Flores (the pair would marry in 2020), a recent convert to the Catholic Church from Seattle. Before moving to Texas, Jacob attended and was confirmed at St. James Cathedral, a parish with a vibrant gay and lesbian community that met every Sunday after Mass for donuts and coffee. As Jacob became more involved with V&F, his experience at St. James inspired a "digitalized international coffee and donuts, where queer folks of faith can come together and just really talk about anything."[70]

V&F launched with a website and social media in late 2018. It was unabashedly queer and Catholic from the start. According to Pat, contributors had no desire to "defend ourselves to the Church" or "play apologetics" but instead to "state that we are very comfortable with our sexuality, and we're very comfortable with our Catholicism, and anybody who wants to can come join."[71] The group introduced itself to the world with a video montage of secular and sacred sites in Rome accompanied by words of welcome: "If you are queer and Catholic you have a new home where your Catholic faith will be affirmed along with your sexuality, your relationships, your humanity, your love. Whether you have been married for years or are just checking things out, you are welcome here."[72]

V&F's first blogpost, "Pat's Queer Catholic Story," was soon joined by several other autobiographies and reflections.[73] The group set out to build a repository of resources that would connect visitors to a worldwide fellowship of queer Catholics. But branching out required fresh perspectives. One early supporter was Zinzy Nev Geene, who hailed from Amsterdam and described herself as "a queer Afropean seminary dropout." Her gift for creating "resonant queer spaces" soon became fundamental to V&F's growth.[74]

By May 2019, V&F's founders recognized the need for a more intentional community structure. Theological and spiritual resources were important, but how could they foster dialogue and be church together in online spaces? Leaders wanted a forum where queer believers could work through their questions and issues in real time. The V&F website explained, "A church which doesn't fully affirm all its members, more than any other, has a need for strong community where we can lean on each other, listen to each other, and learn from one another."[75]

In May 2019, Patrick invited the V&F email LISTSERV to join Slack, a secure social media platform with chatrooms, messaging, and voice and video calls. Since then, more than six hundred people from around the world have logged on. The online community is closed to protect its members from outside abuse. Many who belong to the group are not out of the closet, use anonymous names to protect themselves, and/or live where being openly queer could provoke homo/transphobic violence.

V&F does everything possible to safeguard the physical, emotional, relational, and spiritual well-being of those who participate. To join the Slack community, newcomers must be eighteen years old and complete a questionnaire that assures they are both queer-affirming and Catholic. Community guidelines offer "Ten Commandments" for engagement such as "2. Cultivate a safe and brave space," "3. Do not promote non-affirming stances," and "5. Do not explain a person's reality to them." Some of the guidelines, such "6. Always assume positive intent," are helpful etiquette for all online spaces. Others, such as "Expect to grow," reflect V&F's mission to foster relationships "with people who have experienced lives entirely different from ours."[76]

According to Zinzy, Slack has made it possible for people from innumerable backgrounds to share in the community: "We don't just see lesbian women and gay men, but we also see lots of trans people, non-binary people, and Catholics of color from all over the world. And what's beautiful about that is that it helps us all learn through conversations and the stories we get to read,…from gay white men in Kentucky to transgender women in Nairobi."[77] V&F's commitment to representation became even more evident in April 2020, when Zinzy and Jacob formally joined the leadership team. Since then, the pair have helped the group embrace intersectional approaches to race, gender, ability, and other issues as core elements of its mission.[78]

Integrating Catholic faith and queer identity is hard work, and Slack conversations do much of the heavy lifting. V&F members see the fruits of their labor in real time. Zinzy recalled the experience of one person who came to the community and learned to "grapple with what it means to be a queer cradle Catholic, what it means to be a young adult trying to find their way in the world, and what kind of queer person they want to be." Gender nonconforming and trans folks are also an important part of the conversation. Some come out to others for the first time on message boards. Their pronouns may change, but they find acceptance within a "community that just kind of flows with it."[79]

Community via Slack also brings challenges. There is an abiding tension between the need for honest dialogue and the need to provide a safe and affirming space for everyone. How can the group offer healing for those who have suffered from spiritual trauma or answer difficult questions while ensuring that others are not hurt in the process? Conversations sometimes develop around sensitive issues such as mental health, family, and racism, and community members may have very different perspectives. V&F leaders sometimes censure inappropriate posts and intervene to steer discussions toward safer and more constructive ground.

In addition to their contributions to the Slack community and website, Pat and Jacob began a podcast called *Tabard Inn* in September 2019. Named after the starting point and destination of the pilgrims in Chaucer's *Canterbury Tales*, the podcast's first episode shared V&F's queer ecclesiology:

> The Church is like a group of people gathered together on pilgrimage, or, at least, that's what the Second Vatican Council said. For queer Catholics we can sometimes feel estranged from that community, inside and yet outside at the same time. We are our own pilgrim people within a pilgrim church. This podcast is about some of the stories we tell, the events we talk about along the way until we make it home again.[80]

Through its podcast, Slack community, and other spiritual resources, V&F manifests its leaders' conviction that Catholicism and queerness can be reconciled. Although members are honest about their often brutal struggles with the institutional church, the community is secure in its hope that God is moving to transform Catholicism from the grassroots up. Until affirmation becomes the rule around the world, online ministries such as V&F will provide a vital space for Catholics to celebrate the good fruits of queer relationships and identities.

CONCLUSION

One Body

> There is one body and one Spirit, just as you
> were called to the one hope of your calling.
>
> —Ephesians 4:4

In 1 Corinthians 12, Paul describes Christians as the members of Christ's Body: "For just as the body is one and has many members, and all the members of the body, though many, are one body, so it is with Christ" (v. 12). According to Paul, each believer has a unique role to play in keeping the Body healthy and helping it to grow. In the Body of Christ, a foot cannot disown the eye, and an ear cannot go its own way. For the Body to properly function, all its parts must work together. The Church's well-being depends on each member, irrespective of their position or function. Paul explains,

> But God has so arranged the body, giving greater honor to
> the inferior member, that there may be no dissension within
> the body, but the members may have the same care for one
> another. If one member suffers, all suffer together with it; if
> one member is honored, all rejoice together with it. (1 Cor
> 12:24–26)

LGBTQ people belong to the Body of Christ, and the Church cannot function as God intends without them. Their sufferings and their joys, whether visible in the Church or not, affect everyone else. When they thrive, so does the rest of the Body. When they hurt, the Body feels it. When they go missing, the Church lacks.

For generations, LGBTQ Catholic ministries have sensitized the Body of Christ to its queer members. They have done so in innumerable times and places, employing strategies that reflect changing conditions in society and the Church. Their goal has always been the same: to build a Church better prepared to welcome and care for the queer people of God, whose gifts build up the Body of Christ.

A LONG TRADITION OF SPIRITUAL CARE AND ADVOCACY

More than twenty years before the Stonewall Riots, George Hyde's Eucharistic Catholic Church provided spiritual healing for queer people within the safety of a Catholic faith community. The group's invitation for Christians of all sexual orientations and races to participate in the Lord's Supper was as prophetic then as it is today. Shortly after its founding, Hyde's group affiliated with independent Catholics, because remaining within Roman Catholic institutions would have impeded its mission. Hyde and others embraced gay and lesbian believers by affirming their spiritual gifts and making room for them in the Body of Christ. Throughout the fifties and sixties, the ministry aimed to assimilate gays into Christian faith and broader society by giving them a pathway to spiritual, relational, and vocational flourishing.

By the early seventies, a new model of LGBTQ ministry had emerged. DignityUSA, a predominately lay-led group, had its roots in gay liberation. The ministry organized a powerful, nationwide network that partnered with local parishes to build spiritual homes for gays and lesbians. Members were outspoken about homophobia wherever they found it, whether in secular government or in the Church. Embracing gay pride and demanding change, they were a thorn in the hierarchy's side until the Vatican called for them to be expelled from parishes in 1986. Like the Eucharistic Catholic Church, they became ecclesial outsiders while continuing the work to which God had called them.

Other national ministries began at the behest of men and women religious. New Ways Ministry was founded in 1977 by Sr. Jeannine Gramick, SSND, and Robert Nugent, SDS, as an organization to equip the Church for ministry to gays and lesbians. The pair's popular work-shops and literature acknowledged the Church's traditional teaching but also highlighted the experiences of gay and lesbian believers. Their advocacy was grounded in hope that the Church's approach to homo-sexuality could and would eventually change. Negotiating commit-ments to both their religious vocations and LGBTQ people, Gramick and Nugent spent decades in dialogue with a Church often eager to silence them. Their faithfulness paid off. Under Pope Francis, New Ways Ministry has received praise as a leading voice on LGBTQ issues.

In the early 2000s, families joined the LGBTQ Catholic move-ment. Mary Ellen and Casey Lopata's Fortunate Families provided support for parents, siblings, and others who struggled to integrate Catholicism with their love for queer family members. The minis-try provided theological, spiritual, and relational resources that were grounded in Catholic tradition and, above all, a compassionate com-munity for hurting families. In the 2010s, the network spread across the country, expanding its focus to include issues such as Catholic educa-tion and trans ministry. To this day, Fortunate Families exemplifies the power of allied family members and friends to drive change in the Church.

As broader U.S. society has become more accepting of queer folks, local parishes, too, have joined the cause. In Manhattan, the parish of St. Paul the Apostle has been home to LGBTQ Catholics for decades. During the AIDS crisis, the Gay and Lesbian Catholic Ministry, led by Donald Maher, bridged the gap between the institutional church and activists. In the 2010s, a new generation of ministry emerged from the leadership of Fr. Gil Martinez, who encouraged LGBTQ parishioners to become ministers themselves. Through activities such as its annual Pride Mass and bar nights, Out at St. Paul became one of the most recognizable and innovative LGBTQ Catholic groups in the world. Led by Paulist fathers and lay parishioners, the dynamic community models change in a rapidly evolving church.

In recent years, the public face of LGBTQ Catholic ministry has been Fr. James Martin, SJ. Inspired by the Pulse Nightclub shooting to "build a bridge" between the Catholic hierarchy and LGBTQ com-munity, his advocacy relies on Catholic teaching that calls believers to "respect, compassion, and sensitivity." Martin has found a sympa-thetic ear among Catholics, including Pope Francis, eager to see the Church's relationship with queer people improve. He has used his popularity as a spiritual leader and media figure to amplify LGBTQ voices, communicating their concerns to the highest levels of the hierarchy. Critics accuse Martin of rejecting Catholic tradition, but his steadfast adherence to traditional teaching and obedience to his superiors have allowed LGBTQ advocacy to take root in church spaces where it was impossible before.

WHAT ABOUT YOU?

After generations of struggle, LGBTQ Catholics and their allies are still striving to make their presence felt in the Roman Catholic Church. Today, the Church is learning how to better sense, appreciate, and care for its queer members, but there remains much work to be done. Parts of the Body still maim others while some members are putrid with the gangrene of self-loathing.

As the Church reckons with its sin-sickness, every Catholic has a responsibility in nursing the Body of Christ back to health. Recovery requires great effort and health comes slowly. But the Church is not without God's grace. Paul knew that all the members of Christ's body possess spiritual gifts to help the Church thrive. Early Christian communities were full of apostles, prophets, teachers, miracle workers, healers, helpers, guides, and those who spoke in tongues (see 1 Cor 12:28). Today, these same charisms can build up the Church's ministry to LGBTQ people. As this book has shown, there are endless possibilities for ministry and advocacy.

Whatever your own place and calling in the Church, LGBTQ believers are hurting and need your help. What will you do to heal the wounded Body of Christ?

NOTES

INTRODUCTION

1. Edward Pentin, "Archbishop Chaput: 'LGBT' Should Not Be Used in Church Docs," *National Catholic Register*, October 4, 2018, https://www.ncregister.com/blog/archbishop-chaput-lgbt-should-not-be-used-in-church-docs. Charles Chaput served as the archbishop of Philadelphia until 2020 when, at the age of seventy-five, his letter of resignation was accepted by Pope Francis who appointed Nelson Perez, then bishop of Cleveland, to replace him. Although his five predecessors were named cardinals by the pope, Chaput never received the honor.

2. *Catechism of the Catholic Church*, 2nd ed. (Vatican City: Vatican Press, 1997), §§2357–58.

3. Congregation for Catholic Education, "Instruction Concerning the Criteria for the Discernment of Vocations with regard to Persons with Homosexual Tendencies in View of Their Admission to the Seminary and to Holy Orders," November 4, 2005, sec. 2, https://www.vatican.va/roman_curia/congregations/ccatheduc/documents/rc_con_ccatheduc_doc_20051104_istruzione_en.html.

4. Home page, Courage, https://couragerc.org/.

5. See Mark Jordan's masterful work *The Silence of Sodom: Homosexuality in Modern Catholicism* (Chicago: University of Chicago Press, 2000).

6. Gustavo Gutiérrez, *A Theology of Liberation* (Maryknoll, NY: Orbis Books, 1988), xxix.

7. Harvey Milk, "That's What America Is," speech given to the San Francisco Gay Freedom Day Parade, June 25, 1978.

CHAPTER 1

1. The language used to describe LGBTQ people has changed over time, presenting a challenge for historians working with nomenclature and identities from the past. This book will strive to use historically accurate terms. For more, see Claire Hayward, "Queer Terminology: LGBTQ Histories and the Semantics of Sexuality," *Notches*, June 9, 2016, https://notchesblog.com/2016/06/09/queer-terminology-lgbtq-histories-and-the-semantics-of-sexuality/.

2. George Hyde, interview by J. Gordon Melton, July 6, 2005, transcript, Lesbian, Gay, Bisexual, Transgender, and Queer Religious Archives Network, p. 3, available online at https://lgbtqreligiousarchives .org/media/oral-history/george-augustine-hyde/GHyde.pdf.

3. George Hyde, interview by J. Gordon Melton, 3–4.

4. George Hyde, interview by J. Gordon Melton, 3–4.

5. George Hyde, interview by J. Gordon Melton, 1. For more on Archbishop Gerald O'Hara's life and legacy, see "Archbishop O'Hara Dead at 68; Papal Representative in Britain," *New York Times*, July 17, 1963. For more on St. Mary's of the Barrens Seminary, see Richard J. Janet, "The Decline and Fall of Saint Mary's of the Barrens: A Case Study in Contraction of an American Catholic Religious Order—Part One," *Vincentian Heritage Journal* 22, no. 2 (Fall 2001): 152–82.

6. George Hyde, interview by J. Gordon Melton, 1–3.

7. George Hyde, interview by J. Gordon Melton, 2.

8. Bishop George Hyde, interview by SAGA Spartansburg-Anderson Gay Alliance, August 30, 1975, transcript, Lesbian, Gay, Bisexual, Transgender, and Queer Religious Archives Network, p. 4, available online at https://lgbtqreligiousarchives.org/media/profile/george-augustine-hyde/George%20Hyde%20interview%20Aug%2030 %201975.pdf.

9. George Hyde, interview by J. Gordon Melton, 3.

10. Jodie Talley, "A Queer Miracle in Georgia: The Origins of Gay-Affirming Religion in the South" (PhD diss., Georgia State University, 2006), 41, available online at https://scholarworks.gsu.edu/history _theses/17.

11. Bishop George Hyde, interview by SAGA Spartansburg-Anderson Gay Alliance, 4–5.

12. For more on the history of anti-LGBTQ legal discrimination in the United States, see William N. Eskridge, *Dishonorable Passions: Sodomy Laws in America, 1861–2003* (New York: Viking, 2008).

13. For more on independent Catholics, see Julie Byrne, *The Other Catholics: Remaking America's Largest Religion* (New York: Columbia University Press, 2016).

14. Talley, "A Queer Miracle in Georgia," 52–53.

15. Bishop George Hyde, interview by SAGA Spartansburg-Anderson Gay Alliance, 5.

16. George Hyde, interview by J. Gordon Melton, 5.

17. "Rev. George Augustine Hyde, Oral History," *LGBTQ Religious Archives Network* (September 2004), https://lgbtqreligiousarchives.org/oral-histories/george-augustine-hyde.

18. Talley, "A Queer Miracle in Georgia," 53; Bishop George Hyde, interview by SAGA Spartansburg-Anderson Gay Alliance, 6.

19. George Hyde, interview by J. Gordon Melton, 5–6.

20. Talley, "A Queer Miracle in Georgia," 53; Bishop George Hyde, interview by SAGA Spartansburg-Anderson Gay Alliance, 5.

21. Bishop George Hyde, interview by SAGA Spartansburg-Anderson Gay Alliance, 6–7.

22. "Rev. George Augustine Hyde, Oral History"; Bishop George Hyde, interview by SAGA Spartansburg-Anderson Gay Alliance, 7–8, George Hyde, interview by J. Gordon Melton, 7–8.

23. Talley, "A Queer Miracle in Georgia," 53.

24. For more on the Homophile Movement, see Julian Jackson, "The Homophile Movement," in *The Ashgate Research Companion to Lesbian and Gay Activism*, ed. David Paternotte (London: Routledge, 2016), 31–44.

25. George Hyde, interview by J. Gordon Melton, 9.

26. Bishop George Hyde, interview by SAGA Spartansburg-Anderson Gay Alliance, 7.

27. Advertisement, *ONE Magazine* 2, no. 10 (December 1954): 32 cited by Heather White, "'The Ecclesiastical Wing of the Lavender Revolution': Religion and Sexual Identity Organizing in the USA, 1946–1976," in *New Approaches in History and Theology to Same-Sex Love and Desire*, ed. Dominic Janes and Mark D. Chapman (London: Palgrave Macmillan, 2018), 142.

28. George Hyde, interview by J. Gordon Melton, 9–10.

29. George Hyde, interview by J. Gordon Melton, 6.

186   LGBTQ Catholic Ministry

30. George Hyde, interview by J. Gordon Melton, 9.

31. Byrne, *The Other Catholics*, 272.

32. "Rev. George Augustine Hyde, Oral History."

33. Byrne, *The Other Catholics*, 273.

34. "Bishop Michael Francis Augustine Itkin, Profile," *LGBTQ Religious Archives Network* (December 2002), https://lgbtqreligiousarchives.org/profiles/michael-francis-augustine-itkin.

35. "Rev. Robert Mary Clement, Oral History," *LGBTQ Religious Archives Network* (September 2004), https://lgbtqreligiousarchives.org/oral-histories/robert-mary-clement.

36. Byrne, *The Other Catholics*, 273–74.

37. "Rev. George Augustine Hyde, Oral History."

CHAPTER 2

1. For more on these movements, see M. E. Chamberlain, *Decolonization: The Fall of the European Empires* (London: Wiley, 1999); Thomas Holt, *The Movement: The African American Struggle for Civil Rights* (New York: Oxford University Press, 2021); F. Arturo Rosales, *Chicano! The History of the Mexican American Civil Rights Movement* (Houston, TX: Arte Público Press, 1997); Stephanie Gilmore, ed., *Feminist Coalitions: Historical Perspectives on Second-Wave Feminism in the United States* (Champaign: University of Illinois Press, 2008); and Lillian Faderman, *The Gay Revolution: The Story of the Struggle* (New York: Simon and Schuster, 2015).

2. For more on these movements, see Angie Pears, *Doing Contextual Theology* (New York: Routledge, 2010); Matthew Cressler, *Authentically Black and Truly Catholic: The Rise of Black Catholicism in the Great Migration* (New York: New York University Press, 2017); Mario García, *Católicos: Resistance and Affirmation in Chicano Catholic History* (Austin: University of Texas Press, 2008); and Carla Bittel and Mary J. Henold, *Catholic and Feminist: The Surprising History of the American Catholic Feminist Movement* (Chapel Hill: University of North Carolina Press, 2020).

3. Vatican Council II, *Gaudium et Spes*, http://www.vatican.va/archive/hist_councils/ii_vatican_council/documents/vat-ii_const_19651207_gaudium-et-spes_en.html. For more on the Council, see John W. O'Malley, *What Happened at Vatican II* (Cambridge, MA:

Harvard University Press, 2010), and Ormond Rush, *The Vision of Vatican II: Its Fundamental Principles* (Collegeville, MN: Liturgical Press, 2019).

4. Robert Imbelli and Thomas Groome, "Signposts towards a Pastoral Theology," *Theological Studies* 53 (1992): 128, http://cdn.theologicalstudies.net/53/53.1/53.1.7.pdf.

5. Gustavo Gutiérrez, *An Introduction to Liberation Theology* (Maryknoll, NY: Orbis Books, 1990), xxix.

6. Michael Lee, *Revolutionary Saint: The Theological Legacy of Oscar Romero* (Maryknoll, NY: Orbis Books, 2018).

7. Vatican Council II, *Ad Gentes*, http://www.vatican.va/archive/hist_councils/ii_vatican_council/documents/vat-ii_decree_19651207_ad-gentes_en.html.

8. "Our Founder," Dignity/San Diego, https://www.dignitysd.org/about_us.

9. Joseph Gilgamesh Killian, "Dignity: The Early Years," *DignityUSA Newsletter* 21, no. 4 (Summer 1989): 1.

10. Patrick Roche, "DignityUSA History," DignityUSA, https://www.dignityusa.org/history.

11. Heather Rachelle White, "Proclaiming Liberation: The Historical Roots of LGBT Religious Organizing, 1946–1976," *Nova Religio: The Journal of Alternative and Emergent Religions* 11, no. 4 (May 2008): 111.

12. "All Right—Who Started It?," *Insight: A Quarterly of Gay Catholic Opinion* 2, no. 1 (Fall 1987): 6.

13. Dignity Constitution, cited by Gregory Baum, "Catholic Homosexuals," *Commonweal*, February 15, 1974, 14.

14. Killian, "Dignity: The Early Years," 1.

15. White, "Proclaiming Liberation," 111.

16. Cited by Mark Jordan, *The Silence of Sodom: Homosexuality in Modern Catholicism* (Chicago: University of Chicago Press, 2000), 250. The full statement can be found inside the front cover of Gramick, Nugent, and Oddo, *Homosexual Catholics: A New Primer for Discussion* (Los Angeles: Dignity, 1980).

17. Gramick, Nugent, and Oddo, *Homosexual Catholics*, inside front cover.

18. Killian, "Dignity: The Early Years," 1.

19. See, e.g., Fr. Michael Donahue, "Letter to Dignity NY President Timothy Coughlin," October 13, 1986, which outlined the dates

and fees for Dignity's use of space at St. Francis Xavier parish, Box 2, File 28, Collection #74 DIGNITY/NEW YORK RECORDS, The Lesbian, Gay, Bisexual, Transgender, and Queer Community Center (LGBTQCC) Archives, New York City.

20. Steve Warren, "Dignity USA Convening in San Francisco," *San Francisco Sentinel*, August 31, 1989, 10.

21. Diane Pawlowski, "Dignity: The Organization" (master's thesis, University of Windsor, 1990), 4, 20.

22. Killian, "Dignity: The Early Years," 1.

23. Jordan, *The Silence of Sodom*, 249.

24. Killian, "Dignity: The Early Years," 1.

25. Hank Stuever, "Spurned by the Archbishop of L.A., Members of Dignity, an Organization of Gay Catholics, Maintain Their Allegiance to the Church but...They Pray Alone," *Los Angeles Times*, August 29, 1990.

26. Bob Fournier, "Our Cause: The Gay Catholic," *Dignity: A Monthly Newsletter* 2, no. 1 (March 10, 1971): 1, 3.

27. White, "Proclaiming Liberation," 112.

28. "Next Meeting," *Dignity: A Monthly Newsletter* 2, no. 1 (March 10, 1971): 1.

29. Patrick McArron, interview by author, Zoom, April 24, 2020.

30. "Membership Report," *Dignity: A Monthly Newsletter for Catholic Homophiles and Concerned Heterophiles* 3, no. 1 (March 5, 1972): 3.

31. John J. McNeill, "The Christian Male Homosexual," *Homiletic and Pastoral Review* 70 (1970): 667–77, 747–58, 828–36. See also James P. McCartin, "The Church and Gay Liberation: The Case of John McNeill," *U.S. Catholic Historian* 34, no. 1 (Winter 2016): 125–41.

32. Marianne Duddy-Burke, "Memorial Reflection of John McNeill by Marianne Duddy-Burke," November 14, 2015, https://www.dignityusa.org/page/memorial-reflection-john-mcneill-marianne-duddy-burke/.

33. John McNeill, "Reflections on the Fiftieth Anniversary of My Ordination to the Priesthood," https://www.dignityusa.org/article/reflections-fiftieth-anniversary-my-ordination-priesthood.

34. John McNeill, *Both Feet Firmly Planted in Midair* (Louisville, KY: Westminster John Knox Press, 2004), 82.

35. Dignity/NY, "Calendar," *Insight: A Monthly Newsletter for Dignity NY Chapter* 2, no. 5 (May 1976).

36. Roche, "DignityUSA History."

37. NFPC Justice and Peace Committee Resolution 74–20, "Civil Rights of Homosexual Persons," in *Gay and Lesbian Issues: A Reference Handbook*, ed. Church Stewart (Santa Barbara, CA: ABC-CLIO, 2003), 185.

38. Robert Nugent and Jeannine Gramick, *Building Bridges* (Mystic, CT: Twenty-Third Publications, 1992), 69.

39. For more on *Humanae Vitae*, see Richard Gaillardetz, "*Humanae Vitae* and Its Ecclesial Consequences," *Theological Studies* 93 (July 2019): 841–63.

40. Bob Fournier, *Dignity: A Monthly Newsletter* 2, no. 1 (March 10, 1971): 3.

41. Fr. Tom Oddo, "The Spirit Calls Us Anew—Labor Day Weekend, 1974," *Dignity: A National Publication of the Gay Catholic Community* 5, no. 9 (September 1974): 2–4; Roche, "DignityUSA History."

42. Catholic Theological Society of America, *Human Sexuality: New Directions in American Catholic Thought* (New York: Paulist Press, 1977), 211, 214.

43. Gregory Baum, "Catholic Homosexuals," *Commonweal*, February 15, 1974, 14–17.

44. "Resources," *Dignity: A National Publication of the Gay Catholic Community* 6, no. 3 (March 1975): 6.

45. Dignity/NY, "Calendar," *Insight*, August 1976, The Lesbian, Gay, Bisexual, Transgender, and Queer Community Center Archives, Box 3, File 62, New York City.

46. John D'Emilio, "Activist Catholics: Dignity's Work in the 1970s and 1980s," in *Queer Legacies: Stories from Chicago's LGBTQ Archives* (Chicago: University of Chicago Press, 2020), 57.

47. "Dignity Celebrates Its 20th Year!," *Gay and Lesbian Catholics: DignityUSA* 21, no. 6 (Fall 1989): 1.

48. Pawlowski, "Dignity: The Organization," 34–35.

49. David Bird, "Thousands Hold March to Back Homosexuals," *New York Times*, June 25, 1984, B3.

50. *Gay and Lesbian Catholics: DignityUSA* 22, no. 4 (May/June 1990): 12, 18–19.

51. "Minutes of the Fifth Dignity Elected Board of Directors Meeting New York–New Jersey," September 23, 1973, Box 1, File 2,

Collection #74 DIGNITY/NEW YORK RECORDS, LGBTQCC Archives.

52. Roche, "DignityUSA History"; *Dignity/NY Service Committee Report*, November 1982, Box 1, File 13, Collection #74 DIGNITY/NEW YORK RECORDS, LGBTQCC Archives.

53. Leather and Levi Club Statement of Goals, December 9, 1981, Box 4, File 117, Collection #74 DIGNITY/NEW YORK RECORDS, LGBTQCC Archives.

54. Dignity/NY Newsletters, 1974–1990 and Dignity, Inc. Newsletters (1971–1989), Box 3, Files 60-71, Collection #74 DIGNITY/NEW YORK RECORDS, LGBTQCC Archives.

55. "Dignity Fire Island Pines Chapter Forming August 1979," Box 3, File 82, Collection #74 DIGNITY/NEW YORK RECORDS, LGBTQCC Archives.

56. Marianne Duddy-Burke, email with author, January 8, 2021.

57. Dignity Task Force on Sexual Ethics, "Sexual Ethics: Experience, Growth, and Challenge; A Pastoral Reflection for Lesbian and Gay Catholics," August 1989, https://www.dignityusa.org/content/sexual-ethics.

58. Dignity Task Force on Sexual Ethics, "Sexual Ethics."

59. Patti O'Kane, Letter to the Editor, *Gay and Lesbian Catholics: DignityUSA* 22, no. 4 (May/June 1990): 2.

60. Salvatorian Gay Ministry Taskforce, *Ministry/USA: A Model for Ministry to the Homosexual Community* (Milwaukee: National Center for Gay Ministry, 1974).

61. Acceptance, "History: The Story of Acceptance Sydney," accessed July 8, 2022, http://www.gaycatholic.com.au/history.

62. For more on the Global Network of Rainbow Catholics, visit http://rainbowcatholics.org/. For more on Equal Future, visit https://equalfuture2018.com/.

63. Marianne Duddy-Burke, interview by author, Zoom, January 10, 2020.

64. Roche, "DignityUSA History."

65. NY–NJ Chapter of Dignity, "Steering Committee Minutes," January 25, 1973, Box 1, File 2, Collection #74 DIGNITY/NEW YORK RECORDS, LGBTQCC Archives.

66. Eleanor Blau, "Vatican Disputed by Homosexuals," *New York Times*, February 22, 1976, 26.

67. John Rash letter to Dignity/NY Board of Directors and Committee Members, May 8, 1985, Box 2, File 21, Collection #74 DIGNITY/NEW YORK RECORDS, LGBTQCC Archives.

68. Roche, "DignityUSA History."

69. Dignity, Inc. Newsletter, February 1981, Box 3, File 71, Collection #74 DIGNITY/NEW YORK RECORDS LGBTQCC Archives.

70. Roche, "DignityUSA History."

71. Marianne Duddy-Burke, interview by author.

72. Jordan, *The Silence of Sodom*, 250; "Paper Is Assailed by a Homosexual," *New York Times*, August 11, 1974, 27.

73. Nancy Manser, "Dearden Firm on Homosexual Stand," *The Detroit News*, August 21, 1974, B5, B7; Brian McNaught, "Brian's Column," *Insight: A Quarterly of Gay Catholic Opinion* 4 (Summer 1974); Pawlowski, "Dignity: The Organization," 30–34.

74. "Dignity/New York Meets with Representatives of the Brooklyn and the New York Ordinaries," *Insight: A Monthly Newsletter for Dignity NY Chapter* 2, no. 2 (May 1975): 1, 3.

75. Dignity/NY, "Calendar," *Insight: A Monthly Newsletter for Dignity NY Chapter* 2, no. 9 (September 1976): 1.

76. Blau, "Vatican Disputed by Homosexuals," 26.

77. National Conference of Catholic Bishops, "Principles to Guide Confessors in Questions of Homosexuality" (Washington, DC: USCCB, 1973).

78. "Dignity Reaches Out to National Conference of Bishops," *Dignity: A National Publication of the Gay Catholic Community* 6, no. 7 (July 1975): 5.

79. Paul Diederich, "From the National President," *Dignity: A National Publication of the Gay Catholic Community* 6, no. 11 (November 1975): 1–2; "Good News from Washington," *Dignity: A National Publication of the Gay Catholic Community* 6, no. 12 (December 1975): 3–5.

80. Call to Action Conference, Detroit, Michigan, Work Papers, October 21–23, 1976, Box 20, File 11, Dignity/USA Records, ONE National Gay & Lesbian Archives, USC Libraries, University of Southern California, Los Angeles, California.

81. For more on the outcome of the 1976 Call to Action meeting, see Bradford Hinze, *Practices of Dialogue in the Roman Catholic Church* (New York: Continuum, 2006), 64–89.

82. "Calendar," *Insight: A Publication of Dignity/New York Inc.* 2, no. 8 (August 1976): 1; Roche, "DignityUSA History."

83. Anonymous, "John Paul's Visit: The Ecstasy and the Agony," *Bridges: Bay Area Dignity* 7, no. 11 (November 1979): 1.

84. Roche, "DignityUSA History," and Marianne Duddy-Burke email with author, January 8, 2021.

85. Roche, "DignityUSA History."

86. Roche, "DignityUSA History."

87. John Pineda, "Gays March Carrying Signs," *The Miami Herald*, June 27, 1977; Roche, "DignityUSA History."

88. Roche, "DignityUSA History." For more on the march, see Amin Ghaziani, "Breakthrough: The 1979 National March," *Gay and Lesbian Review Worldwide* 12, no. 2 (2005): 31–32.

89. Lawrence K. Altman, "Rare Cancer Seen in 41 Homosexuals," *New York Times*, July 3, 1981.

90. Roche, "DignityUSA History."

91. Center for Disease Control, "HIV and AIDS—United States, 1981–2000," accessed July 8, 2022, https://www.cdc.gov/mmwr/preview/mmwrhtml/mm5021a2.htm.

92. See varia in "Dignity/NY AIDS Ministry," Box 2, File 44, Collection #74 DIGNITY/NEW YORK RECORDS, LGBTQCC Archives; Fr. Gardiner, SA, "Greenwich Village Hosts AIDS' Healing Service," *The Tablet*, October 7, 1983.

93. For more on Dignity's role in the AIDS crisis, listen to Michael O'Loughlin's *Plague: Untold Stories of AIDS and the Catholic Church*, America Media, podcast series, December 2019–November 2021, https://www.americamagazine.org/plague/. The first episode, "Surviving the AIDS Crisis as a Gay Catholic," tells the story of David Pais, then a member of Dignity/NY.

94. Marianne Duddy-Burke, email with author, January 8, 2021.

95. Marianne Duddy-Burke, email with author, January 8, 2021.

96. No author, handwritten outline for Dignity/NY program on HIV/AIDS, Box 2, File 44, Collection #74 DIGNITY/NEW YORK RECORDS, LGBTQCC Archives.

97. John McNeill, "A Theological Statement on AIDS," n.d., Collection #74 DIGNITY/NEW YORK RECORDS, LGBTQCC Archives LGBTQCC Archives, Box 2, File 44.

98. For more on the Catholic Church's response to the AIDS crisis, see Michael O'Loughlin, *Hidden Mercy: AIDS, Catholics, and the*

Untold Stories of Compassion in the Face of Fear (Minneapolis, MN: Broadleaf Books, 2021).

99. For more on the expulsion of Charles Curran from the Catholic University of America, see his autobiographical work, *Loyal Dissent: Memoirs of a Catholic Theologian* (Washington, DC: Georgetown University Press, 2006).

100. Congregation for the Doctrine of the Faith, "Letter to the Bishops of the Catholic Church on the Pastoral Care of Homosexual Persons," October 1, 1986, no. 3, http://www.vatican.va/roman _curia/congregations/cfaith/documents/rc_con_cfaith_doc_19861001 _homosexual-persons_en.html.

101. Congregation for the Doctrine of the Faith, "Letter to the Bishops of the Catholic Church on the Pastoral Care of Homosexual Persons," no. 7.

102. Congregation for the Doctrine of the Faith, "Letter to the Bishops of the Catholic Church on the Pastoral Care of Homosexual Persons," no. 8.

103. Congregation for the Doctrine of the Faith, "Letter to the Bishops of the Catholic Church on the Pastoral Care of Homosexual Persons," no. 10.

104. Gene Burns, "Abandoning Suspicion: The Catholic Left and Sexuality," in *What's Left? Liberal American Catholics*, ed. Mary Jo Weaver (Bloomington: Indiana University Press, 1999), 78.

105. Bruce Buursma, "Vatican Targets U.S. in Blast at Homosexuality," *Chicago Tribune*, October 31, 1986, 1.

106. Roche, "DignityUSA History."

107. DignityUSA, "What Jesus Said about Homosexuality '…'," *Newsweek*, April 27, 1987.

108. Michael O'Loughlin, "Surviving the AIDS Crisis as a Gay Catholic," in *Plague: Untold Stories of AIDS and the Catholic Church*, America Media, starting at 13:59.

109. Warren, "Dignity USA Convening in San Francisco," 10.

110. Roche, "DignityUSA History."

111. Jordan, *The Silence of Sodom*, 251.

112. Patrick Roche, interview by author.

113. Dignity/USA, "Statement of Position and Purpose," no. 2, cited by Leonard Norman Primiano, *Gay Religion* (Lanham, MD: Alta Mira Press, 2005), 26.

114. Warren, "Dignity USA Convening in San Francisco," 10.

---

115. Warren, "Dignity USA Convening in San Francisco"; Patrick Roche, interview by author.

116. Religious News Service, "Break with Catholic Church: Dignity 'Manifesto' Calls Gay Sexuality a 'Holy Gift,'" *Los Angeles Times*, September 16, 1989.

117. See, e.g., DignityUSA's response to the CDF's 2021 prohibition on blessings for same-sex couples, "Vatican Statement Denying Blessings to Same-Sex Couples 'Exacerbates Pain and Anger' for Gay Catholics Says DignityUSA," March 15, 2021, https://www.dignityusa .org/news/vatican-statement-denying-blessings-same-sex-couples-%E2 %80%9Cexacerbates-pain-and-anger%E2%80%9D-gay-catholics.

118. Marianne Duddy-Burke, interview by author.

119. Bill Kenkelen, "Dignity Leaders Take up Cudgels after Evictions," *National Catholic Reporter*, January 30, 1987, 24.

120. The Cathedral Project divided Dignity/NY members, with some pursuing an activist course of action and others seeking reconciliation with the archdiocese. This led to a decades-long split of the local group into two separate organizations. See Jeff Stone, "LGBT Pride Reflection: 40th Anniversary Pride Liturgy of Dignity/New York," June 23, 2012, https://www.dignityny.org/sites/default/files/Pride%202012 %20Reflection.pdf.

121. "Cathedral Project" and "Cathedral Project Clippings," Box 4, Files 115 and 116, Collection #74 DIGNITY/NEW YORK RECORDS, LGBTQCC Archives; Rita Giordano, "Demonstration in the Cathedral: 11 Arrested in Gay Protest against O'Connor," *Newsday*, December 7, 1987. For more on ACT UP and the Catholic Church, see Thomas F. Rzeznik, "The Church and the AIDS Crisis in New York City," *U.S. Catholic Historian* 34, no. 1 (Winter 2016): 143–65.

122. Patricia Lefevere, "Gay, Catholic Struggle Moves into N.Y. Courts: Fight Seen as 'Act of Faith,'" *National Catholic Reporter*, April 15, 1988.

123. Associated Press, "U.S. High Court Backs Protests at St. Patrick's," *New York Times*, March 10, 1987, 3.

124. "Is DignityUSA (DUSA) an Accepting and Welcoming Church for Transgender and Non-binary Persons and Does It Actively Oppose the Catholic Church's (Church) Teachings?," DignityUSA, https://www.dignityusa.org/faq/dignityusa-dusa-accepting-and -welcoming-church-transgender-and-non-binary-persons-and-does-it.

125. Jordan, *The Silence of Sodom*, 252–53.

CHAPTER 3

1. Cf. Matthew 13:1–23; Mark 4:1–20; and Luke 8:4–15.

2. "Co-Founders," New Ways Ministry, archived from the original on September 2, 2017, accessed July 8, 2022, https://web .archive.org/web/20170902184654/http://www.newwaysministry.org/ co-founders.html/.

3. Ralph Cipriano, "Dominic Bash, Hairdresser Who Helped AIDS Victims," *The Philadelphia Inquirer*, January 27, 1993, http:// articles.philly.com/1993 01 27/news/25960643_1_aids victims dignity -s-aids-unconditional-love.

4. Paul Collins, *The Modern Inquisition: Seven Prominent Catholics and Their Struggle with the Vatican* (New York: The Overlook Publishers, 2002), 116.

5. New Ways Ministry, "Book of Memory and Thanksgiving" (2002), 8, https://www.newwaysministry.org/wp-content/uploads/2021/ 03/Book_of_Memory.pdf; Caryle Murphy, "Judgment Day for a Priest," *Washington Post*, August 7, 1999, C1.

6. Howell Williams, "Homosexuality and the American Catholic Church: Reconfiguring the Silence, 1971–1999" (PhD diss., Florida State University, 2007), 35–37.

7. Elaine Woo, "The Rev. Robert Nugent Dies at 76; Priest Who Supported Gays, Lesbians," *Baltimore Sun*, January 5, 2014, https:// www.baltimoresun.com/sports/orioles/la-me-robert-nugent-20140105 -story.html.

8. Robert Nugent and Jeannine Gramick, *Building Bridges: Gay & Lesbian Reality and the Catholic Church* (Mystic, CT: Twenty-Third Publications, 1995), 196.

9. "The Gays and the Church, a Priest and a Nun Tell Why They Minister to Homosexuals," *Ottawa Journal*, February 2, 1978, reprinted in NWM's *Bondings* (Fall 1978): 4.

10. Nugent and Gramick, *Building Bridges*, 195.

11. Woo, "The Rev. Robert Nugent Dies at 76."

12. Jeannine Gramick and Robert Nugent to supporters, April 1978, Box 2, Folder 54, Records of Dignity/NY President Michael J. Olivieri, The Lesbian, Gay, Bisexual, and Transgender Community Center Archives, New York, NY.

13. Bishop Francis J. Mugavero, "Sexuality: God's Gift," Diocese of Brooklyn, NY, February 11, 1976, available online at https://mysticalrose.tripod.com/mugavero.html.

14. Williams, "Homosexuality and the American Catholic Church," 39.

15. New Ways Ministry, "California Workshops Draw 200," *Bondings* (Fall 1978): 1.

16. Rita Gillmon, "Gays' Ministry Role Is Studied," *San Diego Union*, September 1, 1979, reprinted by New Ways Ministry, *Bondings* (Fall 1979): 3.

17. NWM, "Book of Memory and Thanksgiving," 6–7.

18. NWM, "Book of Memory and Thanksgiving," 6.

19. Sr. Eileen J. Cehyra, FMI, to Jeannine Gramick, October, 1 1984, S5 Box 1: Bevilacqua, Bp. Anthony J. (Bishop of Pittsburgh) Correspondence 1984, NWM Collection, Marquette University Library, cited by Williams, "Homosexuality and the American Catholic Church," 47.

20. Robert Nugent, Jeannine Gramick, and Thomas Oddo, *Homosexual Catholics: A Primer for Discussion* (Dignity, 1975); Nugent and Gramick, *Building Bridges*, 200.

21. Robert Nugent and Jeannine Gramick, eds., *A Time to Speak: A Collection of Contemporary Statements from U.S. Catholic Sources on Homosexuality, Gay Ministry and Social Justice* (Mt. Rainier, MD: New Ways Ministry, 1978); New Ways Ministry, "New Ways Publishes Booklet on Church Statements," *Bondings* (Fall 1978): 1.

22. Robert Nugent and Jeannine Gramick, eds., *Voices of Hope: A Collection of Positive Catholic Writings on Gay and Lesbian Issues* (Mt. Rainier, MD: New Ways Ministry, 1995).

23. Robert Nugent, ed., *A Challenge to Love: Gay and Lesbian Catholics in the Church* (New York: Crossroads, 1983).

24. Jeannine Gramick and Pat Furey, eds., *The Vatican and Homosexuality: Reactions to the "Letter to the Bishops of the Catholic Church on the Pastoral Care of Homosexual Persons"* (New York: Crossroads, 1988).

25. Jeannine Gramick, ed., *Homosexuality and the Catholic Church* (Mt. Rainier, MD: New Ways Ministry, 1983).

26. Nugent and Gramick, *Building Bridges*.

27. Nugent and Gramick, *Building Bridges*, back cover.

28. Robert Nugent and Jeannine Gramick, "Homosexuality: Protestant, Catholic, and Jewish Issues; A Fishbone Tale," *Journal of Homosexuality* 18, no. 3–4 (1989): 7–46.

29. Jeannine Gramick, "Social Discrimination of Lesbians and the Church," *Concilium* 194 (1987): 72–78; Nugent and Gramick, *Building Bridges*, 206.

30. Robert Nugent, "Homosexuality and the Hurting Family," *America*, February 18, 1981, 154–57.

31. Robert Nugent, "Courage Curbs Gays," *National Catholic Reporter*, January 18, 1985, 10.

32. New Ways Ministry, *Bondings* (Fall 1979).

33. New Ways Ministry, "Research on Gay Women," *Bondings* (Fall 1979): 3.

34. Nugent and Gramick, *Building Bridges*, 74.

35. New Ways Ministry, "First Lesbian Retreat Held," *Bondings* (Winter 1978–79): 2.

36. "Origins and Past," Catholic Lesbians.org, http://www.catholiclesbians.org/pages/origins.html, cited by Williams, "Homosexuality and the American Catholic Church," 189.

37. Williams, "Homosexuality and the American Catholic Church," 50–54.

38. Jeannine Gramick, "An Invitation to Continue Dialogue among Lesbian Religious," New Ways Ministry, accessed July 11, 2022, https://www.newwaysministry.org/issues/religious-life-2/religious-life/an-invitation-to-continue-dialogue-among-lesbian-religious/.

39. New Ways Ministry, "Religious Life—Women," accessed July 11, 2022, https://www.newwaysministry.org/issues/religious-life-2/religious-life/.

40. For a full bibliography, see New Ways Ministry, "Religious Life—Women," https://www.newwaysministry.org/issues/religious-life-2/religious-life/#toggle-id-2.

41. Adam Rogan, "Archdiocese Denounces Siena Center 'Gay Priest' Retreat," *The Journal Times*, August 24, 2018, https://journaltimes.com/news/local/archdiocese-denounces-siena-center-gay-priest-retreat/article_341459f9-f645-5d0c-8e26-3eef65363c7f.html.

42. Heidi Schlumpf, "Animosity, Attacks against LGBT Catholics Create 'Toxic Atmosphere,'" *National Catholic Reporter*, November 2, 2018, https://www.ncronline.org/news/justice/animosity-attacks-against-lgbt-catholics-create-toxic-atmosphere.

43. Rogan, "Archdiocese Denounces Siena Center 'Gay Priest' Retreat."

44. Gramick, *Homosexuality and the Catholic Church*, 11.

45. Nugent and Gramick, *Building Bridges*, 201.

46. Williams, "Homosexuality and the American Catholic Church," 78–79.

47. Williams, "Homosexuality and the American Catholic Church," 35–36.

48. Jeannine Gramick, Testimony, S1 Box 1: Baltimore City Council Bill on Discrimination Correspondence and Info, 1980, NWM Collection, Marquette University Library, cited by Williams, "Homosexuality and the American Catholic Church," 70.

49. Nugent and Gramick, *Building Bridges*, 197.

50. New Ways Ministry, "Catholic Support in Dade County," *Bondings* (Fall 1978): 1.

51. Williams, "Homosexuality and the American Catholic Church," 65.

52. New Ways Ministry, "Catholic Support in Dade County," *Bondings* (Fall 1978): 2.

53. Williams, "Homosexuality and the American Catholic Church," 69.

54. NWM, "Book of Memory and Thanksgiving," 11.

55. New Ways Ministry and Pax Christi, "A Catholic Pledge to End Violence against Gay and Lesbian People," *New York Times*, December 30, 1998.

56. CDF, "Some Considerations Concerning the Response to Legislative Proposals on the Non-discrimination of Homosexual Persons," no. 13, July 24, 1992, https://www.vatican.va/roman_curia/congregations/cfaith/documents/rc_con_cfaith_doc_19920724_homosexual-persons_en.html.

57. New Ways Ministry, "A Time to Speak—Catholics for Lesbian and Gay Civil Rights," ad for *National Catholic Reporter*, November 13, 1992; Gustav Niebuhr, "2 Bishops Sign Ad Backing Gay Rights; Clerics Join in Public Statement Responding to the Vatican's Stand," *Washington Post*, November 1, 1992, A4.

58. Brief for New Ways Ministry et al. as *Amici Curiae* Supporting Plaintiff, *Koenke v. Saint Joseph University*, 2:19-cv-04731-NIQA (E.D. Pa. Mar. 5, 2020); New Ways Ministry, "A Home for All: A Catholic

Call for LGBTQ Non-discrimination," August 9, 2021, https://www
.newwaysministry.org/homeforall/.

59. New Ways Ministry, "New Ways Consultant for Bishops'
Committee," *Bondings* (Fall 1979): 4. And John D'Emilio, "Activist
Catholics: Dignity's Work in the 1970s and 1980s," in *Queer Legacies:
Stories from Chicago's LGBTQ Archives* (Chicago: University of Chi-
cago Press, 2020), 58.

60. Catholic Council for the Church and Society (The Neth-
erlands), "Homosexual People in Society: A Contribution to the
Dialogue within the Faith Community," trans. Bernard A. Nachbar
(Mt. Rainier, MD: New Ways Ministry, 1980, Dutch ed. 1979); "U.S.
Group Issues Dutch Statement on Homosexuality," *National Catho-
lic Reporter*, March 7, 1980, as reprinted in *Bondings* (Winter 1979–
80): 1. And Williams, "Homosexuality and the American Catholic
Church," 55.

61. "'New Ways' Distributes Document," *The Catholic Review*,
May 1, 1981, as reprinted in *Bondings* (Spring–Summer 1981): 1.

62. Nugent and Gramick, *Building Bridges*, 200; and Williams,
"Homosexuality and the American Catholic Church," 25.

63. New Ways Ministry, "Fall Activities," *Bondings* (Fall 1979): 4.

64. Williams, "Homosexuality and the American Catholic
Church," 96.

65. Collins, *The Modern Inquisition*, 131.

66. Chuck Colbert, "Rome's No Doesn't Stop Mass at New Ways
Conference," *National Catholic Reporter*, March 22, 2002.

67. New Ways Ministry, "Book of Memory," 26.

68. Giovanni Panettiere, "Heed Francis' Example: Bishop
Thomas Gumbleton Speaks on LGBT Issues," *National Catholic
Reporter*, April 13, 2019, https://www.ncronline.org/news/justice/heed
-francis-example-bishop-thomas-gumbleton-speaks-lgbt-issues.

69. Williams, "Homosexuality and the American Catholic
Church," 105–6.

70. New Ways Ministry, "Book of Memory," 5.

71. New Ways Ministry, "Book of Memory," 5–6.

72. Nugent and Gramick, *Building Bridges*, 198.

73. Nugent and Gramick, *Building Bridges*, 200–201; Williams,
"Homosexuality and the American Catholic Church," 89.

74. Williams, "Homosexuality and the American Catholic
Church," 89–91.

75. Nugent and Gramick, *Building Bridges*, 201–2.

76. Nugent and Gramick, *Building Bridges*, 202–5.

77. Nugent and Gramick, *Building Bridges*, 203.

78. Nugent and Gramick, *Building Bridges*, 204.

79. Ari Goldman, "Catholics Meet on Gay Role in Clergy," *New York Times*, September 28, 1989, B2.

80. Nugent and Gramick, *Building Bridges*, 203–4.

81. "Letter from Archbishop Vincent Fagiolo of the Congregation for Religious and Secular Institutes to Nugent and Gramick Regarding the Commission," Rome, July 23, 1988, available online at http://www.natcath.org/NCR_Online/documents/fagiolo.htm.

82. Collins, *The Modern Inquisition*, 132–34.

83. Robin Edwards, "Ministry to Gays Investigated," *National Catholic Reporter*, May 27, 1994, 5.

84. Collins, *The Modern Inquisition*, 133–36.

85. Archbishop Adam J. Maida, Msgr. James J. Mulligan, and Dr. Janet E. Smith, "Report of the Findings of the Commission Studying the Writings & Ministry of Sister Jeannine Gramick, SSND, and Father Robert Nugent, SDS," October 4, 1994, available online at http://www.natcath.org/NCR_Online/documents/gn03.htm.

86. For an in-depth look at the Maida Commission proceedings, see Collins, *The Modern Inquisition*, 132–54.

87. Francis DeBernardo, "Sister Jeannine, Cardinal Ratzinger, New Ways Ministry, and Solidarity with LCWR," New Ways Ministry, May 11, 2012, https://www.newwaysministry.org/2012/05/11/sister-jeannine-cardinal-ratzinger-new-ways-ministry-and-solidarity-with-lcwr/.

88. Tom Roberts, "At Call to Action, Stories Show Softer Side to Disputes," *National Catholic Reporter*, November 19, 1999, https://natcath.org/NCR_Online/archives2/1999d/111999/111999i.htm.

89. CDF, "Notification Regarding Sister Jeannine Gramick, SSND, and Father Robert Nugent, SDS," Rome, May 31, 1999, https://www.vatican.va/roman_curia/congregations/cfaith/documents/rc_con_cfaith_doc_19990531_gramick-nugent-notification_en.html.

90. Pamela Schaeffer, "Gramick Says No to Vatican Silencing, Expects Dismissal," *National Catholic Reporter*, June 16, 2000, 4.

91. Tom Roberts, "Gramick Seeks to Overturn Ruling," *National Catholic Reporter*, October 1, 1999, 7.

92. Tom Roberts, "Gramick on Conscience in Lincoln," *National Catholic Reporter*, May 5, 2000, 6.

93. Matt Kantz, "Gramick Confers with Superiors on Response to Vatican Order," *National Catholic Reporter*, September 17, 1999, 6.

94. Schaeffer, "Gramick Says No to Vatican Silencing, Expects Dismissal."

95. Woo, "The Rev. Robert Nugent Dies at 76."

96. Woo, "The Rev. Robert Nugent Dies at 76."

97. RNS Blog Editor, "Maryland Nun Plans to Defy Latest Vatican Ban regarding Gay Ministry," *Religion News Service*, May 31, 2000, https://religionnews.com/2000/05/31/rns-daily-digest2662/.

98. Sisters of Loretto, "Our History," https://www.lorettocommunity.org/about/history/.

99. "Gramick Leaves Order to Join Loretto Sisters," *National Catholic Reporter*, September 14, 2001, 8.

100. Patrick O'Neill, "Living with Silencing," *National Catholic Reporter*, January 5, 2001, 9.

101. J. Lester Feder, "Meet the Nun Who Battled One Pope over LGBT Ministry and Now Welcomes Another," *Buzzfeed News*, September 22, 2015, https://www.buzzfeednews.com/article/lesterfeder/meet-the-nun-who-battled-one-pope-over-lgbt-ministry-and-now.

102. Teresa Malcom, "Bishop Forbids Retreat," *National Catholic Reporter*, October 3, 1997.

103. Pamela Schaeffer, "Cardinal Bars Pax Christi Meeting," *National Catholic Reporter*, April 30, 1999, 5.

104. Chuck Colbert, "Rome's No Doesn't Stop Mass at New Ways Conference," *National Catholic Reporter*, March 22, 2002, 3; Dennis Cody, "Nun's Reception Cancelled," *National Catholic Reporter*, February 11, 2005, 4.

105. Matt Kantz, "NCCB Head Issues Defense of Gramick, Nugent Ban," *National Catholic Reporter*, December 3, 1999, 8.

106. "New Ways Ministry Not Approved by Catholic Church, Cardinal George States," *Catholic News Agency*, February 14, 2010, https://www.catholicnewsagency.com/news/18668/new-ways-ministry-not-approved-by-catholic-church-cardinal-george-states.

107. Sr. Camille D'Arienzom, "New Ways Ministry Director: Laypeople Need to Proclaim the Gospel with Their Lives," *National Catholic Reporter*, July 8, 2014, https://www.ncronline.org/blogs/

conversations-sr-camille/new-ways-ministry-director-laypeople-need
-proclaim-gospel-their-lives?site_redirect=1.

108. D'Arienzom, "New Ways Ministry Director."

109. Francis DeBernardo, "New Ways Ministry's LGBT Catholic Pilgrims Get VIP Seats at Papal Audience," New Ways Ministry, February 19, 2015.

110. Jeannine Gramick, "This Pope Gives Me Hope," *Global Sisters Report*, May 7, 2015, https://www.globalsistersreport.org/column/ equality/pope-gives-me-hope-24876.

111. Jeannine Gramick, "The Pope and New Ways Ministry," *Loretto Circle Newsletter* (August/September 2021), 4; and Robert Shine, "Pope Francis Writes to New Ways Ministry: 'Thank You for Your Neighborly Work,'" New Ways Ministry, December 9, 2021, https://www.newwaysministry.org/2021/12/09/pope-francis-writes-to -new-ways-ministry-thank-you-for-your-neighborly-work/.

112. Jim McDermott, "Pope Francis Praises Sister Jeannine Gramick's 50 Years of L G B T Ministry in Handwritten Letter," *America*, January 7, 2022, https://www.americamagazine.org/faith/2022/01/ 07/sister-jeanine-gramick-letter-pope-francis-242157.

CHAPTER 4

1. Deb Word, interview by author, May 26, 2020.

2. Fortunate Families, "Mission Statement," https://fortunate families.com/mission-vision-amp-history.

3. Deb Word, interview by author, May 26, 2020. For more on Word's experience, see Deb Word, "This Catholic Mom: Our Family Outreach," in *More than a Monologue*, vol. 1, ed. Christine Firer Hinze and J. Patrick Hornbeck (New York: Fordham University Press, 2014), 17–25.

4. Mary Ellen and Casey Lopata, "All Are Welcome: All in the Family," New Ways Ministry, January 4, 2012, https://www .newwaysministry.org/2012/01/04/all-are-welcome-all-in-the-family/.

5. Fortunate Families, "Mission Statement."

6. Thomas Fox, "Fortunate Families," *National Catholic Reporter* 45, no. 3 (November 28, 2008). See also Mary Ellen with Casey Lopata, *Fortunate Families* (Victoria, Canada: Trafford Publishing, 2003), 14–15.

7. Casey Lopata, "Can My Son Be Gay and Catholic?," originally published in *Open Hands: A Unique Resource on Lesbian/Gay/Bisexual Concerns in the Church*, Fall 1998, https://lgbtqreligiousarchives.org/media/profile/casey-mary-ellen-lopata/Casey%20Lopata%20article%20in%20Open%20Hands.pdf.

8. Lopata, *Fortunate Families*, 6.

9. Lopata, *Fortunate Families*, 67.

10. Casey Lopata, "Can My Son Be Gay and Catholic?" For more on Casey Lopata's story, see "Church Teaching, Pastoral Care & My Son," in Lopata, *Fortunate Families*, 48–63.

11. Fox, "Fortunate Families."

12. Lopata, *Fortunate Families*, 94.

13. Lopata, *Fortunate Families*, 104–6.

14. Fortunate Families, "History Highlights," accessed July 14, 2022, https://fortunatefamilies.com/mission-vision-amp-history. For more on the Catholic Association of Gay and Lesbian Ministries, see the biography of its founder, Fr. James Schexnayder, a priest of the Archdiocese of San Francisco, at the LGBTQ Religious Archives Network, accessed July 14, 2022, https://lgbtqreligiousarchives.org/profiles/james-schexnayder.

15. For more, see "Rev. James Schexnayder, Profile," LGBTQ Religious Archives Network, accessed July 14, 2022, https://lgbtqreligiousarchives.org/profiles/james-schexnayder. In 2003 and 2004, NACDLGM partnered with the Center for Applied Research in the Apostolate (CARA) at Georgetown University to conduct a survey and publish a special report titled "In Search of Best Practices in Ministry with Gay and Lesbian Catholics," https://cara.georgetown.edu/wp-content/uploads/2018/06/Best-Practices-in-Ministry-with-GL-Catholics.pdf.

16. "Casey and Mary Ellen Lopata, Profile," LGBTQ Religious Archives Network, accessed July 14, 2022, https://lgbtqreligiousarchives.org/profiles/casey-mary-ellen-lopata.

17. Lopata, *Fortunate Families*, 150.

18. Lopata, *Fortunate Families*, 94.

19. NCCB/USCC Bishops' Committee on Marriage and Family, *Always Our Children: A Pastoral Message to Parents of Homosexual Children and Suggestions for Pastoral Ministers*, October 1, 1997, https://www.usccb.org/resources/always-our-children.

20. Mary Ellen and Casey Lopata, "Always Our Children: 20 Years Later," New Ways Ministry, October 1, 2017, https://www.newwaysministry.org/2017/10/01/always-children-20-years-later/. See also Associated Press, "Gay Children Need Support, Bishops Urge," *New York Times*, October 1, 1997.

21. Lopata, "Always Our Children: 20 Years Later." For more on AOC, see Lopata, *Fortunate Families*, 79–89.

22. Lopata, *Fortunate Families*, 9.

23. "Stories by Family Members of LGBTQ," Fortunate Families, accessed July 14, 2022, https://fortunatefamilies.com/stories-by-family-members-of-lgbtq and "Accompanying Family, Friends, and Allies' Stories," accessed July 14, 2022, https://fortunatefamilies.com/accompanying-family-friends-allies-stories.

24. Fortunate Families, "History Highlights."

25. Fox, "Fortunate Families."

26. See Joshua J. McElwee, "Joseph Sullivan, Auxiliary Bishop with Wide Impact on US Church, Dies," *National Catholic Reporter*, June 12, 2013, https://www.ncronline.org/news/people/joseph-sullivan-auxiliary-bishop-wide-impact-us-church-dies; Francis DeBernardo, "Remembering Bishop Sullivan's LGBT Ministry," New Ways Ministry, June 11, 2013, https://www.newwaysministry.org/2013/06/11/rest-in-peace-bishop-joseph-m-sullivan/; and Patricia Coll Freeman, "Retired Anchorage Archbishop Hurley Dies at 88," *Catholic News Service*, January 11, 2016, https://www.ncronline.org/news/people/retired-anchorage-archbishop-hurley-dies-88.

27. Fox, "Fortunate Families."

28. Fox, "Fortunate Families."

29. New Ways Ministry, "Parish Toolkit," from the archives of Jenny Naughton.

30. M. Lucassen, T. Clark, E. Moselen, E. Robinson, and The Adolescent Health Research Group, Youth'12, "The Health and Well-being of Secondary School Students in New Zealand: Results for Young People Attracted to the Same Sex or Both Sexes" (Auckland, New Zealand: The University of Auckland, 2014), www.youthresearch.auckland.ac.nz.

31. Fortunate Families Board of Directors, "Fortunate Families Foundational Statement," revised December 2017, https://d2y1pz2y630308.cloudfront.net/19668/documents/2018/4/Fortunate%20Families%20Foundational%20Statement%20REVSIED.pdf.

32. Equally Blessed, "Who We Are," https://web.archive.org/web/20220307172312/https://www.equallyblessed.org/about/.

33. Fortunate Families, "History Highlights."

34. Deb Word, interview by author, May 26, 2020.

35. Deb Word, interview by author, May 26, 2020.

36. Jamie Manson, "Fortunate Families Barred from Exhibiting at World Meeting of Families," *National Catholic Reporter*, June 3, 2015, https://www.ncronline.org/blogs/ncr-today/fortunate-families-barred-exhibiting-world-meeting-families.

37. Deb Word remembers a particularly prickly exchange with Archbishop Chaput after she suggested that he follow the lead of Pope Francis, who famously asked, "Who am I to judge [gay people]?" Chaput retorted to Word that she ought to "stop being disrespectful to archbishops." Deb Word, interview by author, May 26, 2020.

38. Deb Word, interview by author, May 26, 2020.

39. Stanley "JR" Zerkowski, interview by author, May 27, 2013.

40. Francis DeBernardo, "Fortunate Families' Director Has 'Seen Miracles' and 'Expects More,'" New Ways Ministry, December 4, 2017, https://www.newwaysministry.org/2017/12/04/fortunate-families-director-seen-miracles-expects/.

41. Stanley "JR" Zerkowski, interview by author, May 27, 2013.

42. Deb Word, interview by author, May 26, 2020.

43. Stanley "JR" Zerkowski, interview by author, May 27, 2013.

44. Stanley "JR" Zerkowski, interview by author, May 27, 2013.

45. Fortunate Families, "History Highlights."

46. Stanley "JR" Zerkowski, interview by author, May 27, 2013.

47. Casey Sullivan, "Fortunate Families Marks a Decade of Helping Gay Catholics," Out Alliance, July 2, 2014, https://outalliance.org/fortunate-families-marks-a-decade-of-helping-gay-catholics/.

CHAPTER 5

1. In the nineties, most LGBTQ people referred to themselves as gay or lesbian. This chapter will reflect the historical nomenclature.

2. Media took note, and in the days afterward, the story spread across the globe. David Dinkins, the mayor of New York City, sent a note of encouragement for the parish's inclusive vision, and President Bill Clinton hailed the service for its healing power. Donald Maher,

"A Catholic Parish's Response to the Lesbian and Gay Presence: A Report on the Gay and Lesbian Ministry of St. Paul the Apostle and the Survey of Its Membership" (New York, 1994), 8–9, in the archives of Brendan Fay.

3. Brendan Fay, interview by author, Zoom, March 25, 2020.

4. Center for Disease Control, "Mortality Attributable to HIV Infection/AIDS among Persons Aged 25–44 Years—United States, 1990, 1991," MMWR Weekly 42, no. 25 (July 2, 1993): 481–86, https://www.cdc.gov/mmwr/preview/mmwrhtml/00021017.htm.

5. Brendan Fay, interview by author.

6. Philip Kayal, *Bearing Witness: Gay Men's Health Crisis and the Politics of AIDS* (New York: Westview Press, 1993).

7. Deborah Gould, *Moving Politics: Emotion and ACT UP's Fight against AIDS* (Chicago: University of Chicago Press, 2009).

8. Anthony Petro, *After the Wrath of God: AIDS, Sexuality, and American Religion* (New York: Oxford University Press, 2015), 91–136.

9 John Voelcker, a thirty-three-year-old Irish American gay man and magazine editor, remarked on participation in the parade: "I'm not asking to have much to do with the Catholic Church, but I do want to be Irish and gay at the same time." Francis Clines, "To Be Irish, Gay and on the Outside, Once Again," *New York Times*, March 13, 1993.

10. Brendan Fay, interview by author.

11. Jerry Gray, "Gay Group Rebuffed in Bid to Join St. Patrick's Parade," *New York Times*, March 8, 1991.

12. Colman McCarthy, "Hibernian Hatred," *Washington Post*, March 30, 1991.

13. The controversy continued over the next few decades as LGBTQ Irish struggled for inclusion in St. Patrick's Day parades around the United States and world. In the United States, ILGO pursued a legal remedy but suffered a series of losses in court. It was only in 2015, after a number of parade sponsors and dignitaries had withdrawn from the parade, that organizers finally relented by allowing an LGBTQ group from NBC Universal to march. A decade and a half prior, Brendan Fay founded "St. Patrick's for All," an annual festival and parade in Queens that has provided an alternative to the Fifth Avenue parade. To this day it regularly welcomes progressive dignitaries and movement leaders. For more on the ILGO affair, see Katherine O'Donnell, "St. Patrick's Day Expulsions: Race and Homophobia in New York's Parade," in *Irish Postmodernisms and Popular Culture*, ed.

Wanda Balzano, Anne Mulhall, and Moynagh Sullivan (New York: Palgrave Macmillan, 2007), 128–40; and Sheila Langan, "Timeline of the NYC St. Patrick's Day Parade's LGBT Controversy," *Irish Central*, March 17, 2018, https://www.irishcentral.com/news/politics/timeline -of-the-nyc-st-patricks-day-parades-lgbt-controversy-photo-video.

14. Brendan Fay, interview by author.

15. Donald Maher, interview by author, Wernersville, PA, December 6, 2019.

16. Fr. Eric Andrews, CSP, interview by author, Zoom, June 18, 2020.

17. Fr. Eric Andrews, interview by author.

18. Brendan Fay, interview by author.

19. Ameena Walker, "Chelsea, Park Slope among NYC's Friendliest LGBTQ Neighborhoods," *Curbed New York*, June 18, 2018, https://ny.curbed.com/2018/6/18/17475492/nyc-lgbtq-friendly -neighborhoods.

20. For more on Isaac Hecker and the Paulists, see Boniface Hanley, *Isaac Hecker, An American Saint* (Mahwah, NJ: Paulist Press, 2008); John Behnke, *Isaac Thomas Hecker: Spiritual Pilgrim* (Mahwah, NJ: Paulist Press, 2017); David O'Brien, *Isaac Hecker, An American Catholic* (Mahwah, NJ: Paulist Press, 1992); and Joseph McSorley, *Isaac Hecker and His Friends* (New York: Paulist Press, 1972).

21. Paulist Fathers, "Our History," accessed July 14, 2022, https://paulist.org/who-we-are/our-history/, and "Our Mission," accessed July 14, 2022, https://paulist.org/our-mission/.

22. Fr. Eric Andrews, interview by author.

23. "Rev. John P. Collins," *San Francisco Chronicle*, May 20, 1987, 36. "Rev Fr John Patrick Collins," Find a Grave, https://www .findagrave.com/memorial/95847485/john-patrick-collins.

24. Fr. Eric Andrews, interview by author.

25. Maher, "A Catholic Parish's Response," 6.

26. Donald Maher, interview by author.

27. William Grimes, "On Stage, and Off," *New York Times*, November 8, 1996, https://www.nytimes.com/1996/11/08/theater/on -stage-and-off.html.

28. Brendan Fay, interview by author.

29. Maher, "A Catholic Parish's Response," 6.

30. Donald Maher, interview by author.

31. Donald Maher, interview by author.

32. Fr. Eric Andrews, interview by author.

33. Brendan Fay, interview by author.

34. Donald Maher, interview by author.

35. Brendan Fay, interview by author.

36. Maher, "A Catholic Parish's Response," 7.

37. Donald Maher, interview by author; Maher, "A Catholic Parish's Response," 9.

38. Maher, "A Catholic Parish's Response," 10.

39. Account taken from Brendan Fay's handwritten notes from the night of the incident. Copy in the archives of Brendan Fay.

40. Maher, "A Catholic Parish's Response," 9.

41. Shankar Vedantam, "Stain of Hatred on Priest's Garb from Antigay Attack during Mass," *Newsday*, June 28, 1993. Fr. Charles Kullmann believed the press overdramatized the event. He recalled, "He got a scratch that bled, but it wasn't a deep flesh wound or anything like that. In my opinion, in hindsight, it was minor." Fr. Charles Kullmann, interview by author, Zoom, June 30, 2020.

42. Brendan Fay, interview by author.

43. Donald Maher, interview by author.

44. John Burger and Steve McDonnell, "'Reprehensible': Cardinal O'Connor Denounces Interruption of Mass, Violence against Homosexuals," *Catholic New York*. From the archives of Brendan Fay.

45. David Miller, "Gays Disrupt Church Service — Priest Hurt in Struggle," *New York Post*, June 24, 1993.

46. Maher, "A Catholic Parish's Response," 10.

47. Neil Graves, "Raucous Fun Fills 5th Ave. Gay Parade," *New York Post*, June 26, 2000, https://nypost.com/2000/06/26/raucous-fun-fills-5th-ave-at-gay-parade/.

48. Morality Action Committee, flyer, no date. Copy in the archives of Brendan Fay.

49. Fr. Charles Kullmann, interview by author.

50. Fr. Charles Kullmann, interview by author.

51. Donald Maher, interview by author.

52. Katherine Wrightson, "Catholics, Too, Make Room in Pew for Gays, Lesbians on the West Side," *Chelsea Clinton News*, June 13–19, 1996.

53. Fr. Eric Andrews, interview by author.

54. Fr. Charles Kullmann, interview by author.

55. Fr. Charles Kullmann, interview by author.

56. Maher, "A Catholic Parish's Response," 12–13.

57. Donald Maher, letter to John Cardinal O'Connor, December 24, 1994. From the archives of Brendan Fay.

58. Donald Maher, interview by author.

59. Fr. Eric Andrews, interview by author.

60. Donald Maher, interview by author. Maher remembers being taken aback by a throne in the archbishop's residence.

61. Mike Allen, "Cardinal Sees Marriage Harm in Partners Bill," *New York Times*, May 25, 1998.

62. Maher, "A Catholic Parish's Response," 15.

63. GLCM, "A Proposal for the Ministry's 7th Year," n.d. From the archives of Brendan Fay.

64. Brendan Fay, interview by author.

65. Donald Maher, Letter to Editor, "Mass Disruption," *Catholic New York* 12, no. 44 (July 29, 1993): 14.

66. According to Donald Maher, years after Fr. Kullmann's arrival, the priest remarked that the gay ministry was the "single best adult education program in the parish." Donald Maher, interview by author.

67. Wrightson, "Catholics, Too, Make Room in Pew," 23.

68. Wrightson, "Catholics, Too, Make Room in Pew," 23.

69. Donald Maher, interview by author.

70. Brendan Fay, interview by author.

71. Donald Maher, interview by author.

CHAPTER 6

1. Jim Yardley and Laurie Goodstein, "Pope Francis Met with Kim David," *New York Times*, September 30, 2015, https://www.nytimes.com/2015/09/30/us/county-clerk-kim-davis-who-denied-gay-couples-visited-pope.html.

2. Paulist Fathers, "Paulists InFormation Ep 4—Father Gil Martinez, CSP," February 25, 2015, https://www.youtube.com/watch?v=BqGp-o8JotA.

3. Paulist Fathers, "Paulists InFormation Ep 4—Father Gil Martinez, CSP."

4. Mike Hayes, "Busted: Fr. Gilbert Martinez, CSP, One Paulist's Journey from Park Ranger to Priest to Immigration-Rights Activist,"

Busted Halo, July 18, 2007, https://bustedhalo.com/features/busted-fr
-gilbert-martinez-csp.

5. Fr. Eric Andrews, CSP, interview by author, Zoom, June 18,
2020.

6. Fr. Gil Martinez, interview by author, Zoom, June 20, 2020.

7. Robert Siegel, "Churches May Help in Fight against Depor-
tations," *NPR*, May 9, 2007, https://www.npr.org/transcripts/10098237;
Justice Power.org, "New Sanctuary Coalition," accessed July 15, 2022,
https://justicepower.org/project/new-sanctuary-coalition/.

8. Fr. Gil Martinez, interview by author.

9. OSP, 2016 Retreat Video, February 13, 2016.

10. The Gay Catholics group at St. Francis Xavier, e.g., had been
doing ministry for several decades.

11. Fr. Gil Martinez, interview by author.

12. Fr. Gil Martinez, interview by author.

13. Matthew Vidal, interview by author, Zoom, June 27, 2020.

14. Matthew Vidal, interview by author.

15. OSP, 2016 Retreat Video.

16. In the late 2000s and early 2001s, Martinez's vision was con-
fined to gay and lesbian ministry. Many in society and the Church
were still unfamiliar with genderqueer and trans issues, which meant
they could be a lightning rod with church authorities and critics. Fr.
Martinez tread lightly as he watered the grassroots network.

17. Matthew Vidal, interview by author.

18. Matthew Vidal, interview by author.

19. Fr. Gil Martinez, interview by author.

20. OSP member who preferred to remain anonymous, interview by author, telephone, June 28, 2020.

21. OSP, 2016 Retreat Video.

22. Fr. Mark-David Janus, CSP, interview by author, Zoom, July
20, 2020.

23. Fr. Gil Martinez, interview by author.

24. Fr. Gil Martinez, interview by author.

25. OSP member who preferred to remain anonymous, interview by author.

26. Fr. Gil Martinez, interview by author.

27. Fr. Gil Martinez, interview by author.

28. See, e.g., Marie Cartier, *Baby, You Are My Religion: Women,
Gay Bars, and Theology before Stonewall* (New York: Routledge, 2013),

and Patrick Sisson, "How Gay Bars Have Been a Building Block of the LGBTQ Community," Curbed, June 17, 2016, https://www.curbed .com/2016/6/17/11963066/gay-bar-history-stonewall-pulse-lgbtq.

29. Marie Smithgall, interview by author, Zoom, June 2, 2020.

30. Fr. Gil Martinez, interview by author.

31. Email, Out at St. Paul, December 1, 2009. From the archives of Matthew Vidal.

32. Matthew Vidal, interview by author.

33. Fr. Mark-David Janus, interview by author.

34. Email from Matthew Vidal to Fr. Gil Martinez, November 23, 2009. From the archives of Matthew Vidal.

35. Edward Poliandro, interview by author, Zoom, July 31, 2020.

36. Fr. Eric Andrews, interview by author.

37. Matthew Vidal, interview by author.

38. Marie Smithgall, interview by author.

39. See Out at St. Paul, accessed July 15, 2022, https://www.out atstpaul.org/; and Apostolist, accessed July 15, 2022, https://apostolist .org/.

40. Santiago Rivera, interview by author, Zoom, May 29, 2020.

41. Michael Tomae, interview by author, Zoom, May 25, 2020.

42. Marianne Palacios, interview by author, Zoom, May 22, 2020.

43. OSP, 2016 Retreat Video.

44. Marie Smithgall, interview by author.

45. Michael Roper, interview by author, Zoom, August 5, 2020.

46. Fred Negem, interview by author, New York City, May 29, 2017.

47. Mitchell Gold and Mindy Drucker, *Crisis: 40 Stories Revealing the Personal, Social, and Religious Pain and Trauma of Growing Up Gay in America* (Austin, TX: Greenleaf Book Group, LLC, 2008).

48. Fred Negem, interview by author.

49. Larry Holodak, interview by author.

50. Alan Downs, *The Velvet Rage* (New York: Perseus Books Group, 2006).

51. OSP member who preferred to remain anonymous, interview by author.

52. OSP member who preferred to remain anonymous, interview by author.

53. Patrick Manning, interview by author, Zoom, August 25, 2020.

54. Interparish Collaborative, accessed July 14, 2022, http://www.lgbt-ipc.org/.

55. See, e.g., Susan Brinkmann, "NYC Catholic Church to Participate in Gay Pride March," Women of Grace, June 24, 2010, https://www.womenofgrace.com/blog/?p=5041; and Michael Voris, "Bishop Dolan Cheers Gay Groups at Jesuit Parish Rededication," Church Militant, July 14, 2010, https://lesfemmes-thetruth.blogspot.com/2010/07/bishop-dolan-cheers-gay-groups-at.html.

56. Susan Candiotti and Vivienne Foley, "New York Church Maintains Gay Pride Presence, but with Blank Banner," CNN, June 27, 2010, https://www.cnn.com/2010/US/06/27/new.york.church.gay.pride/index.html.

57. Santiago Rivera, interview by author.

58. Fr. Gil Martinez, interview by author.

59. Fr. Gil Martinez, interview by author.

60. In July 2019, e.g., Lifesite News condemned Martinez for the Pride Mass and encouraged its followers to file a complaint with Cardinal Timothy Dolan's secretary. See Martin Barillas, "WATCH: Priest in Rainbow Colors Celebrates 'Pride' Mass outside Stonewall Inn's Gay Bar," Lifesite News, July 5, 2019, https://www.lifesitenews.com/news/watch-priest-in-rainbow-colors-celebrates-pride-mass-outside-stonewall-inns-gay-bar.

61. Fr. Gil Martinez, interview by author.

62. Fr. Mark-David Janus, interview by author.

63. Fr. Gil Martinez, interview by author.

64. Fr. Gil Martinez, interview by author.

65. Fr. Gil Martinez, interview by author.

66. Matthew Vidal, interview by author.

67. Fr. Gil Martinez, interview by author.

68. Fr. Gil Martinez, interview by author.

69. Fred Negem, interview by author.

70. Matthew Vidal, interview by author.

71. Fr. Mark-David Janus, interview by author.

72. Philip Pullella, "Vatican Attacked for Opposing Gay Decriminalization," Reuters, December 2, 2008, https://www.reuters.com/article/us-vatican-homosexuals/vatican-attacked-for-opposing-gay-decriminalization-idUSTRE4B13QA20081202.

73. Matthew Vidal, interview by author.

74. OSP member who preferred to remain anonymous, interview by author.

75. Walter Kasper, *Mercy: The Essence of the Gospel and the Key to Christian Life* (Mahwah, NJ: Paulist Press, 2014).

76. Michael Tomae, interview by author.

77. Michael Tomae, interview by author.

78. Fr. Mark-David Janus, interview by author.

79. Fr. Gil Martinez, interview by author.

80. Fr. Gil Martinez, interview by author. After the difficult meeting, Fr. Mark-David Janus spoke with Cardinal Kasper about what transpired. Hearing how his words had been received by the group, his tone drastically changed. Janus recalled, "I mentioned that some of that was difficult for some of the people who had been in long-term relationships to hear. He thought about it and said, 'Send them my blessing. Tell them they have my blessing.'" Fr. Mark-David Janus, interview by author.

81. Santiago Rivera, interview by author.

82. Michael Tomae, interview by author.

83. Patrick Manning, interview by author.

84. "Owning Our Faith," March 9, 2015, https://www.youtube.com/watch?v=a2vDJRj7AuQ.

85. See owningourfaith.com.

86. Kira Brekke, "This Priest Hand-Delivered a DVD to Pope Francis about LGBT Catholics," *Huffington Post*, September 18, 2015, https://www.huffpost.com/entry/pope-francis-lgbt-equality_n_55fc1bd0e4b0fde8b0cde025?ncid=tweetlnkushpmg00000055.

87. Michael Tomae, interview by author.

88. Marianne Palacios, interview by author.

89. Marie Smithgall, interview by author.

90. Fr. Mark-David Janus, interview by author.

91. Larry Holodak, interview by author.

92. Michael Roper, interview by author.

93. Michael Tomae, interview by author.

94. Marianne Palacios interview by author.

95. OSP member who preferred to remain anonymous, interview by author.

96. Larry Holodak, interview by author.

97. Santiago Rivera, interview by author.

98. Michael Tomae, interview by author.

99. Michael Tomae, interview by author.

100. Patrick Manning, interview by author.

101. Patrick Manning, interview by author.

102. Chip Davy, email to author, August 13, 2020.

103. Fr. Mark-David Janus, interview by author.

104. Marie Smithgall, "OSP Advent—Sunday, December 1, 2019," email to Out at St. Paul LISTSERV, author's archives.

105. Fr. Gil Martinez, interview by author.

106. Marie Smithgall, interview by author.

107. Marie Smithgall, interview by author.

108. Marianne Palacios, interview by author.

109. Marianne Palacios, interview by author.

110. Fr. Mark-David Janus, interview by author.

111. Michael Roper, interview by author.

CHAPTER 7

1. Trudy Ring, "Pope Shows 'Care for LGBT People' in Meeting with Ally Rev. James Martin," *The Advocate*, October 1, 2019, https://www.advocate.com/religion/2019/10/01/pope-shows-care-lgbt-people-meeting-rev-james-martin.

2. Lucas Grindley, "The Advocate's Person of the Year: Pope Francis," *The Advocate*, December 16, 2013, https://www.advocate.com/year-review/2013/12/16/advocates-person-year-pope-francis.

3. Gerard O'Connell, "Pope Francis Meets with Father James Martin in Private Audience," *America*, September 30, 2019, https://www.americamagazine.org/faith/2019/09/30/pope-francis-meets-father-james-martin-private-audience?page=1.

4. Inés San Martín, "Fr. James Martin: Pope Was 'Attentive, Welcoming, and Warm' during Meeting," *Crux*, October 1, 2019, https://cruxnow.com/vatican/2019/09/fr-james-martin-pope-was-attentive-welcoming-and-warm-during-meeting/.

5. Francis DeBernardo, "Father James Martin, Advocate for LGBTQ Catholics, Received by Pope Francis at Vatican," New Ways Ministry, September 30, 2019, https://www.newwaysministry.org/2019/09/30/father-james-martin-advocate-for-lgbtq-catholics-received-by-pope-francis-at-vatican/.

6. John Gehring, "Pope Francis Is Fearless," *New York Times*, October 4, 2019, https://www.nytimes.com/2019/10/04/opinion/pope-francis-catholic-church.html.

7. James Martin, SJ, Twitter, September 30, 2019, https://twitter.com/JamesMartinSJ/status/1178663907084455936.

8. James Martin, *In Good Company: The Fast Track from the Corporate World to Poverty, Chastity, and Obedience* (New York: Sheed and Ward, 2010), 176, e-book edition.

9. James Martin, SJ, email to author, February 10, 2021.

10. For a fuller biography of Fr. James Martin, SJ, see Jon Sweeney, *James Martin: In the Company of Jesus* (Collegeville, MN: Liturgical Press, 2020).

11. Sweeney, *James Martin*, 136–37.

12. For more on John McNeill, see John McNeill, *Both Feet Firmly Planted in Midair* (Louisville, KY: Westminster John Knox Press, 1998), and James McCartin, "The Church and Gay Liberation: The Case of John McNeill," *U.S. Catholic Historian* 34, no. 1 (Winter 2016): 125–41.

13. James Martin, SJ, email to author, February 10, 2021.

14. James Martin, SJ, email to author, February 10, 2021.

15. James Martin, "An Interview with Camille Paglia," *America* 171, no. 15 (November 12, 1994): 10–20.

16. Neil MacFarquhar, "'Corpus Christi' Has a Preview, and Protesters," *New York Times*, September 23, 1998, 3.

17. James Martin, "Of Many Things," *America* 179, no. 11 (October 17, 1998): 2.

18. James Martin, "Of Many Things," *America* 179, no. 14 (November 7, 1998): 2.

19. James Martin, SJ, email to author, February 10, 2021.

20. James Martin, "The Church and the Homosexual Priest," *America* 183, no. 14 (November 4, 2000): 12.

21. James Martin, "The Church and the Homosexual Priest," 14.

22. James Martin, "The Church and the Homosexual Priest," 14–15.

23. James Martin, "The Church and the Homosexual Priest," 15.

24. Matt Carroll, Sacha Pfeiffer, and Michael Rezendes, ed. Walter V. Robinson, "Church Allowed Abuse by Priest for Years," *Boston Globe*, January 6, 2020.

25. Tom Gjelton, "As Catholic Sex Abuse Crisis Deepens, Conservative Circles Blame Gay Priests," *All Things Considered*, NPR, September 19, 2018, https://www.npr.org/2018/09/19/647919741/sex -abuse-scandal-deepens-divide-over-gay-priests/.

26. See, e.g., the scholarship of Fred Fejes, *Gay Rights and Moral Panic: The Origins of America's Debate on Homosexuality* (New York: Palgrave MacMillan, 2008).

27. James Martin, "Of Many Things," *America* 187, no. 20 (December 16, 2002): 2.

28. Congregation for Catholic Education, "Instruction Concerning the Criteria for the Discernment of Vocations with regard to Persons with Homosexual Tendencies in View of Their Admission to the Seminary and to Holy Orders," sec. 2, November 4, 2005, http://www .vatican.va/roman_curia/congregations/ccatheduc/documents/rc_con _ccatheduc_doc_20051104_istruzione_en.html.

29. AP, CNS, RNS, Staff and other sources, "Signs of the Times," *America*, May 23, 2005, https://www.americamagazine.org/issue/532/ news/signs-times; and James Martin, SJ, email to author, February 10, 2021.

30. Sweeney, *James Martin: In the Company of Jesus*, 91.

31. Tom Roberts and John L. Allen Jr., "Editor of Jesuits' *America* Magazine Forced to Resign Under Vatican Pressure" *National Catholic Reporter*, May 6, 2005, https://natcath.org/NCR_Online/archives2/ 2005b/052005/052005a.php.

32. Sweeney, *James Martin: In the Company of Jesus*, 93.

33. James Martin, "The Vatican and Gay Priests," *Commonweal*, January 9, 2006, https://www.commonwealmagazine.org/vatican-gay -priests-0.

34. James Martin, "The Vatican and Gay Priests."

35. Ian Urbina, "D.C. Council Approves Gay Marriage," *New York Times*, December 15, 2009, https://www.nytimes.com/2009/12/ 16/us/16marriage.html.

36. Fr. James Martin, "What Should a Gay Catholic Do?," *America*, November 13, 2009, https://www.americamagazine.org/faith/ 2009/11/13/what-should-gay-catholic-do.

37. Jay Lindsay, "Mass. Catholic School Won't Admit Lesbians' Son," *Associated Press*, May 12, 2010, http://archive.boston.com/ news/education/k_12/articles/2010/05/12/mass_catholic_school_wont _admit_lesbians_son_1273691291/?comments=all&csort=desc.

38. Erica Meltzer, "Denver Archbishop Defends Sacred Heart of Jesus' Decision on Lesbians' Children at Boulder Preschool," *Daily Camera*, March 9, 2010, https://www.dailycamera.com/2010/03/09/denver-archbishop-defends-sacred-heart-of-jesus-decision-on-lesbians-children-at-boulder-preschool/.

39. James Martin, "Same-Sex on the South Shore: The Archdiocese of Boston's Pastoral Decision," *Huffington Post*, May 18, 2010, https://www.huffpost.com/entry/same-sex-on-the-south-sho_b_579659.

40. Tracy Gordon, "Pope Calls Abortion, Gay Marriage 'Insidious and Dangerous Threats,'" *Religion News Service*, May 13, 2010, https://religionnews.com/2010/05/13/pope-benedict-xvi-on-thursday-may-13-called-abortion-divorce-and-same-sex-m/.

41. The piece, titled "Hingham, Same-Sex Marriage, and Life Issues," was originally published on *America*'s blog on Monday, May 17, 2010. It has since been taken down. See "Jesuit Magazine Editor: Pope's Comment on Same-Sex Marriage Is Bizarre," *Catholic News Agency*, May 18, 2010, https://www.catholicnewsagency.com/news/jesuit-magazine-editor-popes-comment-on-same-sex-marriage-against-the-gospel; and Martin, "Same-Sex on the South Shore."

42. James Martin, "Gays and the Church: Two Stories from Today," *America*, June 3, 2011, https://www.americamagazine.org/content/all-things/gays-and-church-two-stories-today.

43. James Martin, "Respect, Compassion, and Sensitivity," *America*, June 12, 2012, https://www.americamagazine.org/content/all-things/respect-compassion-and-sensitivity.

44. Martin, "Respect, Compassion, and Sensitivity."

45. USCCB Public Affairs Office, "Supreme Court Decision on Marriage 'A Tragic Error' Says President of Catholic Bishops' Conference," June 26, 2015, https://www.usccb.org/news/2015/supreme-court-decision-marriage-tragic-error-says-president-catholic-bishops-conference.

46. James Martin, SJ, Facebook, June 26, 2015, https://www.facebook.com/FrJamesMartin/posts/10152861164141496. See also David Gibson, "A Catholic Priest's Viral Facebook Post on Gay Marriage, and What It Means," *Religion News Service*, June 29, 2015, https://religionnews.com/2015/06/29/a-catholic-priests-viral-facebook-post-on-gay-marriage-and-what-it-means/#sthash.dxVR3CkL.dpuf.

47. James Martin, "'A Prayer for When I Feel Hated': Helping Prevent Gay Teen Suicide," *Huffington Post*, May 25, 2011, https://www.huffpost.com/entry/a-prayer-when-i-feel-hated_b_754165.

48. Martin, "A Prayer for When I Feel Hated."

49. Joseph Cardinal Bernadin, *The Seamless Garment: Writings on the Consistent Ethic of Life* (Maryknoll, NY: Orbis Books, 2008).

50. Trevor Project, "Facts about Suicide," accessed July 19, 2022, https://www.thetrevorproject.org/resources/guide/preventing-suicide/.

51. James Martin, "When LGBT Issues Are Pro-Life Issues," *America*, June 12, 2018, https://www.americamagazine.org/faith/2018/06/12/father-james-martin-when-lgbt-issues-are-pro-life-issues.

52. James Martin, "Will Catholics Rejoice Over the Repeal of DADT?," *Huffington Post*, May 25, 2011, https://www.huffpost.com/entry/will-catholics-rejoice-ov_b_800730. This piece was originally published as a blog by America Media but has since been removed.

53. CDF, "Some Considerations Concerning the Response to Legislative Proposals on the Non-discrimination of Homosexual Persons," Foreword, July 24, 1992, http://www.vatican.va/roman_curia//congregations/cfaith/documents/rc_con_cfaith_doc_19920724_homosexual-persons_en.html.

54. CDF, "Some Considerations Concerning the Response to Legislative Proposals on the Non-discrimination of Homosexual Persons," Foreword, nos. 10–12; emphasis added.

55. For a more comprehensive list of LGBTQ people fired from Catholic institutions, see Robert Shine, "Employees of Catholic Institutions Who Have Been Fired, Forced to Resign, Had Offers Rescinded, or Had Their Jobs Threatened because of LGBT Issues," New Ways Ministry, https://www.newwaysministry.org/issues/employment/employment-disputes/. For particular examples, see the stories of Margie Winters (Chris Brennan, "Firing of Teacher in Same-Sex Marriage Roils Catholic School," *Philadelphia Inquirer*, July 8, 2015, https://www.inquirer.com/philly/education/20150708_Firing_of_teacher_in_same-sex_marriage_roils_Catholic_school.html#disqus_thread) and Travis Loeffler (Brian Roewe, "Minnesota Parish Rallies around Gay Musicians Ousted by New Priest," *National Catholic Reporter*, December 22, 2017, https://www.ncronline.org/news/parish/minnesota-parish-rallies-around-gay-musicians-ousted-new-priest).

56. James Martin, SJ, Twitter, October 23, 2017, https://twitter.com/JamesMartinSJ/status/922461135722426368?s=20.

57. James Martin, SJ, Twitter, September 30, 2018, https://twitter.com/JamesMartinSJ/status/1046460723587665921.

58. James Martin, SJ, Twitter, October 16, 2019, https://twitter.com/JamesMartinSJ/status/1184460376785739777.

59. James Martin, *Building a Bridge*, exp. and rev. ed. (New York: Harper One, 2018), 46–50.

60. James Martin, SJ, Twitter, March 27, 2019, https://twitter.com/JamesMartinSJ/status/1110913458973880321.

CHAPTER 8

1. Ariel Zambelich and Alyson Hurt, "3 Hours in Orlando: Piecing Together an Attack and Its Aftermath," *NPR*, June 26, 2016, https://www.npr.org/2016/06/16/482322488/orlando-shooting-what-happened-update.

2. James Martin, *Building a Bridge*, exp. and rev. ed. (New York: HarperOne, 2018), 15.

3. James Martin, SJ, email to author, February 10, 2021.

4. Most Catholic bishops do not use the word *gay* because the term connotes social affirmation for what they believe are sinful sexual practices. Instead, most Catholic leaders employ archaic and pathologizing medical language such as "homosexual" or "same-sex attracted." Understood this way, people who experience homosexuality/same-sex desire cannot claim that it is a fundamental part of their being that comes from God, but a condition akin to a sickness that must be managed and treated.

5. James Martin, "Standing in Solidarity with Our LGBT Brothers and Sisters," Facebook, June 13, 2016, https://www.facebook.com/watch/?v=10153544268041496.

6. Jon Sweeney, *James Martin: In the Company of Jesus* (Collegeville, MN: Liturgical Press, 2020), 125.

7. "New Ways Ministry's Bridge Building Award," 2016, https://www.newwaysministry.org/programs/what-we-do/new-ways-ministry-bridge-building-award-rev-james-martin/.

8. Congregation for the Doctrine of the Faith, "Notification Regarding Sister Jeannine Gramick, SSND, and Father Robert Nugent, SDS," May 31, 1999, vatican.va/roman_curia/congregations/cfaith/documents/rc_con_cfaith_doc_19990531_gramick-nugent

-notification_en.html; James Martin, "USCCB Condemns New Ways Ministry; Gay Ministry Responds," *America*, February 26, 2010, https://www.americamagazine.org/content/all-things/usccb-condemns-new-ways-ministry-gay-ministry-responds.

Judy Roberts, "Father James Martin Explains His Vision Regarding 'LGBT' Catholics," *National Catholic Register*, July 10, 2017, https://www.ncregister.com/news/father-james-martin-explains-his-vision-regarding-lgbt-catholics.

10. Roberts, "Father James Martin Explains His Vision Regarding 'LGBT' Catholics."

11. James Martin, "We Need to Build a Bridge between LGBT Community and the Catholic Church," *America*, published online October 30, 2016, https://www.americamagazine.org/faith/2016/10/30/james-martin-sj-we-need-build-bridge-between-lgbt-community-and-catholic-church.

12. See, e.g., "Pope Suggests Trump 'Is not Christian,'" *CNN*, February 18, 2016, https://www.cnn.com/2016/02/18/politics/pope-francis-trump-christian-wall/index.html.

13. Robert Nugent and Jeannine Gramick, *Building Bridges* (Mystic, CT: Twenty-Third Publications, 1992).

14. Martin, "We Need to Build a Bridge."

15. Martin, "We Need to Build a Bridge."

16. Martin, "We Need to Build a Bridge."

17. Sweeney, *James Martin: In the Company of Jesus*, 125–26.

18. Sweeney, *James Martin: In the Company of Jesus*, 125.

19. See, e.g., James Martin, "Use Your Imagination: A Prayer Tip from St. Ignatius," *The Word Among Us*, https://www2.wau.org/resources/article/re_use_your_imagination/.

20. Martin, *Building a Bridge*, 11.

21. Martin, *Building a Bridge*, 11.

22. Lauren Markoe, "Why I Kept My Questions for the Rev. James Martin to Myself," *Religion News Service*, February 1, 2018, https://religionnews.com/2018/02/01/why-i-kept-my-questions-for-the-rev-james-martin-to-myself/.

23. Jamie Manson, "Can Fr. James Martin's Bridge Hold Up?," *National Catholic Reporter*, July 5, 2017, https://www.ncronline.org/blogs/can-fr-james-martins-bridge-hold.

24. Manson, "Can Fr. James Martin's Bridge Hold Up?"

25. Xorje Olivares, interview with author, February 9, 2021.

26. The Spiritual Friendship movement explores ways that gay and lesbian Catholics can have fulfilling relationships outside of sexual intimacy.

27. Eve Tushnet, "The Challenge of Being Both Gay and Catholic," *Washington Post*, June 1, 2017, https://www.washingtonpost.com/news/acts-of-faith/wp/2017/06/01/the-challenge-of-being-both-gay-and-catholic/.

28. David Cloutier, "The Ignatian Option," *Commonweal*, June 15, 2017, https://www.commonwealmagazine.org/ignatian-option. The irony lost on many of his critics was not only that Martin had not challenged Church teaching on chastity, but that he was also living it, as part of his Jesuit life.

29. Archbishop Charles Chaput, "A Letter to the Romans," *Catholic Philly*, July 6, 2017, https://catholicphilly.com/2017/07/archbishop-chaput-column/a-letter-to-the-romans/.

30. Cardinal Robert Sarah, "How Catholics Can Welcome LGBT Believers," *Wall Street Journal*, September 1, 2017, https://www.wsj.com/articles/how-catholics-can-welcome-lgbt-believers-1504221027.

31. Jim Russell, "The Insanely Stupid 'LGBT' Rhetoric of Fr. James Martin," *Church Militant*, February 5, 2019, https://www.churchmilitant.com/news/article/the-insanely-stupid-lgbt-rhetoric-of-fr.-james-martin.

32. Brian Roewe, "Fr. James Martin in Social Media Fray over LGBT Conversation," *National Catholic Reporter*, September 17, 2017, https://www.ncronline.org/news/media/fr-james-martin-social-media-fray-over-lgbt-conversation.

33. James Martin, "Father James Martin: 7 Lessons for Ministry I've Learned as a Jesuit," *America*, October 10, 2018, https://www.americamagazine.org/faith/2018/10/10/father-james-martin-7-lessons-ministry-ive-learned-jesuit.

34. Brian Roewe, "Fr. James Martin Uninvited from Talk at CUA Seminary," *National Catholic Reporter*, September 16, 2017, https://www.ncronline.org/news/media/fr-james-martin-uninvited-talk-cua-seminary.

35. Sweeney, *James Martin: In the Company of Jesus*, 138.

36. Martin, *Building a Bridge*, 4.

37. Martin, *Building a Bridge*, 104–6.

38. Martin, *Building a Bridge*, 5–6.

39. Archbishop Charles Chaput, "Father James Martin and Catholic Belief," *Catholic Philly*, September 19, 2019, http://catholicphilly.com/2019/09/archbishop-chaput-column/father-james-martin-and-catholic-belief/. Chaput's gripe was long running. The year before Martin's talk at St. Joseph's University, Chaput had taken issue with him even speaking in the archdiocese where the Jesuit was born, raised, and educated. At an evening talk at Old St. Joseph's, Chaput instructed the parish's Jesuit pastor to read out "official church teaching" on homosexuality before Martin took the podium in front of a packed house, which included his eighty-eight-year-old mother. The pastor did so, but also spoke warmly about gay members of his parish, including a man he had recently anointed at a local hospital who asked him, "Can your church accept my love?" James Martin, SJ, email to author, February 13, 2021.

40. James Martin, "What Is the Official Church Teaching on Homosexuality? Responding to a Commonly Asked Question," *America*, April 6, 2018, https://www.americamagazine.org/faith/2018/04/06/what-official-church-teaching-homosexuality-responding-commonly-asked-question?fbclid=IwAR1grr-v-5Q1X5jF8kdGfUqeWhAXgi-mOB6B4sATtFm4A65B-Lf752ncVdg.

41. James Martin, "Fr. Martin Responds to Archbishop Chaput's Critique," *Catholic Philly*, September 19, 2019, https://catholicphilly.com/2019/09/commentaries/fr-martin-responds-to-archbishop-chaputs-critique/.

42. Michael O'Loughlin, "Cardinal Sarah Offers Critique of L.G.B.T. Book, Father James Martin Responds," *America*, August 31, 2017, https://www.americamagazine.org/faith/2017/08/31/cardinal-sarah-offers-critique-lgbt-book-father-james-martin-responds.

43. James Martin, SJ, Twitter, October 4, 2017, https://www.facebook.com/FrJamesMartin/photos/a.139618381495.120357.46899546495/10154725930241496/?type=3.

44. Martin, *Building a Bridge*, 7.

45 Damian Torres-Botello, "The Courage to Love: On James Martin and the Magnitude of Words," *Jesuit Post*, October 6, 2017, https://thejesuitpost.org/2017/10/the-courage-to-love-on-james-martin-and-the-magnitude-of-words/?utm_content=bufferad301&utm_medium=social&utm_source=twitter.com&utm_campaign=buffer.

46. Emily Reimer-Barry, "Toxic Shame and Sin-Talk: Church Militant Has It All Wrong," *Catholic Moral Theology*, October 7, 2017,

https://catholicmoraltheology.com/toxic-shame-and-sin-talk-church
-militant-has-it-all-wrong/.

47. Bishop Robert McElroy, "Bishop McElroy: Attacks on Father
James Martin Expose a Cancer within the U.S. Catholic Church,"
America, September 18, 2020, https://www.americamagazine.org/
faith/2017/09/18/bishop-mcelroy-attacks-father-james-martin-expose
-cancer-within-us-catholic-church.

48. These themes are explored in several of Martin's works,
including *Together on Retreat: Meeting Jesus in Prayer* (New York:
HarperOne, 2013); *Jesus: A Pilgrimage* (New York: HarperOne, 2016);
and *Learning to Pray: A Guide for Everyone* (New York: HarperOne,
2021).

49. James Martin, SJ, email to author, February 10, 2021. See
also Sweeney, *James Martin: In the Company of Jesus*, 126–27.

50. James Martin, SJ, email to author, February 10, 2021.

51. James Martin, SJ, email to author, February 10, 2021.

52. Sweeney, *James Martin: In the Company of Jesus*, 142–44.

53. James Martin, "Spiritual Insights for LGBT Catholics,"
HarperOne, March 9, 2018, https://www.youtube.com/watch?v=
-NWwKgfYfDE&t=2s.

54. Fr. James Martin, "How Parishes Can Welcome LGBT
Catholics," *America*, August 23, 2018, https://www.americamagazine
.org/faith/2018/08/23/father-james-martin-how-parishes-can-welcome
-lgbt-catholics.

55. Sweeney, *James Martin: In the Company of Jesus*, 145.

56. James Martin, "A Good Measure: Showing Welcome and
Respect in Our Parishes for LGBT People and Their Families,"
Address to World Meeting of Families, Dublin, Ireland, August 23,
2018, https://www.newwaysministry.org/blog/subscribe-bondings-2-0/fr
-james-martin-world-meeting-of-families-2018/.

57. Sweeney, *James Martin: In the Company of Jesus*, 145.

58. Inés San Martín, "Fr. James Martin: Pope Was 'Attentive,
Welcoming and Warm' during Meeting," *Crux*, October 1, 2019,
https://cruxnow.com/vatican/2019/09/fr-james-martin-pope-was
-attentive-welcoming-and-warm-during-meeting/.

59. "LGBTQ Ally Father James Martin Reveals New Detail
about Meeting Pope Francis," *Human Rights Campaign*, April 10,
2020, https://www.youtube.com/watch?v=sBS08SSsM9o.

60. James Martin, SJ, Twitter, September 30, 2019, https://twitter.com/jamesmartinsj/status/1178663907084455936?lang=en.

61. Francis DeBernardo, "Father James Martin, Advocate for LGBTQ Catholics, Received by Pope Francis at Vatican," New Ways Ministry, September 30, 2019, https://www.newwaysministry.org/2019/09/30/father-james-martin-advocate-for-lgbtq-catholics-received-by-pope-francis-at-vatican/.

62. J.D. Flynn, "US Bishops: Pope Francis Talks Fr. James Martin, Euthanasia, at Private Meeting," Catholic News Agency, February 20, 2020, https://www.catholicnewsagency.com/news/us-bishops-pope-francis-talks-fr-james-martin-euthanasia-at-private-meeting-46135.

63. Flynn, "US Bishops: Pope Francis Talks Fr. James Martin, Euthanasia, at Private Meeting."

64. Archbishop John Wester, "Archbishop Wester Responds to Recounting of Pope's Words about Jesuit Fr. James Martin," National Catholic Reporter, February 21, 2020, https://www.ncronline.org/news/people/archbishop-wester-responds-recounting-popes-words-about-jesuit-fr-james-martin.

65. Heidi Schlumpf, "Second Bishop Challenges Anonymous Prelates' Version of Papal Meeting," National Catholic Reporter, February 22, 2020, https://www.ncronline.org/news/people/second-bishop-challenges-anonymous-prelates-version-papal-meeting.

66. James Martin, SJ, email to author, February 13, 2021.

67. Michael Sean Winters, "Some US Bishops Let Their Politics Get in the Way during Visits with the Pope," National Catholic Reporter, February 28, 2020, https://www.ncronline.org/news/opinion/distinctly-catholic/some-us-bishops-let-their-politics-get-way-during-visits-pope.

68. National Catholic Reporter Editorial Staff, "Editorial: The Pope Is NOT Upset with Fr. James Martin," National Catholic Reporter, February 27, 2020, https://www.ncronline.org/news/opinion/editorial-pope-not-upset-fr-james-martin.

69. See, e.g., James Martin, "Listen to the L.G.B.T. Person: A Response to the Vatican's Gender Theory Document," America, June 11, 2019, https://www.americamagazine.org/faith/2019/06/11/listen-lgbt-person-response-vaticans-gender-theory-document.

70. James Martin, SJ, Twitter, October 1, 2019, https://twitter.com/JamesMartinSJ/status/1178974888385581056.

71. Fordham Center on Religion and Culture, "Outreach 2020: Catholic Leaders Speak with the LGBTQ Community," June 18, 2020, https://www.youtube.com/watch?v=SUsBWXiolPo.

72. "God Is on Your Side: A Statement from Catholic Bishops on Protecting LGBT Youth," *Tyler Clementi Foundation*, https://tylerclementi.org/catholicbishopsstatement/.

73. Charles Camosy, "Q&A: Rev. James Martin Contemplates Reaction to His Book on LGBT Catholics," *Religion News Service*, September 13, 2017, https://religionnews.com/2017/09/13/qa-rev-james-martin-contemplates-reaction-to-his-book-on-lgbt-catholics/.

74. Charles Camosy, "Q&A: Rev. James Martin Contemplates Reaction to His Book on LGBT Catholics."

CHAPTER 9

1. Martin Luther King Jr., "Letter from a Birmingham Jail," April 16, 1963, https://www.africa.upenn.edu/Articles_Gen/Letter_Birmingham.html.

2. Cesar Chavez, "An Age of Miracles," in *An Organizer's Tale* (New York: Penguin Books, 2008), 45.

3. Dorothy Day, "Letter to Gordon Zahn," in *All the Way to Heaven: The Selected Letters of Dorothy Day*, ed. Robert Ellsberg (Milwaukee: Marquette University Press, 2010), 351.

4. For a helpful summary of this belief, see USCCB, "Marriage: Love and Life in the Divine Plan," November 17, 2009, https://www.usccb.org/resources/pastoral-letter-marriage-love-and-life-in-the-divine-plan.pdf.

5. For a representative (if unsound) formulation of this teaching, see Congregation for Catholic Education, "Male and Female He Created Them," Vatican City, 2019, http://www.educatio.va/content/dam/cec/Documenti/19_0997_INGLESE.pdf.

6. Mark Jordan, *The Silence of Sodom* (Chicago: University of Chicago Press, 2000), 21–22.

7. Stephen Bullivant, *Mass Exodus: Catholic Disaffiliation in Britain and America since Vatican II* (London: Oxford University Press, 2019).

8. Mark Massa, *The American Catholic Revolution: How the '60s Changed the Church Forever* (New York: Oxford University Press, 2010).

9. Jill Peterfeso, *Womanpriest: Tradition and Transgression in the Contemporary Roman Catholic Church* (New York: Fordham University Press, 2020); Mary Henold, *Catholic and Feminist: The Surprising History of the American Catholic Feminist Movement* (Chapel Hill: University of North Carolina Press, 2008).

10. For representative criticism, see Richard McBrien, "John Paul II: Assessing His Legacy," *Commonweal*, April 15, 2005, https://www.commonwealmagazine.org/john-paul-ii-2.

11. Elizabeth Dias, "'It Is Not a Closet. It Is a Cage.' Gay Catholic Priests Speak Out," *New York Times*, February 17, 2019, https://www.nytimes.com/2019/02/17/us/it-is-not-a-closet-it-is-a-cage-gay-catholic-priests-speak-out.html; Sari Aviv and Anna Matranga, "Gay Priests: Breaking the Silence," ed. Ed Givnish, *CBS News*, March 28, 2021, https://www.cbsnews.com/news/gay-priests-breaking-the-silence/, Andrew Sullivan, "The Gay Church," *Intelligencer*, January 21, 2019, https://nymag.com/intelligencer/2019/01/gay-priests-catholic-church.html. For a scientific study, see Stephan Kappler, Kristin Hancock, and Thomas Plante, "Roman Catholic Gay Priests: Internalized Homophobia, Sexual Identity, and Psychological Well-Being," *Pastoral Psychology* 62 (2013): 805–26. Although a few Catholic priests have come out as transgender or genderqueer, there are no large-scale studies on this issue.

12. Frederic Martel provides a comprehensive account of this dynamic in his investigative work, *In the Closet of the Vatican: Power, Homosexuality, Hypocrisy* (New York: Bloomsbury Publishing, 2019).

13. Heidi Schlumpf, "Conservatives Still Rule the US Bishops' Conference," *National Catholic Reporter*, June 3, 2019, https://www.ncronline.org/news/accountability/conservatives-still-rule-us-bishops-conference.

14. Catholic News Service, "U.S. Bishops: If the Equality Act Is Passed It Will 'Discriminate against People of Faith,'" *America*, February 24, 2021, https://www.americamagazine.org/faith/2021/02/24/us-bishops-equality-act-discrimination-faith-240092.

15. Daniel Horan, "Recent Transphobic Statements from Bishops Make Truth Claims without Facts," *National Catholic Reporter*, September 1, 2021, https://www.ncronline.org/news/opinion/faith

-seeking-understanding/recent-transphobic-statements-bishops-make
-truth-claims.

16. For more, see Enrique Dussel, *A History of the Church in Latin America: Colonialism to Liberation (1492–1979)* (Grand Rapids, MI: Eerdmans, 1981); John Frederick Schwaller, *The History of the Roman Catholic Church in Latin America: From Conquest to Revolution and Beyond* (New York: New York University Press, 2007); and John Lynch, *New Worlds: A Religious History of Latin America* (New Haven, CT: Yale University Press, 2012).

17. For more on base communities, see Leonardo Boff, *Ecclesiogenesis*, trans. Robert Barr (Maryknoll, NY: Orbis Books, 1986), For more on the Christian preferential option for the poor, see Daniel Groody, ed., *The Option for the Poor in Christian Theology* (South Bend, IN: University of Notre Dame Press, 2007).

18. Jon Sobrino, "Extra Pauperes Nulla Salus," trans. Joseph Owens, in *No Salvation Outside the Poor: Prophetic Utopian Essays* (Maryknoll, NY: Orbis Books, 2008), 35–76. Sobrino's use of "gravely ill" to describe civilization came from the thought of Ignacio Ellacuría, a Spanish Jesuit and liberation theologian who was murdered with seven others by the Salvadoran military in 1989. Sobrino, "Extra Pauperes Nulla Salus," 35.

19. José Comblin, cited by Sobrino, "Extra Pauperes Nulla Salus," 51–52.

20. For a history of this belief, see Francis Sullivan, *Salvation Outside the Church? Tracing the History of the Catholic Response* (Eugene, OR: Wipf and Stock, 2002).

21. Sobrino, "Extra Pauperes Nulla Salus," 52.

22. Sobrino, "Extra Pauperes Nulla Salus," 53.

23. Sobrino, "Extra Pauperes Nulla Salus," 59.

24. Human Rights Campaign, "Growing Up LGBT in America," accessed July 20, 2022, https://assets2.hrc.org/files/assets/resources/Growing-Up-LGBT-in-America_Report.pdf?_ga=2.48106407.1482537102.1640609892-1874838799.1640609892.

25. Laura Kann, Emily O'Malley Olsen, Tim McManus, et al., "Sexual Identity, Sex of Sexual Contacts, and Health-Related Behaviors among Students in Grades 9–12—United States and Selected Sites," *Morbidity and Mortality Weekly Report Surveillance Summaries* 65, no. 9 (2016): 1–202. See also Centers for Disease Control and Prevention, "LGBT Youth," https://www.cdc.gov/lgbthealth/youth.htm.

26. Lou Chibbaro Jr., "Anti-LGBTQ Hate Crimes Mostly Unchanged in 2019: FBI," Washington Blade, November 24, 2020, https://www.washingtonblade.com/2020/11/24/anti-lgbtq-hate-crimes-mostly-unchanged-in-2019-fbi/.

27. Human Rights Campaign, "Fatal Violence against the Transgender and Gender Non-Conforming Community in 2020," https://www.hrc.org/resources/violence-against-the-trans-and-gender-non-conforming-community-in-2020.

28. Jeremy Gibbs and Jeremy Goldbach, "Religious Conflict, Sexual Identity, and Suicidal Behaviors among LGBT Young Adults," *Archives of Suicide Research* 19, no. 4 (October–December 2015): 472–88, available online at https://www.ncbi.nlm.nih.gov/pmc/articles/PMC4706071/.

29. James Martin, Facebook, September 28, 2021, https://www.facebook.com/FrJamesMartin/posts/carl-siciliano-of-the-ali-forney-center-which-provides-housing-for-homeless-lgbt/412711456881620/.

30. Carina Julig, "A Young Woman's Suicide Puts Focus on Church's Counseling for LGBT Catholics," *National Catholic Reporter*, February 17, 2020, https://www.ncronline.org/news/people/young-womans-suicide-puts-focus-churchs-counseling-lgbt-catholics; Joyce Calvo, "My Daughter Was a Gay Catholic Who Died by Suicide: Here's How the Church Must Protect LGBTQ+ Catholics," *National Catholic Reporter*, January 13, 2022, https://www.ncronline.org/news/opinion/my-daughter-was-gay-catholic-who-died-suicide-heres-how-church-must-protect-lgbtq. For more on the way the nonaffirming theologies affect LGBTQ Christians, see Cody Sanders, *Christianity, LGBTQ Suicide, and the Souls of Queer Folk* (New York: Lexington Books, 2020).

31. Francis DeBernardo and Robert Shine, "Employees of Catholic Institutions Who Have Been Fired, Forced to Resign, Had Offers Rescinded, or Had Their Jobs Threatened Because of LGBT Issues," New Ways Ministry, accessed July 20, 2022, https://www.newwaysministry.org/issues/employment/employment-disputes/.

32. Robert Shine, "Diocese: Pastors Can Deny Funerals to Married Lesbian and Gay Catholics," New Ways Ministry, October 24, 2017, https://www.newwaysministry.org/2017/10/24/bishop-pastors-can-deny-funerals-married-lesbian-gay-catholics/.

33. James Martin, "Father James Martin: How Parishes Can Welcome L.G.B.T. Catholics," Address to Vatican's World Meeting

of Families, Dublin, Ireland, August 23, 2018, available at https://www.americamagazine.org/faith/2018/08/23/father-james-martin-how-parishes-can-welcome-lgbt-catholics.

34. Elizabeth Edman, *Queer Virtue: What LGBTQ People Know about Life and Love and How It Can Revitalize Christianity* (Boston, MA: Beacon Press, 2013), 3.

35. Justin McCarthy, "Record-High 70% in U.S. Support Same-Sex Marriage," Gallup, June 8, 2021, https://news.gallup.com/poll/350486/record-high-support-same-sex-marriage.aspx.

36. Kristjan Archer and Justin McCarthy, "U.S. Catholics Have Backed Same-Sex Marriage since 2011," Gallup, October 23, 2020, https://news.gallup.com/poll/322805/catholics-backed-sex-marriage-2011.aspx.

37. Pew Research Center, "Views about Same-Sex Marriage," accessed June 14, 2021, https://www.pewforum.org/religious-landscape-study/views-about-same-sex-marriage/.

38. PRRI Staff, "Broad Support for LGBT Rights across All 50 States: Findings from the 2019 American Values Atlas," PRRI, April 14, 2020, https://www.prri.org/research/broad-support-for-lgbt-rights/?fbclid=IwAR1XhRgh7GL0kBgG6Ob3siw0IeYIg66c8RGRPFF_rOyZfU5sQ5wToWb5X40.

39. Ivan Briggiler, interview with author, October 12, 2020.

40. John Vernon, interview with author, April 18, 2021.

41. John Vernon, interview with author.

42. John Vernon, interview with author.

43. "LGBT Catholics and Friends," St. Ignatius of Loyola Church, https://ignatius.nyc/ministry/lgbt-catholics-and-friends/.

44. Fr. Dennis Yesalonia, SJ, "A Letter from the Pastor," St. Ignatius of Loyola Church, June 11, 2017.

45. Their stories were accompanied by a well-designed booklet that included contact information for the group. See LGBT Catholics and Friends, "Our Stories: Being LGBT and Catholic," https://issuu.com/saintignatiusloyola/docs/lgbt_full_booklet__final_.

46. Rose DiMartino, interview with author, October 30, 2020.

47. John Vernon, interview with author.

48. Rose DiMartino, email to author, April 22, 2020.

49. Ivan Briggiler, interview with author.

50. "Community Groups," St. Clement Parish, https://www.clement.org/belong/community-groups.

51. "Gay and Lesbian Catholics," St. Clement Parish, https://www.clement.org/who-we-are/parish-groups/gay-and-lesbian-catholics.

52. Michael Bayer, interview with author, November 23, 2020.

53. Katherine Abel, interview with author, December 4, 2020.

54. Michael Bayer, interview with author.

55. Michael Bayer, interview with author.

56. Katherine Abel, interview with author.

57. "About," Affirmed: LGBTQ+ Ministry Chicago, accessed July 25, 2022, https://www.facebook.com/groups/affirmedchicago/about.

58. Michael Bayer, interview with author, and Katherine Abel, interview with author.

59. Michael Bayer, interview with author.

60. Michael Bayer, interview with author.

61. Fr. James Martin, "What Does a Church Open to L.G.B.T. Catholics Look Like?," *America*, August 30, 2019, https://www.americamagazine.org/faith/2019/08/30/what-does-church open lgbt -catholics-look.

62. Rebecca MacMaster, interview with author, May 6, 2021.

63. Michael Bayer, interview with author.

64. Katherine Abel, interview with author.

65. Katherine Abel, interview with author.

66. See https://vineandfig.co/. The founders of Vine & Fig intentionally embrace the word *queer* as a more inclusive alternative to *LGBTQ*. This section will reflect their chosen nomenclature.

67. "About," Vine & Fig, accessed July 25, 2022, https://vineandfig.co/about.

68. Patrick Flores, interview with author, March 2, 2021.

69. Patrick Flores, "Why We Are Called Vine & Fig," Vine and Fig, June 25, 2019, https://vineandfig.co/blog/2019/why-we-are-called -vine-fig.

70. Jacob Flores, interview with author, March 2, 2021.

71. Patrick Flores, interview with author.

72. "Vine & Fig, An Affirming Space for Queer Catholics," December 3, 2018, https://www.youtube.com/watch?v=jzB7JixybA4.

73. Patrick Flores, "Pat's Queer Catholic Story," Vine & Fig, December 25, 2018, https://vineandfig.co/blog/2018/pats-queer-catholic -story.

74. "About," Vine & Fig.

75. "Community," Vine & Fig, accessed July 25, 2022, https://vineandfig.co/resources/community.

76. "Community Guidelines," Vine & Fig, accessed July 25, 2022, https://vineandfig.co/community/guidelines.

77. "About," Vine & Fig; Zinzy Nev Geene, interview with author, March 2, 2021.

78. "About," Vine & Fig; Zinzy Nev Geene, interview with author; "New Vine & Fig Leadership!," Vine & Fig, April 22, 2020, https://vineandfig.co/blog/2020/new-vine-fig-leadership.

79. Zinzy Nev Geene, interview with author.

80. Patrick Gothman (Flores) and Jacob Flores, "What Matters Most to God?," Vine & Fig, September 11, 2019, https://vineandfig.co/podcast/tabard-inn/1/1/what-matters-most-god.

SELECTED
BIBLIOGRAPHY

Coleman, Gerald. *Homosexuality: Catholic Teaching and Pastoral Practice*. New York: Paulist Press, 1995.

Edman, Elizabeth. *Queer Virtue: What LGBTQ People Know about Life and Love and How It Can Revitalize Christianity*. Boston, MA: Beacon Press, 2013.

Firer Hinze, Christine, and Patrick Hornbeck, eds. *More than a Monologue: Sexual Diversity and the Catholic Church; Voices of Our Times (Catholic Practice in North America)*. New York: Fordham University Press, 2014.

Gallagher, John, ed. *Homosexuality and the Magisterium: Documents from the Vatican and the U.S. Bishops 1975–1985*. Mt. Rainier, MD: New Ways Ministry, 1986.

Godfrey, Donal. *Gays and Grays: The Story of the Inclusion of the Gay Community at Most Holy Redeemer Catholic Parish in San Francisco*. New York: Lexington Books, 2008.

Gramick, Jeannine, ed. *Homosexuality and the Catholic Church*. Mt. Rainier, MD: New Ways Ministry, 1983.

Gramick, Jeannine, and Robert Nugent, eds. *The Vatican and Homosexuality*. New York: Crossroad, 1988.

———. *Voices of Hope: A Collection of Positive Catholic Writings on Gay & Lesbian Issues*. Mt. Rainier, MD: New Ways Ministry, 1995.

Holtz, Raymond, ed. *Listen to the Stories: Gay and Lesbian Catholics Talk about Their Lives*. New York: Garland Publications, 1991.

Jordan, Mark. *The Silence of Sodom: Homosexuality in Modern Catholicism.* Chicago: University of Chicago Press, 2000.

LGBTQ Religious Archives Network. https://lgbtqreligiousarchives.org/.

Lopata, Mary Ellen, with Casey Lopata. *Fortunate Families: Catholic Families with Lesbian Daughters and Gay Sons.* Victoria, Canada: Trafford Publishing, 2003.

Martin, James. *Building a Bridge: How the Catholic Church and the LGBT Community Can Enter into a Relationship of Respect, Compassion, and Sensitivity.* Exp. and rev. ed. New York: HarperCollins Publishers, 2018.

Mascagni, Evan, and Shannon Post, directors. *Building a Bridge.* Executive Producer Martin Scorsese, 2021. https://www.buildingabridgefilm.com/.

McNeill, John. *Both Feet Planted Firmly in Midair.* Louisville, KY: Westminster John Knox Press, 1998.

———. *The Church and the Homosexual.* 4th ed. Boston: Beacon Press, 1993.

New Ways Ministry. "Book of Memory and Thanksgiving." 2002. Available at https://www.newwaysministry.org/wp-content/uploads/2021/03/Book_of_Memory.pdf.

Nugent, Robert, ed. *A Challenge to Love—Gay and Lesbian Catholics in the Church.* New York: Crossroads, 1983.

Nugent, Robert, and Jeannine Gramick. *Building Bridges: Gay & Lesbian Reality and the Catholic Church.* Mystic, CT: Twenty-Third Publications, 1992.

O'Loughlin, Michael. *AIDS, Catholics, and the Untold Stories of Compassion in the Face of Fear.* Minneapolis, MN: Broadleaf Books, 2021.

Rick, Barbara, director. *In Good Conscience: Sister Jeannine Gramick's Journey of Faith.* Out of the Blue Films, Inc., 2006. 82 minutes.

Roche, Patrick. "DignityUSA History." DignityUSA. https://www.dignityusa.org/history.

Schexnayder, James. *Setting the Table: Preparing Catholic Parishes to Welcome Lesbian, Gay, Bisexual, and Transgender People and Their Families.* CreateSpace Independent Publishing Platform, 2011.

Sweeney, Jon. *James Martin, SJ: In the Company of Jesus.* Collegeville, MN: Liturgical Press, 2019.

Talley, Jodie. "A Queer Miracle in Georgia: The Origins of Gay-Affirming Religion in the South." PhD diss., Georgia State University, 2006. Available online at https://scholarworks.gsu.edu/history_theses/17.

Trujillo, Yunuen. *LGBTQ Catholics: A Guide to Inclusive Ministry.* Mahwah, NJ: Paulist Press, 2022.

Williams, Howell. "Homosexuality and the American Catholic Church: Reconfiguring the Silence, 1971–1999." PhD diss., Florida State University, 2007.

Zerkowski, Stan "JR." *Coming Out and Coming Home.* Louisville, KY: Butler Books, 2022.

INDEX

and CDF, 52, 58–59; and
CICLSAL, 57, 59–60; civil
rights, LGBTQ, 50–52; and
CPN, 68–69; and CRSI,
56–57; and DignityUSA, 40,
47; disobedience of Gramick,
60–61; education, 44–45,
46; and Francis, 62–63; gay
priests, 48–49; and hierarchy,
52, 56–57; and institutional
church, 42, 52; and lesbians,
47–49; and the Lopatas, 68;
Maida Commission, 57–58;
and Martin, 141; and NCCB,
54; publications, 45–47; and
Ratzinger, 58; symposia, 49;
Vatican directive, 58–59;
women religious, 48–49
New York Roundtable of Gay
and Lesbian Ministries, 91
Nidorf, Pat, 19–20, 21, 25
Nugent, Robert, 5, 26, 40, 44,
45–48, 50, 52–61, 142,
181–82

Obama, Barack, 136
Obergefell v. Hodges, 134
O'Connor, John, 26–27, 79–80,
89–90
Oddo, Tom, 26
O'Gorman, Ned, 116
O'Hara, Gerald P., 11–12
O'Kane, Patti, 28
O'Mally, Sean, 132
Ordination, 12–13
Orthodox Catholic Church of
America (OCCA), 15, 16
Out at St. Paul (OSP), 2–3,
94–95; Advent devotional,
119–20; and archdiocese,
107–9; changes in team, 120;
and Covenant House, 112;
demographics, 121;
dialogue, 109–12; events,
104; expansion, 112–13;
family, 115–18; gay bars,
101, 117; and GMHC,
118; growing edges,
121–22; hospitality,
117; intergenerational
relationships, 117–18;
liturgy, 119; Martin, 145;
and Mass, 102–4, 106–7;
and ministries of St. Paul,
101–6; Owning Our Faith,
113; Pride, 106–7; retreat,
105–6; spiritual diversity,
114–15; Supper Club, 118;
and women, 121–22
Outreach 2020, 157

Pais, David, 37
Palacios, Marianne, 103, 114,
116, 121
Parable of the sower, 41–42
Pastoral theology, 4–5
Paul, Apostle, 180
Paulist Fathers, 82–84, 87, 88,
99–100, 120
Paul VI, Pope, 24
Poverty, 164
"Prayer When I Feel Hated,
A," 135
Pride, 18, 106
Pride Mass, 86–87, 106–7,
213n60
Priesthood, 128–30
Pro-life issues, 135–36

Public Religion Research
Initiative (PRRI), 168
Puerto Rico, 86
Pulse Night Club shooting, 119,
139–40
Purtorti, Matthew, 113
Pyle, Garry, 28

Queer ecclesiology,
166, 178
Queerphobia, 167
Quinn, John, 32
Quixote Center, 44

Ratzinger, Joseph, 35, 36, 53, 58,
130, 136–37
Reese, Thomas, 130
Reply of Martin to critics,
148–50
"Respect, Compassion, and
Sensitivity," 133
Rheimer-Barry, Emily, 150
Rivera, Santiago, 103, 107, 117
Roche, Patrick, 21, 38
Rochester's Interfaith Advocates
for Lesbian, Gay, Bisexual,
and Transgender People, 68
Rohr, Richard, 46
Romero, Oscar, 18
Roper, Michael, 104, 115, 122
Ruse, Austin, 147, 149

Sabatté, Frank, 99
Sacred Heart Roman Catholic
Church (Atlanta), 9, 12
St. Brendan (Los Angeles), 20
St. Clement (Chicago), 172
St. Ignatius of Loyola
(Manhattan), 169–72

St. Patrick's Day Parade, 79–80,
207n9, 207n13
St. Paul the Apostle. *See* Church
of St. Paul the Apostle
Salvation, 164, 166–68
Same-sex desire, 1
Same-sex marriage, 131–33
Sarah, Robert, 146–47, 149
Sciences, 19
Schexnayder, James, 68, 204n14
Sciambra, Joseph, 147
Seaman, Paul, 172–73
Seeds of Hope, 69–70
Servant leadership, 99
Sexual abuse, 129
Sexual ethics, 24–26, 27,
146, 148
Sherwood, Clement, 15
Siciliano, Carl, 165
Sisters of Loreto, 60–61
Sisters of Notre Dame and
Salvatorians, 60
Sixties (decade), 17–18
Slack, 177–78
Smith-Bogart, Penny, 71
Smithgall, Marie, 100, 102, 104,
114, 119, 121
Sobrino, John, 163–64
Social media, 112, 126,
140–41, 147
Society of Jesus, 2, 125–26, 127,
151–52, 157–58
"Some Considerations
Concerning the Response
to Legislative Proposals on
the Nondiscrimination of
Homosexual Persons," 136–37
Spirit Day, 135
Spiritual abuse, 9, 14